The
Flexibility
Factor

The Flexibility Factor

Why people who thrive on change are successful, and how you can become one of them.

Jacquelyn Wonder
•
Priscilla Donovan

Doubleday

New York   London   Toronto   Sydney   Auckland

All the stories and examples in this book are based upon
real people in real situations, but in many cases names
and details have been altered to protect their identities.
Some stories are composites of the experiences of several
individuals or organizations.

PUBLISHED BY DOUBLEDAY

a division of Bantam Doubleday Dell Publishing Group, Inc.
666 Fifth Avenue, New York, New York 10103

DOUBLEDAY and the portrayal of an anchor with a dolphin
are trademarks of Doubleday, a division of
Bantam Doubleday Dell Publishing Group, Inc.

LIBRARY OF CONGRESS CATALOGING-IN-PUBLICATION DATA

Wonder, Jacquelyn.
   The flexibility factor: Why people who thrive on change
are successful, and how you can become one of them.
Jacquelyn Wonder and Priscilla Donovan.—1st ed.
      p.   cm.
   Includes index.
   1. Adaptability (Psychology) 2. Adjustment
(Psychology) 3. Change (Business) 4. Career Development
(Personal growth) 5. Organizational change. I. Donovan,
Priscilla. II. Title.
BF335.W59 1989   88-28164
158—dc19   CIP
ISBN 0-385-24443-6

Book design by Patrice Fodero

June 1989
FIRST EDITION

To Jerry Conover:
Your grace under pressure
as you went through changes in your own life
inspired and enabled us
to get on paper what we most wanted to say.
You were always there to listen,
to share your views,
and to rein us in when needed.

Contents

Acknowledgments

So many individuals helped us throughout the evolution of this book, from its inception to completion, that we hardly know where to begin—except at the beginning. Although we have dedicated the book to him, Jerry Conover still must be mentioned under acknowledgments because he was with us from the very beginning and at every step of the way, both with hands-on editorial help and with encouragement and advice.

Special kudos go to business associates who helped us test the book's materials in the best of all laboratories, the work place, and then gave us invaluable feedback. Although there were many, these stand out for their enthusiasm and expertise: David Ratchford, Citibank, Hong Kong; Kathy de Liefde, AT&T, Denver; Nancy Jaye and Roger Sverson, Professional Value Engineers, Minneapolis; Eric McLuhan, McLuhan & Davies Communications, Inc., Quebec; and Laurie Tolleson, MCI, Atlanta, Georgia.

Also involved from the beginning were Dr. Michael A. Solomon, a psychologist who advised and encouraged us to make the connection between psychological theory and work habits. Some of our most creative and enjoyable moments occurred "in session" with him. Diane Olsen, L.S.W.II, also a professional therapist, contributed immensely to the way we have woven psychological theory into the book's thesis. Shari Robertson, as she did with *Whole-Brain Thinking,* generously shared her expertise in human resource management and thereby kept theory grounded in reality.

Academic advice and inspiration came from Judith McClure, Ph.D., Boston Center for Adult Education; Carl Olsen, Ph.D., University of Denver; Courtney Price, Ph.D., Institute for Creativity and Entrepreneurship, Metropolitan State College, Denver; Eugene Raudsepp, Ed.D., Synectics Institute of Boston; and Phil Shaver, Ph.D., Syracuse University, New York.

It might sound trite, but it is true that without our team of publishing professionals this book would never have come to fruition. Alison Brown Cerier, our editor, is an absolute genius with change—editorial change. She guided us from the beginning of the writing of this book, and when it was finished, she deftly rearranged parts and made the book whole. Our thanks to her son, Alexander, who held off his arrival by one week, thereby enabling his mother to complete her editing of the manuscript. We were most fortunate to have creative and technical assistance from Ted Conover, author of *Rolling Nowhere* and *Coyote.* Barney Karpfinger, our efficient agent, believed in the book at first hearing and helped us define its content so that we were able to target the market we wanted to reach. As he did with our first book, Larry Kessenick, Houghton Mifflin, Boston, was a valued source of publishing advice and encouragement. Final touches of professionalism were added by Jerry Hunter, truly a writer's computer expert, and Curt Brogren, a quick and clever graphics designer.

Among family, certain individuals were especially helpful in providing information, feedback, and ideas in specific areas: Beth Conover, Julian D. Conover, Mike Donovan, Dan Mahoney, and Donovan Mahoney. Don Donovan's practical mind and willingness to help increased our flexibility tenfold and enabled us to do the impossible many times.

Other family members and friends stood by us through days and weeks when we were absorbed in "the book." Although we were often distracted and unavailable during much of the year it took to write the book, they continued their loving support.

And there were friends who were particularly diligent in feeding us many ideas, impressions, articles, and examples that are interwoven throughout the book. These cheerleaders and active contributors are: Jon Adams, Kurt Burghardt, Tom Cole, Sherry Dorward, Nan Fogel, Maurina Hickman, Nancy Martin, Pat McClearn, Chip Newell, Eric Skjei, Abe Wagner, and Patricia Wellingham Jones.

There were the hundreds of test takers who helped us fine-tune the book's Change-Friendly Quotient Survey, the T.E.A.M. Test, and the Corporate Change-Friendly Test. Their input vastly improved these instruments and made them more valuable to our research and more revealing to those who now take them in final form. These test takers are primarily from: ABN Banks, American Express Travel, AT&T, American Television and Communications Corp., Ball Corp., Celestial Seasonings, Coors Brewery, Citicorp, Dow-Corning, Gates Rubber Co., Hewlett-Packard, IBM, Kaiser Foundation Health Plan, Martin-Marietta, Mile-Hi Cable, Mountain States Employers Council, MCI, Neo Data, Petroleum Information, Premium Beverages, Professional Education Group, Rockwell International, Society for Value Engineers, Solar Energy Research Institute, Standard & Poor's, Storage Technology, Sundstrand Aviation, United Airlines, U.S. Forestry Service, and U.S. West.

Assessing the Change-Friendly Quotient Survey and our data were more than fifty professionals: psychiatrists, psychoanalysts, social workers, career counselors, human resource managers, and educators who helped us refine and verify our research.

There are those who inspired us without realizing it. Their views and published works informed and stimulated us in our quest to understand change. While there were many of these sources, those who were of special inspiration include: Drs. Barbara Brown, Marion Diamond, Erik Erikson, Alice Miller, Richard Restak, and Daniel Stern; researchers Thomas H. Budzynski, Ph.D., and Ned Herrmann; and authors Rosabeth Kanter and Judith Viorst.

At the risk of sounding like excited Academy Award winners, we would like to include the whole world in our acknowledgments. After all, it is the dynamic energy of *all* people we have noted and written about. It is their flexibility that has taught us what we know about successful change. It is the interaction between these varied peoples everywhere that keeps us changing—and, as we see it, improving.

Preface

When the winds of change blow, some people hunker down, batten the hatches, and try to ride out the storm. Others sniff the breeze, raise their sails, and lean into the powerful forward momentum. These and other ways of handling change came to our attention soon after our first book was published in 1984.

We were fascinated by the way different people handled the same kind of change with different levels of comfort and success. We asked: Why were some more resilient in the face of change? How do some people become so flexible? But soon we were so submerged in change ourselves that the answers wafted away. We felt thrilled by the success of *Whole-Brain Thinking* but distracted by the upheavals it created in our lives.

As the demand for workshops, speaking engagements, interviews, and consultations increased, we sought to handle them by going our separate ways. Separately, we pursued answers to the same questions: What is the nature of change and how can we use change rather than be used by it? Jacquelyn focused on change and the individual, and Priscilla explored many topics related to the brain's role in personal flexibility.

It was not until 1986 that we began to realize that we were again interested in the same phenomenon and that perhaps we had discovered the same answers guised in different terms. We took a fresh look at what we could do together. We established a new relationship based on a sincere appreciation for the talents we each have. We practiced within ourselves and on each other the techniques for making true change.

We are a case study in the value of flexibility in responding to radical change, in adapting to gradual change, and in initiating successful change. We know that the techniques we've described in this book work because we have lived them.

As we began to work together again, we realized that change itself was changing. Mergers, takeovers, and downsizing were sweeping the country; the global marketplace became a reality overnight; our beliefs about economic theory, ethics, and practices were under assault. We felt that individuals all over the country were in disarray over the effects of this new kind of change on their lives. We felt it ourselves and saw it all about us. We knew there was a need for practical ways to deal with change.

There were a number of good books about the effects of change on organizations, but we could find nothing to help us or others in the day-by-day struggle with plant closings, retraining, deregulation, and expansions. We witnessed the anxiety in clients facing these changes, and we experienced it ourselves. So we decided to write a book, not on the big picture of change, but about how individuals—how *you*—can develop the flexibility needed to gain from change.

This book is the result of what we learned about change and flexibility. It contains our perceptions and experiences and stories about the friends and clients we've encountered. You can learn something significant from each one of their stories. From them you can find new attitudes that will help you look at change in a positive way. You will get specific techniques that can help you handle change more effectively.

The first part of the book will help raise your awareness of change and how you handle it. In Chapter 2, you will get a measure of your "change-friendliness." You'll discover whether you deal with change in the manner of a Risker, Relater, Refocuser, or Reasoner. You'll learn about four successful change-makers: how they experienced everything from a dreadful accident to a humiliating surprise yet found opportunity in change. In this section you'll also learn about pseudochange, an intriguing human frailty that occasionally gets in the way of making productive change.

Part 2 focuses on how psychological flexibility develops within you. There is a survey to help you evaluate where you might have barriers to change. In Chapter 7, through a drama of the mind called "The Wickersham Dilemma," you learn what actually happens in the brain when you decide to change or are made to change. You'll also discover what kinds of activities help you be more flexible in your thinking. You'll end the chapter with an amusing exercise that will reach many parts of your brain.

In the next part, you'll get specific techniques for change. First, you'll tune up your intuition and other anticipation skills, then move on to ways for responding to sudden changes and for adapting to gradual change. Finally you'll tackle initiating change. All these techniques are illustrated by the stories of real people. For example, you'll discover how a forty-year-old, slightly-decrepit, out-of-work developer became a city's most popular man and how a company survived, even thrived, after losing a fortune *and* its charismatic leader.

The fourth section of the book focuses on organizations. What you learned in the earlier sections about personal change is paralleled at the organizational level. You'll find that companies suffer loss and renewal, growth and decline. And you'll discover that the techniques individuals in our workshops found so effective can also be used successfully by companies, institutions, firms, and agencies.

The Flexibility Factor is a map to guide you in increasing your flexibility and mastering change. It is drawn from the experiences of many explorers including the authors. But developing the flexibility to master change is a do-it-yourself project. As you begin your journey, take heart in knowing that others have passed this way before you and succeeded. You will gain confidence and momentum with each step you take.

PART ONE

The Nature of Change and Changemakers

1

The Kairos in Change

Memory implants and genetic manipulation. Doctors threatened by malpractice suits. Seven-year-old computer whizzes. Fast-food restaurants on every corner. Grandmas bicycling through Europe. Lawyers and hospitals using Madison Avenue techniques to sell their services. Cellular phones and answering machines. Fiber optics and superconductors. Russia's glasnost and perestroika. Fathers taking maternity leave.

On the more personal side: You lose your job. You have a child. A friend confides he's been exposed to AIDs. You buy your first pair of bifocals. You get a big promotion. Your company starts a fabulous on-site day-care center. Your close friends are retiring. You're suddenly the oldest person in your social set.

At work, your company is in turmoil after a hostile takeover. You have to plan a year ahead, but your current best-selling product will be antiquated in six months. You are a training manager who has to prepare employees for jobs that don't yet exist.

How does the human spirit survive and even thrive in such chaos? The answer lies in flexibility—the ability to bend without breaking. Flexibility makes it possible to adapt or respond to change, to be influenced, to make modifications and variations.

Flexibility is a characteristic vital to all forms of life, to structures, and to systems. In nature, the species that adapt to changes in the environment are the ones that grow stronger. And manmade structures that survive, are likewise flexible. The following page from history shows flexibility in both people and their works.

Learning from Shock

The view from San Francisco's forty-three hills was grim on April 18, 1906. Amid fire, collapsing buildings, and lurching landscapes, seven hundred people died in an earthquake that registered 8.3 on the Richter scale. The fires raged for three days and destroyed the city's entire core.

San Francisco rebuilt quickly and *differently.* Engineers hunted for clues in the city's surviving structures. They studied the construction methods of Japan, a country perched on a giant earthquake epicenter. They found one factor common to buildings that survive: flexibility in design. Thus emerged techniques for earthquake-proof construction with built-in flexibility. These improvements feature a strong inner core surrounded by sections that are connected by expandable wires. When wind, quakes, and explosions occur, these sinews accommodate the violent expansions and contractions.

And so, the horror and devastation of San Francisco's great earthquake provided an impetus for advances in architectural design and safer building codes.

A parallel can be drawn to great upheavals in our lives. In fact, all the major theories of adult development recognize that there is a predictable growth that occurs with crisis. Without crisis, no growth occurs. But without flexibility, crisis can lead to destruction. Those of us who are flexible not only can survive life's disruptions but can also gain from them. Every tremor we experience offers us a chance to change for the better in the spirit of *kairos,* a Greek word meaning "auspicious moment for opportunity."

Is this Greek perception of change new to you? What does change mean to you? The following words are those most frequently associated with change. Please circle the ones that express your view of it:

improve	upheaval	evolving	disrupt
alter	pennies	new	replace
exchange	aging	action	substitute
modify	transfer	vary	act on
transform	better	transition	shake
exciting	initiate	fun	young
challenge	risky	birth	opportunity
sunset	daybreak	heavy	awesome
different	learn	stress	convert
deteriorate	redress	switch	fearsome
redo	wonder	opportunity	chance

Look at the words you circled and see if there's a pattern. Are most of them pleasant reflections of change? Are they troublesome? Are they neutral?

To some of us, change is all positives. To others, it has negative connotations. Still others regard change as a mix of positives and negatives. If your experiences with change usually have brought defeat, change will seem burdensome. If you've had great results with change, you'll see it through rose-colored glasses. Actually, both views are valid and valuable, because avoiding unproductive change is nearly as important as welcoming change.

People often say they want to change, but in reality we all resist it a lot more than we realize. As Moms Mabley, the television comedian, sang: "Everybody wants to go to heaven, but nobody wants to die." That is, we all want the positive results which change may bring, but we resist the often painful process that gets us there.

In more than sixty organizations we've worked with since 1984, the key ingredient we've seen in successful operations is flexibility. Flexibility in management style and policies. Openness to new ideas and technology. A willingness to adapt to changing demographics. An appreciation for variety in how people think and behave.*

Such flexible attitudes were easy to observe in our creativity workshops. We paired people with different abilities and thinking styles and found that those most open to the ideas of unlike partners produced the most unique and useful solutions to problems. Even those who initially resisted hearing out others and trying new methods were eventually able to produce better plans with unlike partners than when working alone or with like-minded partners.

At the personal level, those who were more flexible were able to handle change most successfully. For example, in a year's time, one corporation manager negotiated the coming out of his gay child, the dissolution of the company he founded, and sizable stock market losses from Black Monday. Not only did he cope with these changes, he grew from them. While he'd always been sensitive to discrimination, he is now a firm but gentle advocate for the rights of all. And his new company is a model in equal opportunities where all employees own and participate in running the organization.

As you begin to negotiate change in your life, keep in mind that you're entitled to disorganization and confusion. They are signs of health. Sometimes they are the side effects that make you resistant to a change, even though you earnestly want the final outcome.

---

*What characteristics are key to success in various professions? The studies below all include "flexibility" or some version of it: *Journal of Police Science and Administration* (1983) states, "The success of this type of police organization lies with its flexibility and adaptability to changing conditions . . ." And in *Hospital and Community Psychiatry* (1979): "The lack of administrative flexibility led to increased conflicts and decreased community and political support." Again: "Flexibility and the ability to tolerate frustration are prime personality requirements" (*Mental Health Administration Journal,* 1986). From the American Medical Association by-laws: "Flexibility in rules is needed." Eight issues of *The Harvard Business Review* (May–June 1977 to May–June 1988) observe that "significant increases in productivity are found where management has free rein to deploy workers in the most flexible manner."

But such blocks can be overcome by successful experiences that give you faith in your ability to be flexible and an appreciation for the good it can bring.

Once you have success with change, you will realize you need not be its helpless victim—you can be an agent for positive change.

Changing can be a way of taking charge, of getting in the driver's seat, and of predicting your life's path while everything around you is unpredictable.

Radical Change

How do you get in the driver's seat? First, it helps to understand the dynamics of change.

People change in three different ways. The first is through the shock of *radical* or imposed change. The second is through *adaptive* or gradual change. The third is through *initiated* or self-directed change.

Radical change comes in many forms: You get a divorce, you lose your job, you have a heart attack—all forcing you to change. These are crises that shake you mentally, physically, and emotionally. But the shock can also be an awakening and an opportunity —if you are listening.

Some of these shocking changes are so sudden and cruel they literally take your breath away. Doris Lake, thirty-eight, gave five years of her life to her job, and her company gave her a five-minute lay-off speech and half an hour to be out the door. "And don't take anything confidential with you," her supervisor said in parting.

Even a year later, there was still shock and disbelief in her voice as she described the scene: "In five minutes' time, five years were written off." Doris is a short, sturdy, dark-haired woman who looks invincible until she talks about being fired from her job as a systems analyst for cost control in a Tucson bank.

"I suddenly felt like I was in a refrigerator. I was chilled to the bone and could barely breathe. I laid in bed the entire first day trying to get warm," she said, her blue eyes filling with tears.

"I was literally in a state of shock . . . and felt that way for a long time afterward. There were days I'd do nothing, other times I'd race around frantically trying to find a job. My mood swings went from the peaks (when I thought I had a job prospect) to the pits. Not hearing back after job interviews added insult to injury. It drained my energy and confidence."

Finally, she sought counseling and took a change test at an Arizona women's resource center. After taking the Change-Friendly Quotient Survey that we had devised, she realized how restrictive her work environment at the bank had been. She began to see that the job had actually been an impediment to her personal growth and happiness.

"I started thinking of the other talents and interests I have," she says today. "I realized I had an entrepreneurial instinct and a wealth of business smarts. Combining these with my systems experience, I set up my own computer consulting business to serve individuals and small companies. Now I'll never need to depend on a corporate employer for my job security again."

In a more reflective moment, she concluded, "I like being in charge of my own life. Getting fired from the bank is the best thing that ever happened to me."

Doris developed this take-charge attitude as a result of the rude shock of being laid off. She found inner resources she didn't know existed, and she's a happier, more confident person as a result. After initial suffering and counseling, she found a new career opportunity in the change that had rocked her life.

Adaptive Change

The second kind of change, one we experience daily, is a more gradual and evolving process. Flexible people respond to it quite naturally. They look around and see new events and relationships, and they adjust almost automatically.

The changing environment itself supplies the motivation for change and provokes positive action. A case in point is Nigel Thomas, a tall, slender Houston lawyer who devoted most of his seventy-hour weeks to providing services to oil and gas clients.

"Nigel wasn't the kind of guy you 'howdyed' up to," recalls an office neighbor. "In fact, people used to tiptoe past his office door rather than be caught in the vortex of his busy-ness and sometimes biting humor."

Nigel had grown up in Oklahoma in a family of professionals. Their high standards produced in him a glow of intensity and energy. He was mostly work and no play. His analytical style and feeling of responsibility to clients led him to focus on every conceivable legal detail, to identify every possible problem, and to omit nothing. At times, his clients would become alarmed by the sheer number of issues he spotted.

However, when the energy boom faded in Houston, Nigel's work tapered to half of what it had been the year before. He found himself with fewer client deadlines and more time on his hands —time to think about his working style, his values, and his future.

"I was uncomfortable without work," he said recently, "and yet I felt a sense of freedom I'd not had since college days. I'd stare out my office window and notice the funny things people did as they walked by. I began working out at the Y down the street.

"I made adjustments at the office. I dropped my parking space and rode the bus or bicycled to work. I sublet half of my office space and gave up one of my telephones. I cut back on memberships and magazines. These and other reductions in my overhead really reduced the pressure on me," Nigel observed.

"Actually, the extra time has changed the way I do business. Since I have more time to spend with each of my clients, I'm getting to know them as *people,* not just billable resources. Now I *rate* their concerns, pointing out which are the most important to them. I'm sure I do a better job now that I understand more about my clients. Besides, working with people, not just legal issues, is much more satisfying.

"It's funny how one change gradually leads to another. The reduction in my work hours means I'm spending more time with my family—doing things spontaneously like playing catch with my eleven-year-old son or going for a walk."

Nigel became more approachable and more aware of the opportunities around him. A year later, he met a Houston news anchorman and was reminded of his teenage ambition to be a radio announcer. He began listening to the local stations to find out where he might fit in.

Today, Nigel has an auxiliary career hosting a talk-show program on law that allows him to display his fine voice, ready wit, and legal expertise. It adds joy and variety to his week and clients to his practice, which has now broadened to many different, interesting areas.

"Once I had a little air in my schedule, all sorts of new options opened up to me," he says today, four years later. "I'll never return to that old, rigid way of life."

Apparently, Nigel was more flexible than he had appeared to his office neighbors. His ability to adapt to the downturn in business led to his discovery of the possibilities inherent in change.

Initiated Change

People such as Nigel, with a high flexibility factor, are ready for the third and most sophisticated level of change—initiated change. An example of such a person is Mary O'Brien, a vibrant woman of thirty-two whose tasteful wardrobe and slim figure advertise her career in clothes merchandising.

"I'm a clotheshorse by breeding. My parents and grandparents *loved* clothes," she joked recently. "So when Rob, my husband, entered medical school at Georgetown University, my first thought was to work at the mecca of retail fashion, Bloomingdale's."

Her enthusiasm for clothes and retailing served her well. When Rob finished school, they moved to Rochester, N.Y., for his internship. Her experience got her instant employment with a New York–based clothing store chain. She advanced rapidly and soon was buying for a line of designer clothing.

When she and Rob bought their first home in the Park Avenue area and financed a second car, their lives stabilized for the first time. When her sister and sister-in-law and friends started families, Mary felt a yearning for children of her own. Suddenly, she saw babies and pregnant women everywhere. Her parents' hints for grandchildren became wishes for her own children.

But she felt a conflict between career and family. "Both Rob and I always wanted children when we could afford them, but when the time came, I was reluctant to lose my toehold in a career I very much enjoy." Furthermore, she dreaded tampering with the satisfying companionship she and Rob enjoyed as DINKS (Double Income, No Kids).

But it wasn't until she participated in our Change Workshop that she was able to resolve the conflict and get on with starting her family. A workshop technique enabled her to see how she would like her life to be in three years:

1. I'd like to be mother of a six-month-old infant.

2. I'd like to coordinate my interests in motherhood and children with my career.

3. I'd like to be my own boss but still have a circle of business associates to talk shop with.

4. I'd like to have at least the earnings I now have.

5. I'd like to be recognized as an authority on clothing trends.

Quite an order—but Mary achieved all of it and more. The tiny tremors going on in Mary's psyche furnished the impetus for her to *initiate* change. Whenever she traveled, Mary made it a point to pop into children's and maternity stores. She felt fabrics and noted styles. She discussed wearing apparel and equipment for babies and mothers with her friends and family. She looked for trends in baby clothes to see if they paralleled those of adults.

Soon Mary realized that while every area of adult clothing design was covered, there was a huge gap in meeting the needs of children (and their parents). Most of the baby clothes lacked the pizzazz young people were accustomed to in their own wardrobes. Items that did have the designer touch were short on convenience. They didn't have snaps for easy diapering, and the natural fabrics required hours of ironing.

As Mary immersed herself in this world, she began to fantasize how a store would look that catered to infant, toddler, and preschool children's needs as well as their mothers'. She saw her relatives working there, the store's color scheme and floor plan, and, finally, a franchise operation.

To date, Mary has a good start on her new way of life. She has a baby, Philip Andrew, and a business plan for her Mother-Baby Shoppe. She's negotiating for test sites in Rochester and working with a marketing specialist. She's currently in touch with a Japanese investment firm and several venture-capital investors.

Mary found she could have a family and an even more satisfying career than she'd thought possible. "I'm eating my cake and having it too," she says smilingly these days.

People like Mary are pretty change-friendly. If you've had similar successes, you are to be congratulated on your ability to initiate productive change.

Step by Step to Greater Flexibility

You are several chapters from learning details of the process that helped Mary resolve to change her life and find fulfillment in doing so. But you are just one step away from beginning the journey that can help you become more adaptable and flexible in the way you think and behave. This first step is to recognize whether the current change in your life is a radical, imposed one; an evolving, gradual, adaptive one; one you are initiating; or all three at one time (for example, a car wreck may force you to adapt to life without your driver's license and to initiate an effort to decipher your city's bus schedules).

The next chapter measures how change-friendly you and your environment are. You will then learn your changemaking strengths and weaknesses and how to build on those strengths. The information in Part 2 will clarify what change does to you physically and psychologically, and Part 3 provides techniques for implementing change. Part 4 applies the same principles to organizations. Somewhere along the way, you will feel the thrill of kairos. You'll discover a moment of auspicious opportunity and use it!

The fact that you are reading a book on change suggests you may be facing some unsettling experiences that open you to change and make you willing to consider new ways of handling it. Such a willingness to examine your own skills indicates a potential for flexibility. Often this openness goes hand in hand with the discipline necessary to become an effective changemaker. You have made a good beginning and can make important changes in your life.

The Flexibility Factor gives you a clear, practical guide for accomplishing these changes. Although change by nature is uncomfortable, this book will make the process stimulating and beguiling. And the process begins now: Each chapter of the first two parts ends with a brief summary that suggests specific activities to help you use what you have learned. This way, you are actually reviewing and practicing the main idea of the chapter. Step by step, you are changing as you go.

Step 1: Identify specific instances in your life when you have experienced the three kinds of change: radical, adaptive, and initiated. Your awareness of change is the first step toward successful changemaking.

2

Your Change-Friendly Quotient

Jessica Turner saw herself as a *very* change-friendly person. She prided herself on being in the forefront of new ideas, techniques, and skills. As a management consultant, she met with different clients, representing different products in different places every day. "I like change," she often said. "It's stimulating, exciting. I thrive on it!"

Then one day at her regular tennis drill, her coach said: "Jessica, the only way I'm going to get you to change your grip is to tape your hand to the racquet." He had repeatedly tried to shift her grip from a handshake position to topside so that her serve would be more difficult to return. "It seemed like a workable solution, but frankly, I was irritated," she confessed.

Driving to work that morning, Jessica reflected on his comment. "Gee, I guess I'm not as open to change as I thought."

Jessica is no different from the rest of us. Most of us have areas in our lives where we are very flexible and other areas where we are not.

The test that follows will help you discover how open you are to change at present.

HISTORY OF THE CHANGE-FRIENDLY QUOTIENT SURVEY

The Change-Friendly Quotient Survey was refined over a four-year period as we researched how individuals respond to and initiate change. Part 1 is based on a 1984 version that loosely correlated left/right brain style to one's ability to create and change. It was administered to 680 health-care professionals. Based on feedback from this test, revisions were made and the test was used with 280 workshop participants and clients during 1986. In 1987 we made changes to include the work of Dr. Milton Rokeach regarding dogmatism* and Dr. Silvano Arieti's correlations among flexibility, mental health, and creativity.† We also consulted with Dr. Michael A. Solomon in the final wording of Parts 1, 2, and 3. Early in 1988, the survey took its present form with the addition of the home and work checklists. Since then, it has been administered to approximately one thousand workshop participants. Thirty professionals in mental and health care, education, and business have taken the survey and consider it a useful, viable method for determining a person's flexibility in managing change.

*Rokeach, Milton, *The Open and Closed Mind* (New York: Basic Books, 1960).
†Arieti, Silvano, *Creativity, the Magic Synthesis* (New York: Basic Books, 1976).

The Change-Friendly Quotient Survey

PART 1: YOU

In the situations described below, four reactions or coping methods are given. Put yourself in each scene and check all those responses you would actually use, leaving blank the ones you would rarely or never use. Also, write the number "1" by your favorite response.

1. If I were asked to choose the designs I find pleasing from those below, I would select:
   a. _____ b. _____ c. _____ d. _____

2. If my company reduced our insurance benefits package, I would:

   a. _____ talk to the benefits officer about it.
   b. _____ discuss it with others to see if they feel as I do about it.
   c. _____ seek additional insurance to compensate for lost benefits.
   d. _____ wonder if my company is in financial trouble; review my career options.

3. If a friend/colleague canceled our luncheon at the last possible moment, I would:

   a. _____ confront the person about his or her behavior.
   b. _____ ask around to see if this person has canceled with others.

    c. _____ think what to do with the free time and how it affects my schedule.

    d. _____ assess whether there was a good reason for canceling.

4. If I were sent for training in a field totally new to me, I would:

    a. _____ look forward to learning something entirely new.

    b. _____ get information from others who've had the training.

    c. _____ bone up on information that would help me with it.

    d. _____ evaluate how useful it would be to me.

5. If I were transferred to another city, I would:

    a. _____ picture myself living and working there.

    b. _____ find out more about the place by talking to everyone.

    c. _____ call a realtor to settle the housing issue.

    d. _____ review the social, personal, and financial pros and cons.

6. If I were to notice one of my parents' health declining, I would:

    a. _____ contact my parent's doctor for an opinion.

    b. _____ talk it through with parents, relatives, and friends.

    c. _____ read up on the illness and its symptoms.

    d. _____ try to determine how serious it really is.

7. If an important relationship suddenly ended to my surprise, I would:

    a. _____ become more active socially, plunge into new interests; develop a new skill.

    b. _____ join support group on breakups; talk to others who've "been there."

    c. _____ transfer my energy to areas of my life that are going well.

     d. ____ figure out what caused the breakup and, perhaps, consult an expert.

8. If my favorite newspaper columnist were dropped, I would:

     a. ____ call the editor and ask for an explanation.
     b. ____ read the replacement column and compare with my favorite.
     c. ____ begin a letter-writing campaign to get the column reinstated.
     d. ____ recall past columns to find reasons for the cancellation.

9. If a project I had devised were rejected, I would:

     a. ____ protest and try to dissuade objectors.
     b. ____ confer with others, then go "back to the drawing board."
     c. ____ give it up if objections seem legitimate and move on.
     d. ____ study the project design for possible flaws.

10. If a friend wore an inappropriate outfit, I would:

     a. ____ smile and say "more power to you."
     b. ____ ask others for their reactions to it.
     c. ____ caution him or her about wearing it to work.
     d. ____ worry about my friend but do nothing.

11. If I were delayed in traffic thirty minutes on my way to an important appointment, I would:

     a. ____ try to find a shortcut or new route.
     b. ____ rehearse explanations in my mind.
     c. ____ try to find a phone to notify someone of my delay.
     d. ____ assess how to turn the situation to my advantage.

12. If I were asked twenty minutes before a meeting to describe a project for which I'm responsible, I would:

a. ____ welcome the chance to make an impact; dream up a dramatic way to present it.

b. ____ ask others on my team for their input; conceptualize a brief overview.

c. ____ tune out everything going on around me; outline the essential information.

d. ____ decline until I have time to prepare more fully.

13. If I were challenged when discussing a topic I know well, I would:

a. ____ relish the controversy if the challenger is witty and friendly.

b. ____ ask the challenger to say more about his or her views, then paraphrase to further clarify.

c. ____ compare our points of view and attempt to get consensus.

d. ____ review how I came to my conclusions; wonder if the challenger has more data.

____   ____   ____   ____
  a   b   c   d

To score, add the number of *first* choices you checked in a, b, c, and d and enter above.

Now, enter the grand total of all the responses you checked: _____.

*   *   *

What's in Part 1?

You have just completed the first section of a three-part survey that helps you determine your overall flexibility in managing change. This section is composed of questions that tease out your attitudes toward various kinds of change.

As you review this first section, you can see that it includes everything from a measure of your taste in design to how you cope with minor and major changes in your routine.

Four different reactions are offered for each situation. All of them are valid, normal, and effective ways of managing change. Therefore, checking all four alternatives indicates that you are very flexible in the type of situation described and have many options in dealing with that kind of change.

KNOW Your Change Style

Can you see a pattern in your first choices? Each line (a, b, c, or d) represents a style for responding to change. If most of your first choice answers were in line a, your change style is usually enthusiastic, spontaneous, and daring. We call someone in line a the Risker.

If most were in line b, you rely on your friends, family, and others for information and advice in processing change. Because you relate to others so well, line b represents the Relater.

If your responses were in c, you focus your energies and like to finish one thing at a time. So line c stands for the Refocuser.

If most were in d, your attitude toward change is studied and careful, your style logical and orderly. This style is for the Reasoner.

How might people with the different styles approach the same kind of task? For example, how might each person learn to ski? Risker just jumps in and skis. He makes the most progress under pressure, so he constantly challenges himself. He learns by doing.

A Relater learns best by getting tips on techniques from advanced skiers or instructors and responds best to sensory hints. For example, to improve Relater's turns, you'd say, "To carve your turns and keep them in control on ice, press down with your feet and pretend you're squeezing an orange half beneath your skis."

Refocuser tunes out everything else and tunes into all the visual sensations and every contour on the slope. His approach is concentrated and intense.

Reasoner first conducts a thorough investigation of the sport and purchases state-of-the-art equipment. She wants step-by-step instructions and is forever on the lookout for ways to make it easier to ski.

Risker

If most of your first choices are in line a, you are a Risker, someone who is decisive about making change. You are a risk-taker either mentally or physically (and sometimes both). You are the leader who has learned to lead by leading, the changemaker who has learned how to do by doing. Your comfort with risk allows you to make great leaps forward when massive changes are required. Generally an extrovert, you are visual and action-oriented and may find yourself being impatient with gathering details. Your energy and intuition will often help you handle changes easily, but when you make an error, it can be a whopper.

Relater

If most of your first choices are in line b, you are a Relater and are rather like a poll-taker. Since you relate well to people, when faced with change you will seek out the opinions of others instead of researching facts and focusing on details. You alter your own attitudes in response to others. Because of your sensitivity to people, you are especially successful in influencing others to change. You consult with professionals, friends, family, and the person on the street. This approach is effective as long as you stop at some point and actually make the necessary change. But excessive poll-taking can leave you confused and dispirited; if you get too many conflicting views, the task of sorting them out can become overwhelming.

Re-Focuser

A preponderance of first choices in line c means that you are a goal-oriented Refocuser. While you have strongly held attitudes towards change, you periodically review and revise your way of doing things, usually in response to a problem. When involved in change, you are practical and focus on achieving tangible benefits. Even when interrupted or offered a pleasant diversion, you can quickly refocus on your task. Your intense concentration makes you extremely effective in getting things done and unshakable even under pressure. But occasionally you may overlook important details or circumstances. You might behave like the plumber who was so intent upon installing the new plumbing and appliances during a kitchen renovation that he failed to notice clues that the water heater was building pressure. Just as he completed the beautiful designer kitchen, the hot water tank blew up, spattering the pristine white decor with rusty water.

REASONER

Line d is most often checked by the analytical Reasoner, who approaches change thoughtfully. If you are a Reasoner, you base your attitudes and responses to change on past experiences and on information you carefully search out. Before undertaking change, you spend a great deal of energy on this research, making sure you have a thorough understanding of all the implications of the change. You are particularly skillful in dealing with change that requires organization. If you were planning a cross-country move, you'd have inventories and flowcharts for each phase. While others find this kind of planning for change tedious, you thrive on it. Your tendency to over-plan can be a pitfall when you irritate those you're working with or when you become so enamored with information-gathering that you never act.

For a vivid, colorful way of remembering the distinctions among these four types of changemakers, you might relate each to a popular television news host or interviewer:

Risker—Sam Donaldson
Relater—Barbara Walters
Refocuser—Ted Koppel
Reasoner—George Will

Sam Donaldson typifies the Risker in the way he interviews. As a White House reporter, he is well known for his probing, blunt questions and forthright challenges to the President and his staff. He is always polite, but he frequently manages to push those he interviews to the very edge of outright anger. He is witty but uses humor to provoke ad lib answers. Although he is well versed in the facts, he asks his questions with reckless abandon, perfectly willing to be chastised by the President or anyone else he is interviewing.

The media Relater is Barbara Walters, who specializes in getting big stories by grazing through many topics with each interviewee. She is famous for her ability to ask personal questions that elicit information her guest may never have meant to reveal. Evidence of her penchant for poll-taking is the title of a book she wrote, *How to Talk with Practically Anybody About Practically Anything* (Doubleday, 1983). Quite often, she weaves information from several interviews into one large, colorful tapestry. She uses a classic Relater method for change: talking to many people and melding her findings into one grand outcome.

The format of Ted Koppel's interview program, *Nightline,* has a Refocuser approach. It dissects one topic each night and features different experts on a specific topic. In a polite but persistent manner, Koppel keeps his guests on target with "But, sir, you haven't answered my question." He controls the interview to ensure in-depth coverage of that night's topic. The next evening, he shifts to another topic and gives it the same thorough attention.

George Will looks like a Reasoner. His glasses and oval face give him an owlish look. His formal clothes and soft-spoken, carefully researched questions and opinions all fit perfectly with the data-gathering change style of the Reasoner. When you look more deeply at this studious looking fellow, you will see the lighter side of a Reasoner: the ability to turn a clever phrase, a fast and intellectual wit, and a passion for baseball and family life.

Most likely, all four of these successful broadcasters use all four change styles at times. They may have one style at home and another for work. Most of us do. This enables us to keep balance in our lives. If you are a Reasoner at work, you need some Relater and Risker experiences during the weekend to keep your attitude flexible, to keep the creative juices flowing, and to accommodate the needs of your family.

In a syndicated column he wrote after attending the play *Les Misérables,* George Will describes just such a shift from his usual Reasoner style to the Risker: "One half of your brain—the sober, rational conservative half—says of the production: This is mawk-ish, sub-Dickensian sentimentality and pernicious twaddle, and we are being shamelessly manipulated. The squishy liberal side of your brain says: Yeah, and isn't it fun!"‡

Those who handle great change successfully seem to shift automatically to their primary style but have an overall balance between styles. Here are some examples from our workshops:

- Of 120 volunteers for a Florida association that had lost its funding, forty-five were Relaters and forty were Refocusers, twenty Riskers and fifteen Reasoners—a good balance for overcoming their financing problems.

- Fifty-one percent of a group of 160 judges were balanced as individuals in all four change categories on the test—not surprising for those whose career requires valuing all points of view.

- Forty-two out of fifty engineers and computer technicians working for AT&T in the early years of divestiture tested out as half Refocuser and half Relater—a useful combina-tion for restructuring products for a competitive market.

- Each person in a group of female engineers and resource managers at Martin Marietta scored 25 percent in each change style category—an indication of a team of truly balanced individuals.

- Sixty percent of the new managers hired by the Allied Bank of Netherlands were Refocusers—an indication that the bank had found the leaders it needed to change direction.

From these examples of the four broadcasters and the Change-Friendly Quotients for successful changemakers, you can see that all four categories offer viable ways of dealing with change but that optimum performance comes from using many styles. A company can achieve this by balancing the team. You can start to reach this

‡Will, George, *Washington Post* Writers' Group, *Rocky Mountain News,* Jan. 8, 1987.

same kind of balance at the personal level by noticing which categories need your attention. The ideal configuration for this part of the test shows a favorite style but also includes an ability to use the other three styles comfortably. As you look at this gauge of your personal flexibility, notice where you might start flexing your change muscles.

Two more sections of the Change-Friendly Quotient Survey follow and assess home and work influences on your flexibility. Part 2 looks at your home life, and Part 3 surveys your work environment.

PART 2: HOME

Check all options that apply to you at home:

1. Household tasks

    _____ I perform chores that are nontraditional for my sex.
    _____ My spouse/roommate shares household tasks with me.
    _____ Other persons in my household help with these duties.
    _____ I hire regular household help.
    _____ I sometimes use food delivery services (pizza, groceries).
    _____ I usually have the latest household appliances.

2. Vacations

    _____ I sometimes vacation alone.
    _____ I sometimes visit relatives and/or friends.
    _____ I have a scheduled vacation each year.
    _____ I vacation with my spouse/roommate regularly.
    _____ I sometimes add vacation excursions to my business trips.
    _____ I sometimes go on the spur of the moment.
    _____ I have a place to retreat to (mountains, shore).
    _____ I travel abroad.

3. Transportation

    _____ I drive to and from work alone.
    _____ Because work and shopping are nearby, I can bicycle there.
    _____ Train, bus, and/or rapid transit are available and affordable.
    _____ I can carpool to work.
    _____ I can share transportation with friends for errands.
    _____ I have a company car (or company carpool, etc.).
    _____ My schedule allows me to travel to work when traffic is light.

_____ I am not responsible for transporting children, relatives, or friends.

4. Finances

_____ There are other income earners in my household.
_____ I have income other than my working wages.
_____ My income has some incentive features.
_____ I could earn money from non-job activities (crafts, singing).
_____ My career is on the upswing.
_____ My spouse's career is on the upswing.
_____ I normally have a comfortable margin of discretionary income.
_____ I am eligible for a retirement plan.
_____ I get money from such sources as alimony, vet's benefits, etc.
_____ I have investments.
_____ Credit and/or venture capital are accessible to me.

5. Meals

_____ I eat a wide variety of foods from simple meals to ethnic dishes, to gourmet.
_____ Menus are not the same as they were five years ago.
_____ Other members of the household usually like to try new things.
_____ Because I frequently dine alone, I am free to eat what I like.
_____ More than one person prepares meals in my household.
_____ I have a variety of cooking methods (oven, microwave, barbecue, crockpot).
_____ I sometimes dine out and use fast food, take-out, and food delivery services.
_____ I sometimes use caterers.

6. Social occasions

_____ My entertainment frequently involves ideas from new friends.

_____ Holidays include many traditional family customs.
_____ I have a wide variety of friends from many backgrounds.
_____ I like to plan outings that are different (tennis-barbecue party or an old-time movie review with popcorn and Popsicles).
_____ My spouse/roommate has friends whom we entertain frequently.
_____ I'm comfortable in most social groups.
_____ I usually decide on my own which social events to attend.

7. Communication with my spouse, significant other, or best friend

_____ We clearly and directly state our needs to each other.
_____ We use humor to communicate.
_____ We use sarcasm and teasing to communicate.
_____ We often understand each other intuitively.
_____ We have specific times to catch up on each other's activities and thoughts.
_____ I have reliable friends for rap sessions.

How many options did you check in this section? _____ (add 5 points if you live alone).

PART 3: WORK

Check all options that relate to you at work.

1. Work tasks

_____ Roles change frequently.
_____ Whoever brings up an idea gets to follow through.

_____ Job descriptions are frequently stretched to fit the situation.
_____ We have employees who job share.
_____ We are able to use outside consultants when needed.
_____ We do a lot of cross-training.
_____ Each staff member has a variety of skills.

2. Work hours

_____ We/I vary work schedules.
_____ Schedules can be changed fairly easily.
_____ We are task/time-oriented in crunches, self-directed otherwise.
_____ We/I adapt schedules to individual needs when possible.
_____ We/I have part-time employees.
_____ We are on flex-time.

3. Meetings

_____ We take turns in conducting the meeting.
_____ We have agendas, but they're not sacrosanct.
_____ We are all consulted about the agenda.
_____ There are very few mandatory meetings.
_____ If someone is up against a deadline, he or she need not attend.
_____ Anyone who is concerned about an issue may call a meeting.

4. Management style of my workplace

_____ There are always several people authorized to make decisions.
_____ Our CEO has an open door policy.
_____ I make 90 percent of the decisions about my work without consulting with a superior.
_____ When I've made mistakes, management has backed me to the hilt.
_____ We/I have a suggestion box or something similar.
_____ We have a company newsletter.
_____ We/I have functions such as sport events, celebrations, and retreats.
_____ Lines of communication are unrestricted.

5. Problem solving

    ____ The company is open to taking risks.
    ____ No idea is too silly to be considered.
    ____ There is time for pet projects.
    ____ We/I brainstorm regularly.
    ____ Resources for new projects are available.
    ____ New products and techniques have high priority.
    ____ Extra effort and innovation are rewarded.

6. Work setting

    ____ We/I have ample and up-to-date office equipment.
    ____ Conveniences such as restaurants and banks are accessible.
    ____ Office decor is up to the individual.
    ____ There is work space/room for special projects.
    ____ There is space for relaxation and/or exercise.

7. Benefits

    ____ There is an adequate training budget.
    ____ Work-related expenses are reimbursed.
    ____ Vacation and sick leave policies are flexible.
    ____ Convenient company parking is available.
    ____ My company is well known and respected.

How many options did you check in this section? ____ (add 5 points if you are self-employed).

You now have evaluations for three aspects of your Change-Friendly Quotient. Transfer those totals to this chart. Double your score for Part 1 (You).

Part 1 – You _____ /104
Part 2 – Home _____ /54
Part 3 – Work _____ /44
Total _____ /202

The total is your Change-Friendly Quotient.

If you have a high total score (170 or more), you are Change-Friendly and have many options for dealing with change. To interpret your overall score, use the following guideline:

170–202—You are extremely flexible. You can use the test results to build on existing strengths.

130–170—You have a fair degree of adaptability. You can look to the test to identify secondary styles.

100–130—You will want to focus on the one area where you can most easily increase your flexibility.

Under 100—You may have a restrictive environment and might want to develop more personal flexibility to compensate.

*   *   *

What's in Parts 2 and 3?

The more statements you check in Part 2, the more flexibility you have in your home life. For example, if you are married and your spouse is very flexible about meals, schedules, and housekeeping, your home environment score will be high. However, if your spouse is picky about food, has rigid standards for cleanliness, and lives by the clock, your home environment is less change-friendly.

If you live alone, your scores on personal flexibility and home environment will often be at the same level. Since you need not consult with someone else on matters of day-to-day living, your behavior at home reflects your own attitudes toward change. For example, you can eat what you want, when and where you feel like it.

If your score in home environment is proportionately much lower than in the two other sections of the test, you'll know that this area is prime for expansion.

Part 3 makes the same kind of diagnosis of your work environment. If your scores in Parts 1 and 2 are proportionately much higher, you will know that your work environment is the place to start your expansion efforts.

It's fairly obvious that the flexibility of your work environment is very much dependent upon the management style of your boss or major client, the policies and financial health of your company, and the skills and attitudes of your coworkers.

If you are self-employed, an entrepreneur, or the executive

officer, then your work environment is more likely to reflect your own attitudes toward change. When you're calling the shots in your work environment, then the two scores, personal and work, are apt to be similar.

Here again, being on your own does not automatically invest you with maximum flexibility. The one-man-band retailer is often too busy to find new and helpful resources and ways of doing things, so the Mom and Pop store is twice as adaptable. But the supermarket with strong financial backing that offers flowers, videotapes, and hardware provides even more retailing flexibility.

The 3-Way Stretch

The Change-Friendly Quotient Survey was designed to give you a quick reading of your overall flexibility in dealing with change. It includes both your personal attitude toward change and some factors in your work and private life that affect the way you deal with change. You might be open to new ideas and challenges, but a rigid office policy or a restrictive home life might temper your zest for and ability to change.

To understand how this interaction works, envision a rubber band. The thin, tan kind is very resilient—it expands and contracts readily. Other kinds are thicker. These are more difficult to stretch out, and they snap back into place with a smack. Still others, usually the red ones, are thin and brittle; they break with one or two expansions.

Now picture two poles with a rubber band stretched between them. One pole is your work environment, one your home environment. Sometimes the poles are rigid and set in concrete; sometimes they are supple and set in sand. The rubber band is your personal flexibility. If you're a stretchy, tan one, you can stand a lot of change even with inflexibility at home and work. If you are the thick band, you won't stretch as far, but you're also not likely to break. Finally, if you are the brittle one, the two poles of your life will need to move and bend until you develop some personal elasticity. A rubber band might become more flexible if it were warmed up or perhaps if it were slowly stretched out. And even the most rigid pole loosens over time. Luckily, human beings have many more ways than rubber bands to stretch, contract, expand, and maneuver.

These three parts of your Change-Friendly Quotient (personal flexibility and home and work environments) influence each other greatly. When you get a new boss, her new policies might change your attitude about marketing procedures, which in turn might lead to your traveling more, thus affecting your home life. Or if your spouse is promoted or working her way up in her career, you'll learn a great deal about management theory, production factors, etc., and thereby increase your knowledge and attitudes.

Using the survey to identify the three aspects of your change-friendliness can be remarkably helpful in solving problems that seem hopelessly tangled and complex. Sue Ann, for example, a young professional encountered two proposals in a month's time: one, of marriage, the other, of a new job. Sounds exciting and promising, doesn't it? But . . . there are always buts. Her would-be fiancé, Vince, owned a business in the northwest section of Milwaukee. The job offer was in Waukegan, Wisconsin, fifty miles south of Milwaukee. Seasoned commuters from such metropolitan areas as New York City or Los Angeles might consider a fifty-mile commute a breeze. But Sue Ann hated driving in traffic and, even more, hated the idea of spending precious daylight hours in her car. Besides, her potential boss said during her interview: "Here's the way we operate. If we decide to have a meeting on a Saturday, we may not be able to tell everyone until Friday night, and we expect everyone to be there together on Saturday."

So it seemed that the two posts holding Sue Ann's rubber band were pretty inflexible and that all the "give" would have to come from Sue Ann. There didn't seem to be much room to maneuver.

But love and personal flexibility won out for Sue Ann and Vince. The strength of their romance motivated them to find flexibility. Because of her upbringing, Sue Ann was timid and indirect. But after taking the Change-Friendly Quotient Survey, she screwed up her courage and asked Vince to move closer to her work. It was a big risk for her—and she was pleasantly surprised that he agreed so readily. They found a home in the southernmost suburb of Milwaukee, eliminating more than ten miles of the most disagreeable part of Sue Ann's commute.

Her easy success in being direct with her fiancé encouraged Sue Ann to press the company to keep Saturday meetings to a minimum and to excuse her from any meeting not scheduled one week in advance. Furthermore, she was able to negotiate a four-day work week at ten hours a day.

As for her attitude toward driving (the rubber band), Sue Ann is now enthusiastically involved in an audio-tape program to "Learn French While You Drive." Her listening fare on the way home is lighter: all the romantic novels on tape that she never had time to read. In further analyzing her Change-Friendly Quotient, Sue Ann saw minor changes she could make in her personal attitude, her home life, and her work life. Her overall goal for marriage and career seemed more attainable. Each small success built her confidence and enabled her to achieve major improvements in her life. What initially seemed to her like an overwhelming change became manageable when she was able to identify specific tasks to undertake.

Look at your own Change-Friendly Quotient score now and think of a problem you are currently experiencing. What small change might you make in your home environment that would improve the situation? In your work environment? How might you stretch your attitudes to help you solve your problem? Identify several unchecked items under Parts 2 and 3 that you can convert to options. For instance, under Home Environment, order in pizza once a month. Fix that old bike in the garage, then ride it to the grocery or to do other errands twice a month. Under work environment, you might suggest cross-training on your jobs with an agreeable colleague. To test the waters for a four-day work week, try going to work an hour early and leaving an hour late for several weeks.

Next, think about the four categories of changemakers. Can you use an approach different from your usual one to eliminate the problem or to turn it into an opportunity? If you are a Reasoner, look at the options in another column and resolve to try some of those choices the next time such a situation occurs. Adding options now will give you a head start in applying the techniques in the second section of the book.

Again, look at those four styles of changemakers. Does one really fit you to a T? The minute you read it, did you recognize yourself? If not, you may be a combination of several types, or you may behave in one mode in your everyday work activities but be quite different in your private life. You may have recognized yourself at previous times but now have moved into a more complex pattern.

Most of us have times when we behave like the Reasoner, Refocuser, Relater, or Risker. What causes these shifts and how many of us combine several approaches is clarified in the next chapter.

Step 2: To get a picture of how the three elements of your change-friendly quotient interrelate, shadow in your scores for Parts 2 and 3 on the poles below. Each tick mark represents five units of your flexibility score. As you shade in your score for each, it will become visually apparent in which areas you are most flexible and in which you'll want to expand your flexibility.

The Flexibility Factors

HOME   WORK

3

Four Flexible Changemakers

"Play it, Sam."—Humphrey Bogart's choked request for "As Time Goes By." He copes manfully with heartbreak by smoking another cigarette.

Paul Henreid lights two cigarettes and wordlessly passes one to Bette Davis. The smoldering look between them speaks volumes about the intensity of their romance.

Such scenes from the movies of the forties and fifties show what a prominent role the cigarette played in our perception of romance and sophistication in those times. This picture has prevailed in movies, in novels, on television, and in advertising ever since. As recently as four years ago, smoking was an inalienable right. Today, it is under siege in stores, restaurants, airplanes, and the workplace.

Many view this radical change as desirable. But if you are a smoker, you might mourn the loss of the good old days when romantic scenes on television and movie screens were always aswirl in smoke . . . when the Marlboro man was bigger than life . . . and when women came a long way, baby, by smoking Virginia Slims. Smokers today are uncomfortable and somewhat resentful. Nonsmokers are feeling pleased and a bit self-righteous.

If you were the CEO at RJR-Nabisco, formerly the R. J. Reynolds Tobacco Co., you would be looking for ways to combat this crucial change in how smoking is perceived—or for products to replace traditional cigarettes. J. Tylee Wilson personifies the kinds of change the Reynolds firm has undergone in the past few years. He is not one of the good ole boys who used to run Reynolds like benevolent plantation owners. But he is courtly and traditional compared to his successor, F. Ross Johnson, the hard-driving CEO who rode out the history-making 24-billion-dollar takeover of RJR–Nabisco.

Although Reynolds has yet to admit that smoking is a health hazard, major changes in policy show that the problem has been duly noted. Reynolds has diversified, broadened its base of operations, and launched research that holds great promise. It has developed a "smokeless cigarette" and other tobacco alternatives. In 1985, Reynolds merged with Nabisco while its chief competition, Philip Morris, joined forces with General Foods and Kraft. This industry trend toward marketing food also can be seen in Reynolds' purchase of Kentucky Fried Chicken.

To cope with flagging cigarette sales, Reynolds stepped up research efforts on filtered cigarettes and looked for a new "star" product that could replace the old, tainted one. As part of its research, chemical analysts and other company researchers scheduled our creativity Seminars and even investigated the smoking habits of right- and left-brained thinkers.

The sudden change in consumer attitudes forced this staid southern company to move into the fast lane. From polite, mint-julep garden parties, it shifted to hardnosed negotiations in skyscrapers overlooking the Hudson River.

Reynolds' leaders met radical, imposed change, and while they haven't totally conquered it, many welcome the outcomes. A highly placed executive confessed, "I've been dreading this for years. I knew eventually the statistics on smoking would affect sales and the way we do business. To tell you the truth, I'm glad it happened. It has given the company a whole new lease on life. We've had to get with the times and face the reality of smoking's effects. Broadening our base and continuing efforts to improve the product have revitalized the entire company. We've lowered tar and nicotine content and developed filters that have been used by firefighters and as dust protectors as well as for cigarettes. I'm once again proud to work for R. J. Reynolds."

In this smoky scene, do you detect the sweet smell of kairos? The change that all had dreaded finally arrived, and it proved to be an opportunity for positive change.

The remainder of this chapter is devoted to four individuals who also experienced disturbances in their lives that led to new opportunities. From reading their stories, you'll learn how radical change rocks the lives of ordinary people and provokes them to make extraordinary advances in their lives. At chapter's end, you'll find a blueprint for your own successes in change.

From Brawn to Books

The old snapshot of Tom Gable shows him as quite a different person from the one he is today. Today he heads the library of a major university in New England. At fifty-five, he sports a trim beard, wears campus tweeds, and has the mien of a sensitive intellectual. In the old picture, he was a muscled, wide-smiling outdoorsman, clad in blue jeans and checkered shirt.

The most apparent difference, however, is his right hand —actually the lack of a right hand. Today he has a hook that glistens intriguingly.

"It happened just after that picture was taken. I worked for the Haines Construction Company in Lynchburg, Virginia, getting experience in all areas of their operation, which was extensive. It included a chain of building supply stores, design and production facilities, plus sales and marketing.

"I had gone to work for Haines after college on the recommendation of my roommate. His grandfather was the company's founder. I wasn't thrilled with the job, but I wanted to make big money fast so I could go to graduate school. I'd majored in Phys Ed in college because I had a baseball scholarship, but what I really wanted to be was a librarian.

"From the time I was eight years old, I'd loved libraries. I lived on a ranch in Idaho and during one of our infrequent trips to town, someone took me to the local library. I couldn't believe that they actually loaned you books! The library seemed to me like the most wonderful place in the world. I'd spend every trip to town there. I'd first pick out the six books I was going to check out, and then browse through the shelves and read at the big oak library tables. The library and its books had a special, comforting aroma that I can still smell today. I'd get lost in those books until Dad or one of my brothers came back to take me home.

"Dad was pretty upset about my wanting to become a librarian. 'Only sissies work in libraries—besides, you'll never be able to make a decent living,' he warned.

"Truthfully, what Dad said didn't have much impact on me—but Aubrey did. She was old man Haines' niece, and I fell madly in love with her the first time we met at a company picnic. From that point forward, my whole life revolved around Aubrey —and working at Haines was a surefire way to get close to her. Within ten months we were engaged, and I was making great progress toward management at Haines.

"That's when the accident happened. I was setting up a subsidiary company to make roof trusses. While working on an improvement in the layout of lumber, my right hand got caught in a 3-foot-diameter swing saw.

"I remember being surprised by how quickly it happened. One minute my hand was there, the next gone—and with it went the life in which I'd immersed myself. Suddenly, I felt alone. I withdrew. I felt deprived, and though everyone was very supportive, I nearly became a recluse.

"It was particularly painful to be around Aubrey, and I was a real pill. Her attentiveness actually irritated me. She visited me twice a day through rain, sleet, and hail. It seemed like she was on a schedule, being professionally cheerful, bringing me magazines, records, fruit, or something thoughtful each time.

"Finally, one day I threw one of the magazines she'd brought across the room and told her to stop playing 'Candy Striper' to me. I yelled at her—called her a phony—and told her to get out. She left without a word and later mailed her engagement ring to me.

"I was sorry almost immediately, but couldn't muster the energy to try to reconcile. Then, as I weighed the pros and cons, I decided this really was for the best.

"All this happened during the dawn of the Space Age. I watched everything available on television and read a lot of newspapers. I started compiling files on all types of careers, technology, and the future . . . just to distract myself. When JFK responded to the Russian's launch of Sputnik, I applauded—not an easy thing for a one-handed man to do.

"I began to rethink my future. President Kennedy called for drastic improvements in our educational system. I remembered how important libraries had been to my childhood and education and noticed in the statistics I'd gathered that librarians' salaries were making substantial gains. For the first time since the accident, I felt interested in something. I began to list my options and analyze my chances for getting a scholarship or a grant in order to earn my master's in library science.

"About that time a library position opened in Madison Heights, a suburb of Lynchburg, and I took it. I knew I needed to get moving in some direction. I just couldn't continue to mope around. I could get my master's later.

"As I was packing to leave, I debated about calling Aubrey . . . the pluses and the minuses. Finally, I decided to call her just to say goodbye. Well, there was no hesitation or barriers. We just talked like crazy, catching up on each other's news. Suddenly, somewhere in the middle of it all, I asked, 'Would you consider being a librarian's wife?' A week later we were married and living in Madison Heights.

"Before the accident, I didn't have enough confidence in myself or faith in the profession to become a librarian. Once I got in the field, I found plenty of opportunities. There were lots of scholarships and grants available and jobs were plentiful. The year we moved up North, I had three other offers, but Aubrey and I wanted to live in New England.

"The accident precipitated the right move for me. I might not have made the move without it. What's more, it helped me marry Aubrey—not the Haines family.

"Another rather strange outcome is that I feel like a different person. I'd swear that becoming left-handed changed and expanded my personality, my interests, my thinking. And frankly, I'm happy with the change. This is the real me.

"I can't say I'd prescribe this particular method of changing, but I am doing many things well that I was never able to do before," Tom concluded.

Big Sales

Edward Sand's superiors at corporate headquarters asked him to fly to New York for a meeting. Ed was jubilant. He was the forty-five-year-old vice president of Burrel Finch's St. Louis office and had just closed the biggest institutional stock trade ever recorded in the history of the New York Stock Exchange. He wondered in what special way they were going to honor him. He thought how this meeting would represent the pinnacle of his career.

As he looked at his trim, tall reflection in the mirror, he felt proud to be so successful in such a demanding field and in such a renowned company. He chose a conservative striped Italian silk tie to highlight his charcoal-gray suit. Did he seem pale only in contrast to the dark clothing, or was his pallor from the two weeks of twelve-hour days he was closeted indoors negotiating his historic deal? "No matter," he thought, "it was worth it."

On the plane ride to New York, Edward speculated about the speeches and awards that would be given to honor his accomplishment. In fact, quite out of character, he fantasized, savoring the accolades and the humorous but dignified acceptance speech he would make.

Understandably, Edward was astonished when he went into the meeting and the first words out of the company manager's mouth were "Buddy, did you ever blow it." He was severely reprimanded in front of the entire Burrel Finch investment committee—because he had not followed company protocol in closing the sale. Since he had circumvented the traditional institutional sales procedures, he was suspended from work for one week.

"I was completely stunned and then outraged that they were so locked into one way of doing things. How could this be happening? I had a fantastic record with Burrel Finch. I'd begun at the bottom and over a period of years worked at seven branches in a variety of positions. At each step, I gave up a little bit of myself. Every time I'd want to cut back at work, I'd see some new challenge. It was something like a hunting expedition. You'd push yourself to the limit, rest a moment, and then continue. So, though

I'd become weary of work and get distracted momentarily, the next morning I was back at it, excited by the smell of the hunt. With each success, I focused more energy on work and less on my home life and personal interests. I missed my kids' birthday parties and recitals; I had no time for movies or traveling for just plain pleasure. The truth is, what I valued was measured in dollars and cents.

"When I first began with Burrel Finch, I had an agreement with myself to leave when I reached two million in net worth. There were lots of other things I wanted to do. But when I reached that level, I felt pulled or challenged to go higher. I stretched myself further and tighter to focus on a higher and larger goal and postpone my departure. I really wanted to set up my own film-making studio, but everything worked so well for me at Burrel Finch that it was hard to see anything else. It wasn't that I needed more money; I just couldn't make the break with this big, reliable institution.

"The meeting ended that. Although I was humiliated and angered, I was too paralyzed with fear to quit. I went home feeling like a whipped dog. As I talked it over with my wife, I began to feel better. During my suspension, we went to afternoon movies, walked in the park, and played golf.

"That's when I realized I had been defining myself by the amount of money I made and by my standing within the company. I wasn't Ed Sand, husband, father, solid citizen, Rotary member. I was Edward Sand, vice president of Burrel Finch.

"When I went back to work, it was with a new attitude about work and the company. This painful episode gave me pause to step back and see what I really wanted in life, and I decided it was to broaden my horizons—to work for more than money."

It took him six months to leave Burrel Finch and become an independent investor in a company that produced films. He then spent another six months learning the process of making films and finally focused on producing educational aids. A friend reported some remarkable differences in his behavior and appearance: "Ed even looked different. He had always dressed rather formally, sometimes wearing a hat and carrying an umbrella, with the obligatory *Wall Street Journal* under his arm. All this and a three-piece suit is definitely not the norm in St. Louis. It was as though he had to personify the good name and image of his company. He was very pleasant of course, but he seemed distant, as though he weren't really there."

"But once he made the break," the friend continued, "he shifted to open-collared shirts and casual slacks. For a while, when he was making a film in the Yucatan, he even wore safari suits! It was fun to watch. But his face changed the most. Even though he has steel-gray hair, his face has that ruddy schoolboy shine to it. Whenever you see him, he's brimming with enthusiasm for some new project he's undertaken."

Today, Edward has his financial interests spread over many fields, including farming, television, and radio. He is a producer of business training videotapes and orientation films for corporations. The film Ed's friend referred to was for the zoological association whose board he chairs. While on a learning sabbatical to the Yucatan and Chiapas, he made a film on lowland and highland animals for the zoological association to use in its funding drive. He combines his creative abilities with business ventures and finds a renewed and heightened love for life.

"I was so successful and comfortable with that one part of my life, I thought that was all there was to me. When I finally broke away from Burrel Finch, I felt like a whole person for the first time. I didn't have to rely on the company for my livelihood or identity anymore."

Big Moves

If you were young and ambitious and lived in Germany during the sixties, it was the "in" thing to emigrate to the United States. In fact, there were specially priced package deals aimed at young people with little money.

Anna and Kurt Kimmel came over in a converted aircraft carrier on just such a thrifty fare. Although the ship had been refitted for passengers, a battleship-gray aura seemed to hang in the air. But the Kimmels were undaunted. They were so excited about their prospects for success and happiness in the United States that they behaved like newlyweds.

They had both become discouraged with life in Europe. They couldn't find an apartment, the cities were swamped with refugees, and the Russian threat was a grim and close companion.

Kurt had made a meager living as a photographer in Germany, but Anna was a meticulous and frugal hausfrau. She accumulated a small nest egg that financed their trip across the ocean and their first six months in the United States.

When they arrived, Anna worked in a bakery and took in sewing. Kurt found a job with a small photography studio in Queens. During the next twelve years, Anna bore three children and devoted herself to making life comfortable for her family. When Kurt was out of work, she'd work at odd jobs to get them through.

As the children became older and more independent, Anna felt restless and looked beyond her home and odd jobs for challenge. She found a secretarial job for a pharmaceutical company where she gained typing and other secretarial skills.

In the mid-seventies many of their friends began to vacation in Colorado and come back with stories of the beauty of the mountains and the benefits of clean air. Although Kurt was discouraged with his photography earnings, Anna was happy about her progress at the pharmaceutical company and didn't want to move. But she relented: It would be good for the children—and maybe her marriage.

Kurt had fantasized that Colorado was a "Switzerland with a New York economy," but reality quickly set in when he looked for work. Though the cost of living was lower in Colorado, the jobs that were available paid much less than the same kind in New York.

As the financial situation grew worse, Anna went job hunting and became a secretary for an engineering firm in a suburban business park. "Everyone seemed so bored—and boring—out there. I hated every minute of it," she recalls. In desperation, she consulted an employment agency. Her counselor said, "If it's stimulation you want, I'll send you to Worldwide Communications," a company that had just been awarded the licensing rights to cable television in Denver and sixty other cities.

When Anna walked into the Worldwide building for the job interview, she stopped short and breathed in the atmosphere. "It was electric," she said later. "The fountain, the waterfall in the middle of the two-story atrium. They were broadcasting Beethoven throughout the complex. There were gorgeous flowers everywhere and the bustle of interesting, energetic people. I knew I wanted the job . . . whatever it was."

"Office manager" was the job title. Anna had thought she'd be applying for another secretarial position. She did not have even a high school diploma and had absolutely no formal management experience, so the prospect of applying for such a position was especially shocking to her.

"But I knew I could do it. I gulped down my fears and completed the application form. I must have said something right, because the interviewer called the top executive, talked to him about me for a few minutes, and I was hired."

She adjusted easily to the job but was uneasy about discussing it at home. "I didn't want to compete with Kurt for family breadwinner, but on the other hand, I was tired of low-level jobs that didn't require commitment. And I was ready to leave the role of understudy."

Anna soon learned that her boss was an executive who delegated; she found herself immersed in making decisions about office policies and procedures and she loved it. "Each day was a new shock and thrill. I'd have three phones going at once, the usual man in charge would be out of town, and decisions had to be made. I'd make them, most of the time, with my heart beating wildly. But he always backed me up. Whether the decision was perfect or not, he stood behind it.

"One Monday morning a year later, I walked into the office to find on my desk a newly-engraved brass nameplate: Anna Kimmel, Vice President. There were flowers, champagne, and a string quartet in tuxedos.

"I was ecstatic but frightened. Me, a vice president of an international company. How could I become vice president of a worldwide, multimillion-dollar operation in one year without a formal education? The bottom line was I had no choice. I had to do it.

"I thought of what I was giving up: seeing myself as a homemaker and office 'mom'—to become an international business leader? What qualities had helped me make this huge career shift, and were they more than skin-deep? Did I really deserve the job? Could I handle it? Would other staff members resent me? Would gossips question how I'd earned this promotion? What would Kurt and the girls think?

"It took a while for me to learn the answers to these questions. I operated on nerve the first few months. On the side, I passed the G.E.D. and enrolled in some evening college classes. I lived that job and my schooling sixteen hours a day. Now, four years later, I have my degree, and I am also very confident of myself as vice president. I've earned the support and admiration of my staff and won a few honors along the way from my industry colleagues."

Anna's dramatic job change looked to all those on the outside as a fantastic blessing. But even when the disturbance in your life is a desirable one, it can still temporarily shake your confidence and resolve.

Anna's experiences with challenge ranged from the confusing to the terrifying, but she wouldn't give up any of them. "My attitude and skills have been tempered in the fires of change. I work today not to save a nest egg or to supplement the family income, but because it is intensely satisfying to me."

Out of the Sky

Malcolm S. Sky was torn between his conservative upbringing and his youthful enthusiasm for solving world problems. He was a "Yalie" who had grown up in a wealthy Boston family steeped in tradition and the Republican party. Prospective spouses for members of the Sky clan were screened on the basis of political affiliation rather than race, social status, or religion. Malcolm was not exactly the family black sheep, but he was often a shade of gray. The painful fact was that Malcolm did not fit the Sky mold. He was expelled from prep school for accidentally setting a fire in the chemistry lab. Later, at Yale, he was not pledged by his father's fraternity because of his objections to some hazing practices. When asked what career he was preparing for, he admitted he hadn't the foggiest idea. He changed majors so many times it took him five years to graduate, not all that unusual in the late sixties but unacceptable in the Sky family.

Malcolm's summer jobs were an outright embarrassment to the family. He worked as a roofer, a shag boy for a car agency, a waiter, and finally as a ground maintenance caddie at a rural airport. But most disturbing of all was the trend of his political views. He could be heard sympathizing with flower children, draft dodgers, and welfare moms.

During this period, Malcolm himself felt very uncomfortable at family gatherings, where "knee-jerk liberals" were the object of jokes and scorn. Occasionally, his temper would flare, and he would dig in and defend more extreme liberal viewpoints than he really believed in.

"Frankly, they were ashamed of me . . . and I was ashamed of them. I understood their political viewpoints and agreed with most of them, but they just sounded so negative and overly dramatic about communism and a welfare state. I couldn't hack it anymore."

After graduation, Malcolm got what his father considered a real job with an agriculture organization, but then his father learned that it was a nonprofit foundation set up to improve farming practices in South America. He sighed with resignation.

A year later, barely twenty-three and on his third mission to Costa Rica, Malcolm and his partner were flying over Cuba. The plane was suddenly intercepted by the Cuban air force and forced to land. Malcolm was arrested and held for sixteen days in a Cuban jail.

"A sense of unreality overwhelmed me as six aircraft surrounded our plane. It couldn't be happening! As we got out of the plane, I had sort of a sinking feeling . . . standing there on a foreign tarmac with Cuban soldiers pointing carbines at me. John and I just stared in disbelief. When they took us to jail and separated us, terror set in.

"As the hours passed, I ran the gamut of moods—fear, anger, dullness, and depression. By the third day, I started doing pushups because I felt so antsy. Suddenly, I thought how funny I must look to the Cubans—a big, tall, skinny guy doing pushups in this cell. The jailkeepers were all short, round little tubs with handlebar mustaches.

"Luckily, I spoke some Spanish. I joked with them and told them stories about the United States. It helped me get my head together, and they dropped bits of information that I used to get out of there. It might sound odd to say this, but I learned more about myself in those sixteen days than at any other time in my life.

"I felt genuine, gut-wrenching fear. Even though John and I were treated well by their standards, I was aware it could change at any moment. Most of the guards would casually clobber Cuban prisoners for the most minor offenses. They'd be jolly and interested talking to me, then just turn and brutalize a fellow citizen.

"I discovered skills I didn't know I had—how to figure out a tough situation and conquer it, how to keep my nerve in danger- ous times, and how to manipulate people and systems that were alien to me. Surviving it all gave me a real sense of self-confidence.

"But even more important, I experienced a physical love for my country. Suddenly, the talk I'd heard all my life about the constitution, freedom, and 'the American way' were fleshed out for me. I felt it all—really felt it for the first time.

"I realized I wanted to do something practical for myself and my country. I could see that peasants aren't automatically warm, wonderful people and that having material possessions doesn't automatically make you hard-hearted."

Soon after Malcolm returned from Cuba, he joined a small aircraft company experiencing financial difficulties. He advanced quickly, becoming chief executive officer by the time he was thirty. He went on to other enterprises, eventually earning a reputation as a fix-it man for troubled companies. He also ran for political office and served two terms in the state house of representatives.

Today, he's head of Titan Tectronics, a privately owned sup- plier of parts for nuclear power plants located in San Diego. He believes strongly that the best way to preserve this country and at the same time help third-world countries is through inexpensive energy.

"Energy is the base for economic power. There's a direct correlation between a nation's available energy and its gross national product. Nuclear power provides inexpensive energy, but its gotten a bad name undeservedly. My plant is going to change that perception."

Malcolm Sky discovered his own considerable power in a Cuban jail. He clarified his political convictions and wedded them to his personal goals. He has achieved success as *he* defines it. For him, a frightening ordeal in Cuba was an opportunity for momentous change.

Gaining Through Change

Tom, Edward, Anna, and Malcolm found opportunity in life's disturbances. Anna's "earthquake" was opportunity itself—but, nevertheless, it upset her equanimity, made her uncomfortable, and forced change in her attitudes. So it is not just *negative* change that causes us anxiety and discomfort. *It is how we handle change that regulates the quality of our lives, not the change itself.*

Successful changemakers have some characteristics in common that can serve as a blueprint in your own search for understanding how to deal with imposed, radical change:

1. *They have a primary way of handling change but then are able to move to secondary change styles.*

All of the successful changemakers in this chapter were flexible enough to use a variety of change styles. For example, Malcolm Sky, in spite of his conservative background, was very much a Risker from the beginning. He involved himself in typically liberal causes with little investigation or preparation. He demonstrated his taste for physical risk by flying off to Central America in a small, two-engine plane. But during his Cuban encounter, Malcolm exhibited several other change styles: He behaved as a Reasoner when he analyzed the jailers' behaviors, the possible consequences of his capture and what, if any, options he could exercise. Then, he purposefully moved to a Relater style, using his "people skills" to gather information from his jailers and to gain their friendship. Even though some of his Risker behavior and general flexibility can be attributed to his young age, the path of the career that followed shows clear signs of a willingness to risk first, then use other change styles later.

Each of the others exhibited this tendency to use a favorite change style first, then shift to other ways. Tom, the librarian, was a Reasoner by inclination and tried to deal with his accident by thinking it through. When this failed and he was overwhelmed by depression, he overcame it by refocusing his approach to life.

Edward was a Refocuser who wanted the facts to back up the changes he made but would get stuck all over again on a new approach. When he was finally shocked out of this pattern, he became more varied in his change style and used Relater and Risker characteristics.

Anna was by nature a Relater who wanted to please everyone first before herself. What others said and thought meant much more to her than how she felt about herself. Finally, she used the Risker and Reasoner approaches to help her make the big leap from follower to true leader.

2. *At some point, successful changemakers shift from being acted upon by external forces to acting from an internal conviction or energy.*

Each of our four successful changemakers moved from reacting to external forces to making an internal decision to act. This switch is necessary for real, positive change to occur.

Tom's came when he chose to be a librarian, rich or poor; Edward's when he cut the cord at Burrel Finch; Anna's when she wanted a challenging job more than pleasing everyone; and Malcolm's when his political feelings were his own and not mere reflections of or reactions to his parents.

Before their traumatic experiences, each of them was defined by outside factors. Afterward, each consciously took steps to change. Malcolm got off the fence politically and merged his convictions to his career. Anna took a gigantic leap forward first, then earned a degree for personal satisfaction, not because her job required it. Edward became an innovative entrepreneur, rather than just a representative of a large business entity. Tom embarked on a career of his own choosing.

All four changes were precipitated by external forces that interrupted comfortable patterns. Once they were provoked to feel the need for change, each of these individuals changed forcefully, creatively, and profitably.

3. *Successful changemakers can feel when the time is right, and they choose their moment carefully.*

Although suffering a profound depression, Tom took action when a library job opened up; while licking his wounds, Edward recognized the opportunity for fulfillment open to him; Anna felt unprepared for her moment of opportunity, but grabbed the brass ring anyway; and Malcolm suddenly turned his life around at the young age of twenty-three.

Would the outcome have been different for Tom, Edward, Anna, and Malcolm if these radical changes had occurred at some other time of their lives? Perhaps. There seems to be a rhythm or pattern to the way each of us reacts to change—certain optimal moments for learning from change, and an inner timetable.

Although you can alter the path of your life at almost any time, some moments are more favorable than others. There seems to be a waxing and waning of each person's energies and resources over a lifetime. If you are operating without a safety net, such as financial security or a supportive spouse, you may need to be more restrained in the leaps you make. If you feel reluctant about a change, it may mean you're at a tranquil point in your timetable, happy with how things are, so enjoy your contentment. Or you may simply be unclear about where you want to go and need some time for the picture to clarify. Don't force yourself into changes at these moments. And don't criticize yourself. While it is beneficial to look for the opportunities in change and to attempt continued growth, why expend energy unnecessarily? Look for those times when your efforts are more apt to be productive. As you become more aware of change and your inner timetable, you'll become more adept at finding those auspicious moments for change and avoiding those less favorable times.

At the corporate level, there is a similar timeline. Consider the RJR-Nabisco story that began this chapter. The company had stayed with a predictable growth line, a predictable management style, and a predictable product for fifty years. Discomfort with this pattern began to be felt slightly ten years ago. Then, slowly, external pressures became stronger, and RJR-Nabisco changed.

The time was right. RJR-Nabisco trusted the economy and the market. The company trusted its skills and people. Its directors felt the company was strong enough to be successful in new areas and had the confidence to separate from the long-time identity with the tobacco industry. They had the initiative to act, to develop new products, new processes, and to move to a new plant in a new city. And they knew they had an organization and a system that worked. Having this trust, identity, initiative, and a method allowed the RJR-Nabisco to make and to continue making successful change. You will discover later in the book how these four abilities relate to the larger ability to *manage* change successfully.

We chose these four examples of successful changemaking from the hundreds of participants in our workshops and seminars because we know them well and because they typify kairos. But the successful changes that Tom, Edward, Anna, Malcolm, and Reynolds made did not guarantee a life without further perturbation and pain. Because you make lemonade out of lemons once doesn't mean that your life will be sweet from that day forward. Anna's marriage broke up soon after her promotion, for example, and Malcolm ran unsuccessfully for office several times.

But, rest assured, they dealt with these problems more effectively and with more ease because of their earlier successes.

As you review their experiences, you may recognize similar attitudes and experiences in your own life, and you may realize that you have often used a variety of approaches to change, even though you have a preference for one. You may remember a time when you suddenly took control of external demands for change. You may become conscious of your own timetable for change.

The more awareness you have of your own and others' way of dealing with change, the more apt you are to broaden your change skills and attitudes. And the closer you will be to discovering kairos in the radical and not-so-radical changes in your life.

However, lest you get carried away with the stimulating challenge of change, you need to be aware of the detours and dead-ends that lurk in "pseudochange." This phenomenon is described in the next chapter.

Step 3: Review a change you have made and see if you can identify the three elements of successful change:

- Did you begin with your natural change style (Reasoner, Refocuser, Relater, Risker), then shift to another?
- Did you shift from reacting to outside forces to internal control?
- Did you have a feeling this was the right time to act?

4

Pseudochange

The battle-weary sergeant called his troops into formation after two weeks of intensive combat. They were a dirty, smelly, disheveled lot. He announced:

"I have good news and bad news. The good news is . . . the enemy is on the run. The bad news is . . . we must pursue them. The good news is . . . you're all getting a change of underwear. The bad news is . . . Kelly, you're changing with Jones . . . Bauer is changing with Rea . . ."

Change just for the sake of change is not an improvement. When we feel unsure or scared, disrupted and off balance, we sometimes block change with excessive or misdirected energy. The flurry of activity may look like change, but it actually keeps us from making real change. Sometimes behavior that *looks* change-friendly actually keeps us from making progress.

In the business world, a quick fix can give the illusion of progress. Sales are down, so reshuffle the marketing department; operating expenses are up, so install a new budgeting procedure; the competition is eating into the market, so start a negative advertising campaign against them; accidents are rampant, so broaden the medical plan. But the real problems remain.

Alterations that are superficial may actually impede true change. "Pseudo" means false, spurious, or sham, apparent rather than real or actual. So pseudochange is change that is misdirected and artificial. All of these characteristics are evident in the ironic footnote to the sinking of the *Titanic*. Reportedly, as the ship was going down, the stewards busied themselves with rearranging the deck chairs. The activity made them feel better, but the decrease in their anxiety may have preempted the genuine, useful change which might have helped save lives.

We all indulge in pseudochange at times. We undertake hectic schedules, gargantuan projects, and intense research that give the appearance of openness and flexibility but actually leave us with no time or energy for essential, authentic change. This behavior is easier to see in others than ourselves. Consider these instances:

- The woman who pursues every new self-improvement fad: She seems intent on changing herself but in truth is merely pacifying anxieties about growing older

- The man who jumps from job to job or scheme to scheme: He yearns for financial security. He always believes that the *next* job or project will be the one where he makes a million

- The committee that gathers data and changes directions *ad infinitum:* It is going through the motions of change to avoid making a decision.

All of these people *look* flexible, but they only give the appearance of change. They are practitioners of pseudochange. This is not the kind of change recommended or produced by techniques presented in this book. In fact, this chapter is designed to help you identify and come to grips with the pseudochange in your life.

Ironically, the kind of pseudochange we practice is usually a misuse of our favorite way of managing change. The methods that help make the Reasoner, Refocuser, Relater, and Risker effective changemakers can also become ways for avoiding change. Here's how this transformation works:

The Risker and Pseudochange

When the Risker is avoiding change, he looks the most change-friendly of the four types. He is constantly plunging headlong into one scheme after another. But the exciting idea of yesterday too often is replaced by the even more exciting idea of tomorrow. The risk-oriented person is frequently a "stimulant freak" who finds the possibilities of the future more exciting than the 101 good ideas already underway. He jumps in with both feet, gets things started, but then moves on to another new idea, without allowing time for fulfillment of his present activities.

An example of someone who practices pseudochange is Larry Mulohan, a Montana native with a Ph.D. in economics and a persuasive manner that helped him get a toehold in entrepreneur-ship. In the fifties, he convinced a light beer and canned pop manufacturer to grant him a distributorship for a mere $500 investment. Larry worked hard and emerged at the end of one year with a tidy profit. But he was impatient for big earnings and opted out a few years before canned beer and pop became tremendously popular.

Instead, Larry used his profit to buy land in Montana and became a cattle feeder. He bought the first machine of its kind to convert hay into animal food pellets—a visionary step—but, unfortunately, this prototype still had many bugs in it and did not operate in a reliable way.

Over the next ten years, Larry shifted from the cattle-feeding business to a helicopter service for oil geologists, to prefabricated circular houses, to gold and uranium prospecting. He was more than open to new ideas; he was more than flexible. But he was never content to enjoy moderate gains. He always wanted to up the ante. Larry never benefited substantially from his vision and energy because he was always ahead of his time and too impatient to wait for maximum financial return.

While pseudochange in the Risker seems positive, proactive, and even visionary, lack of commitment often thwarts productive change. If you see signs of the Risker in yourself, you'll want to keep your openness and flexibility and your willingness to take risks. But be sure that your anticipated gains warrant the risk. And be willing to stay with your initiated change long enough for it to bear fruit.

The Relater and Pseudochange

The Relater uses a different technique. This person may consult endlessly with others as an unconscious strategy for postponing or preventing change. As a "people" person, she will interview, discuss, join support groups, conduct polls, and sponsor referendums to get the counsel and support of others. Should consensus ever be reached or specific remedies offered, the Relater who is involved in pseudochange will quickly raise a new issue to stall change once more.

A case in point was the University of Minnesota's Psychiatric Department committee that met (and met and met and met) over a nine-year period to establish an advanced therapy program. The committee was composed of four psychiatrists with high credentials, who were given the power to initiate the program. They gathered information and discussed each detail in great depth —even to the point that they compiled a list of fifty potential faculty members. Finally, it was agreed that these candidates would be given written invitations to apply to the faculty. But then, Dr. Martha Solomon, the head of the committee said, "Dr. Miller is absent tonight; we'd better postpone this until the next meeting."

In frustration, another doctor said, "Every time we're on the verge of implementing our discussions, you call for another delay. What's going on here?" Then, Dr. Solomon realized that she was reluctant to bring the project to closure. It was her "baby," and she really didn't want the process to end or the situation to change.

It is easy to understand why this strain of pseudochange is so virulent in committees and teams. The very nature of group responsibility attracts Relaters. Thus, chances are high that more than one member of a group will have this way of stonewalling against change. They'll toss the issues back and forth for years, introducing new topics for discussion just as old topics are about to be resolved.

This behavior is equally obvious when you observe the individual Relater. Bob Williams, a fifty-four-year-old, second-level administrator for a northeastern Indiana hospital, was constantly polling his colleagues and subordinates for their ideas on his career directions. "Do you think I should take early retirement or hang in another few years?" was just one of his questions. "My raise this year was only 2 percent, and the cost of living went up 8 percent. Maybe I should talk to the board. Do you think I'd do better at another hospital?"

The responses he got mattered little; Bob never really listened to them. He was so absorbed in poll-taking that he never used the information made available to him. In fact, he overlooked the specific changes in hospital policy that terminated early retirement benefits, and he was left with no option except to wait for full retirement benefits at sixty-three.

If you are a Relater, be on the alert to this misuse of your most effective approach to change. Work to get in touch with your internal motivation instead of looking to others for advice. Continue to gather, value, and synthesize the opinions of others, but recognize that you might overdo the relating process when you're feeling anxious or are particularly vested in a situation. By relating too much, you might miss the auspicious moment for successful change.

The Refocuser and Pseudochange

The Refocuser tends to make inappropriate or useless changes. Because his style is intense, solutions often occur one at a time. This task-oriented person becomes preoccupied with a problem and can see only one aspect of it. The more unrelenting the problem, the more fixed he becomes in his approach to solving it.

A home for disturbed boys in Dallas once hired a mental health consultant to discover why its troubled clients showed no improvement after weeks of treatment. This residential school was supposed to foster independence and responsibility in the children so that they could return to their families. But the consultant observed that the home's program concentrated so intently on structure and discipline that there was no opportunity for the boys to develop the independence necessary to function on their own. For example, toothpaste was doled out one dollop at a time and shampoo by the capful; no talking was allowed during mealtimes. From the school policies, the boys were learning only dependence. They continued to be irresponsible and untrustworthy because they had no experience with trust and responsibility. By being so focused on discipline and structure, the school was thwarting the very qualities it sought to develop in its young charges.

On a much larger scale, the *Challenger* shuttle tragedy in 1986 illustrated the same kind of ineptitude that results from overfocusing. All parties involved were so focused on getting the *Challenger* off the ground that they ignored more important considerations. The investigation that followed the disaster revealed that the booster rocket O-rings had frozen in the unusually cold weather and failed to release. What was the solution recommended after a year-long investigation? Redesign the rings and joints. Add a heater to keep the rings from freezing up in cold weather. While this is an innovative approach to solving design problems without having to jettison existing equipment and materials, the underlying breakdown in the decisionmaking process was not addressed. This narrow view of the problem within the organization was noted by the presidential commission also investigating the disaster.

In corporations, the Refocuser's pseudochange behavior is seen often in the workaholic. It is difficult for most of us to fault the worker who is always busy, arrives early, works late, and never takes a break or vacation. Her energy is often admired, but, in truth, much of it is wasted on busy-work.

She feels most comfortable when focused on specific projects because "things are really getting done—and on schedule." Conversely, the typical workaholic feels uneasy about innovation, ambiguity, relaxation, delegation, or new viewpoints because they threaten the busy-work that fills her days.

Take Don Jenkins, president and founder of a CPA firm in Atlanta, who declared his desire to revitalize the firm's approach to management in an age of increasing competition and major consolidation in public accounting. He pleaded earnestly to his colleagues for "progress, growth, and change," while he continued to spend seventy-hour work weeks on behalf of his audit clients.

Members of his firm suggested such creative ideas as a retreat for brainstorming and team-building, a professional advertising and public relations campaign, and a plan for the CPAs to perform public service as a way of heightening the company's image.

But Jenkins remained preoccupied with meeting client deadlines. His focus on personally seeing clients and recording billable time precluded his devoting the time and energy required to implement the change recommendations. While he focused on current engagements, his competitors moved ahead and left his firm behind.

If you are a Refocuser, use your wonderful talent for concentration efficiently. But be sure a project really needs to be done—and that you are the person to do it—before you commit to it. Every task is not your responsibility, every hill is not yours to climb.

Furthermore, if you refocus too quickly, you may exclude important elements of the picture and begin work on the wrong section or with the wrong tools. So step back and take a long, panoramic view of the situation before you zoom in on your tasks, and you can avoid the kind of pseudochange that frequently preys on the Refocuser.

The Reasoner and Pseudochange

While the Refocuser's way of avoiding change is to focus on narrow, short-term goals, the Reasoner's outlook is more distant. When this person is anxious and uncomfortable with an impending change, she will analyze, quantify, and theorize endlessly. Reasoner will be too busy taking things under advisement, validating information, making projections, and estimating costs to actually get things underway. Besides, the time is never quite right to make a move. Procrastination is an outgrowth, but sometimes a distortion, of Reasoner's very real executive abilities.

You can detect such behavior even when Reasoners go on vacation. The engineer who spends a month in France wants to schedule every activity and every hour. Months before the trip, she read a stack of books on the history, culture, and landmarks of

France. She improved her French and compiled a list of sites and people to visit while there. She even arranged to attend three business meetings during this long-awaited getaway.

This preparation can enhance her enjoyment of the trip. What often happens, though, is that Reasoner distorts the process. She gets to her dream place but cannot change into a vacation mode. If she feels compelled to stay on schedule and never vary from the plan, the very purpose of the vacation is frustrated. Instead of a change of pace, she only gets a change of scenery.

Or take, for example, Gretchen Morris, a career woman who, at thirty-three, began to wonder if she should have a child. She conducted a thorough investigation of her prospects for conceiving and having a normal delivery and child. She learned that her chances were quite good on both counts but then shelved the idea because she entered an extremely busy and rewarding period in her work.

When a lull came, she began reading extensively about parenting, maternal and child nutrition, and early childhood education. Her interest and hopes were revived, but then several other interruptions came along. It seemed that each time she had gathered enough information and was ready to take on motherhood, something happened to deter her.

By the time she had completed her research, Gretchen was thirty-nine and too old, she thought, to risk pregnancy. She then turned to adoption but found that her age was considered a hindrance there too. At last word, she was seeking information on private adoptions. Sadly for Gretchen, her reasoned, analytical approach to changing her lifestyle ended up precluding the very change she wanted to initiate.

Form Over Substance

Pseudochange frequently occurs when form is changed but the underlying reality remains the same. Refocusers frequently commit this kind of pseudochange because they miss the forest for one tree; they focus on the wrong issue and completely overlook details and patterns. The Reasoner makes a similar mistake by applying correct information to the wrong situation.

Pseudochange happens in companies, too. George Odiorne's *The Change Resisters* (Prentice-Hall, 1981) describes "activity traps" whereby corporate managers busily change the superficial form of American business without really changing the way things are done. The organization is crippled by the outdated behavior of its own employees.

A telling example of such a situation is in the incredibly wrong-headed system used by Chrysler Corporation's management during the mid-sixties and early seventies. Chrysler sales, products, designs, reputation, and employee morale were dropping precipitously. Management was abuzz with strategies for correcting the problems. Complicated organizational charts were designed to show new areas of responsibility and lines of command and communication. Hopes were that major changes in operations would then take place. However, these organizational charts were revised every two to three years. Divisions and departments were shifted willy-nilly. Reporting relationships were altered; divisions were shuffled. And all the time, nothing improved because nothing really changed. The company continued to operate in exactly the same way it had before the organizational charts were revised. All of this activity made management feel better—and the good feeling itself became a barrier to change.

It was not until Lee Iacocca became Chrysler's CEO that real changes were made. He established a simple, logical organizational chart, made sure every one understood it, and instituted the effective management that has brought Chrysler back to health.

Of course, relieving anxiety with a spurt of activity can be a healthy response to crisis. But beware of habitually using this way of dealing with tension. It can produce pseudochange and serious, long-term outcomes, as in the Chrysler situation.

Conflict and Resolution

Most pseudochange can be attributed to the conflict we all feel in making real change. Most of us face changes with a great deal of ambivalence. On the one hand, we are eager to experience a new opportunity. On the other hand, we are afraid and somewhat sad to lose what we are already comfortable with. For instance, the typical workaholic feels guilty about not relaxing with his family more, but the pull to work nights and weekends, to be productive every possible hour, is so strong that he can't break the pattern.

Similarly, the mother whose children reach school age might really want to return to her job as a medical technician. But she fears that playing the double role of homemaker and careerist will erode her personal pleasures and relationships.

Another case: Part of the budding author wants to finish her first novel, but another part dreads putting it out for public view. She may even demand unrealistic contract terms from publishers, thus sabotaging publication.

What American in 1987 could not observe the conflict apparent in the behavior of presidential candidate Gary Hart? Clearly, his public side showed an ambition to become president of the United States. But trips to Bimini and a challenge to the press to investigate his private life revealed a part of him that must not have wanted the presidency.

Our inner debates keep us from wholeheartedly endorsing change; thus we subvert the change process, often by pursuing pseudochange instead.

Have you ever seen a child rearrange the food on his plate when told: "Finish your dinner or you can't watch TV"? He has not resolved to eat the food. In fact he has resolved *not* to eat it but he would like to please his parent and he would like to watch TV. The resulting inner conflict drives him to hide the meatloaf in his hollowed-out baked potato skin and push the peas across the plate, artfully scattering them under and around the base of the potato. When his mother says, "You haven't touched your dinner," he can honestly say, "Yes, I have."

Adults face the same kind of inner conflict all the time, but find much less direct ways of dealing with it. Understandably so, for when we leave childhood, the penalty for lack of resolution becomes much more severe.

The contrasting styles in testimony of Robert McFarlane and Oliver North during the 1987 Iran-Contra hearings illustrate clearly the difference between being conflicted and resolved over one's actions. Withdrawal of congressional support of the Contra resistance forces in Nicaragua prompted McFarlane and North to change their National Security Council operations from public aid to a covert scheme. As often happens with complex schemes, the new strategy came unraveled, and they were called before Congress to explain.

North became an overnight hero to many because he testified in a very passionate, personal way. It was evident that he had no conflicts over what he had done. He even felt comfortable acknowledging his mistakes. McFarlane, on the other hand, was a picture of unresolved inner conflict. He feared that he had compromised the President, our foreign policy, and his own sense of right and wrong. His distress was evident in his appearance and demeanor and, tragically, in his suicide attempt several months before his testimony.

North's action-oriented approach seems typical of the Risker while McFarlane's is more that of the Reasoner. But both dramatize the effect of presence or absence of conflict in taking action.

Becoming Resolved

You might notice in your own, everyday dealings with others that it is much easier to represent your point of view when you feel strongly about it. You become resolved by taking the time to clarify your *thoughts* to make sure that they match your *feelings*. Here's an inner dialogue that shows how you might move from conflict to resolution:

YOU	YOU-2
This new assignment could be really good for me and the company. If I can just get it completed . . .	
	What a plum! The CEO assigned the whole project to me.
Hmmmmm. The CEO said the plan must be "sold" to the Board of Directors.	

Actually, the plan came to me as I talked with John in Accounting. I wonder if I should include him in the presentation.

I'll really have my day in the sun. I can hardly wait to razzle-dazzle them.

Let's see . . . the costs are fairly straightforward. It's the complex billing I don't understand.

John didn't come up with the plan, he only provoked it. He's sharp on the details. He could back me up on the facts.

Perhaps I should talk to John about this, get an update on the procedure.

The CEO likes take-charge, independent operators . . . but I don't want to be fuzzy on the numbers.

I'd need to get it to him right away. I wonder if he's jammed up now.

John might feel entitled to be in on the project if I ask him for details.

He can be a pain in the rear when he's number-crunching. He's slow and detailed. He's kind of pathetic. Really a nice guy, though.

Time is of the essence. I'd better just go with the information I have. If the CEO asks for something I don't know, I'll just say I'm researching it.

You and You-2 are in conflict here over several matters. On the ethical level, should John get some of the credit for this project? On the practical side, can you spare the time to get John's input? Do you understand the technical aspects of the program well enough to make the presentation by yourself? And your final answer is "Yes, I can."

This is a process that helps you come to resolution, so that you can effect change. The point is, you must be personally resolved about all issues before you go into the meeting. Otherwise, you cannot present your plan persuasively.

Identifying Pseudochange

How do you recognize a desire for real change? How does making real change differ from merely rearranging deck chairs or altering organizational charts? How do you know when you're involved in pseudochange? Here are some questions for determining how you feel when you are in conflict and mired in pseudochange and when you are resolved and making productive change:

FIVE-QUESTION CONFLICT DETECTOR

Think of a change you are currently facing. Now ask yourself the following questions, answering with yes or no.

1. Do you feel obliged or forced to go along with a change instead of making it by choice?

2. Do solutions come easily, with almost no thinking?

3. Do you listen to others' suggestions without defensiveness, are you open to their ideas?

4. Are you anxious a major portion of the time that you're involved in the change?

5. Have you developed new physical illnesses or symptoms, such as migraine headaches or an upset stomach?

6. Do you feel irritated or defensive discussing this change with others?

7. Do you have a general sense of well-being?

8. Do you feel benevolent towards others—even your critics?

9. Are you drinking more? Eating more? Popping pills? Exercising less?

10. Do you feel a release of energy? Are your senses heightened?

*   *   *

If you answered "yes" to two or more of questions 1, 4, 5, 6, and 9, you are experiencing major conflict over the change you're working on. And you may be reacting with pseudochange. Notice the inner conflict in your feelings regarding pseudochange. Notice how comfortable and resolute you feel with real change.

True change may happen gradually, over a long period of time for some and more rapidly for others. The more sensitive you are

to ethical considerations, the feelings of others, and the consequences of your actions, the more likely you are to feel conflict. It
may take you longer and be more difficult for you to be firmly
resolved, but the struggle is worth the effort: Grappling with your
doubts and feelings rather than burying them is a sign of maturity
and strength. You are less likely to be confronted later with
surprises that destroy your plans or fill you with regret. But keep in
mind that continued struggle is also a way of avoiding change.

The knottiest challenge in changemaking is to transform
conflict into resolution and resistance into enthusiasm. Chapter 5
introduces you to the four qualities that enable you to be more
resolute in making change.

Step 4:   Pseudochange comes in many forms and becomes
a way of life when we have doubts about what we're doing.
To determine if you are fully resolved about an upcoming
change, apply the "five-question conflict detector" to it.

PART TWO

The Psychology of Change

5

The Inner T.E.A.M. of Flexibility

Suppose a genie appeared before you at this very moment and promised to award you the four skills essential for success if you could name them. What would you guess?

The answer is the qualities that help you to be most flexible in the face of change:

Trust—in oneself and the world
Ego-identity—a strong and realistic sense of who you are
Action skills—abilities
Method—a way of learning.

These are the **T.E.A.M.** skills that you acquire gradually early in life and then refine throughout your life. Here's what they look like and how they emerge in childhood:

Trust allows us to depend on others and develop close relationships in our lives. It is born in infancy but requires reinforcement throughout all of our years.

Trust is what a child learns when his mother brings him to her breast. Trust is what a two-year-old feels when she allows herself to fall from a platform into her father's loving arms. Later this sort of trust in relationships develops into trust in oneself or self-confidence.

Ego-identity is an awareness that you are separate from your parents, siblings, home, and neighborhood. It's that "I gotta be me" feeling. In fact, you might feel so different from your sister that you come to the conclusion you're adopted. Or you feel unique and special when an adult says, "Oh, you're the Bailey boy, the one who does such good magic tricks." How significant others respond to you is the beginning of a positive sense of self.

Action skills enable you to think your own thoughts and then act on them. You might make a corsage out of wildflowers and tape for your mom or round up the neighborhood kids to dig a cave. Even though this kind of initiative relates to later attitudes toward work, it also has its social side. For example, saving money for a Father's Day present involves getting jobs or doing chores where you can earn money, then planning and purchasing the gift, while walking your first love home from school requires overcoming the fear of rejection and testing new communication skills. These are preparations for making friends and pursuing a mate in adulthood.

Methods for solving new problems without starting at square one each time are indispensable. They enable you to build on each experience and grow from it. You have a base of knowledge that you can revise and use each time you confront a new challenge. Each of us develops a little bag of skills to solve problems, win praise, and influence people; then we generalize and extend it. For example, when you take responsibility for feeding a pet, you then can extend that concern and dedication to looking after brothers and sisters and finally use those same skills to become a capable supervisor.

These qualities—Trust, Ego-identity, Action skills, and a Method for mastery—have roots in childhood, then become more refined throughout life—largely at the provocation of change. Each quality emerges at early stages in life and they build one upon the other. These stages are identified by developmental psychologists* who link "life tasks" to each stage. For example, the degree to which you are able to become an independent person during your ego-identity stage is influenced by how well you did with learning to trust in the earlier stage. Likewise, how successfully you deal with your third task, action, will depend in part on your experiences with the life tasks of the first two stages. It is more than coincidental that the first letters of the skills spell "team"—if you are to be an adult capable of teamwork (on the job, in a relationship, or on behalf of your community), you need to have a fair mastery of each one.

Successful Changemakers and the T.E.A.M. Skills

To see how T.E.A.M. works, look back for a moment to the successful changemakers and see how these four qualities helped them cope with the radical changes they faced. Although all of them used all four at times, each had a special need at the time and therefore focused on a particular skill. Notice, too, that though they had good skills to begin with, the wrenching changes they experienced pushed them to even higher levels.

When Tom lost his right hand in an accident, he was being drawn into a lifestyle that focused on physical and financial success as well as social prominence. His self-trust was shaky. So he had been denying his own wishes. He had opted for security because he did not trust himself or the outside world to provide him with life's essentials. His accident clarified this conflict, and with clarity, he found enough confidence in his own intellectual process and his own instincts to *trust* the world he wanted to live in.

Edward gained *ego-identity* as a result of the disappointment and humiliation he suffered when he was rebuked for his history-

*Erikson, Erik, *Childhood and Society* (New York: Norton, 1950); Maslow, A. H., *The Farther Reaches of Human Nature* (New York: Viking, 1971); Pascual-Leone, J., *Cognitive Development and Cognitive Style* (Lexington, Mass: D. C. Heath, 1976); Rogers, C. R., *On Becoming a Person* (Boston: Houghton Mifflin, 1961); and others.

making stock sale. He had fallen into a strong identification with Burrel Finch. Being vice president of such a large, prestigious company offered him a solid financial base with a nearly unlimited earning potential. Over the years, he had repressed a desire for more challenge and creativity in his work. But when the blow fell, though he was hurt and embarrassed, he realized that the problem was in the company policy, not in his abilities. Furthermore, he soon welcomed the idea of separating from "Big Daddy," the corporate father. And with the separation, his own ego became more secure.

Anna struggled through many changes to accommodate her husband and children. She was always doing something to help others. By the time she had the chance to become vice president, she was ready to *act* on her own behalf. She took the initiative, changed jobs, accepted her own abilities, and overcame her doubts about whether she was truly qualified. She was then able to use her strong executive skills without feeling that her family role and sense of self were threatened.

Malcolm came to appreciate his *method* for solving problems while surviving his stay in a Cuban jail. This frightening time also helped him come to terms with his political beliefs and to incorporate them into his career. He could then focus his attention and energies in a way that pleased him and his parents.

So becoming a successful changemaker depends upon fully learning certain fundamental skills. You'll know you've arrived when you begin to make changes because you want to—not because of an outside force or something thrust upon you.

All four of these successful changemakers moved from being under the control of external forces to internal control. Taking this step is necessary for real, positive change, and it is empowering. You no longer simply react to the forces around you or what seems to be expected of you. You make decisions and you take action because of what you think best.

Anna got her degree because she wanted it. Malcolm pursued a career because of his own political beliefs, not to please or irritate his parents. Tom became a librarian for the love of books, not for security, position, or even Aubrey. Edward worked hard on creative and entrepreneurial projects that brought joy to his life.

While Tom, Edward, Anna, and Malcolm experienced dramatic and radical changes that tested their skills, you need not experience such extreme changes to profit as they did. Each day, we all struggle with disquieting moments from which we can learn and grow.

The T.E.A.M. Test

Think for a moment about some of the experiences you've had and evaluate how you handled them. Did you, indeed, handle them or were you "a helpless pawn"? Was the outcome successful for you?

As you think about your experiences, do you find clues to which of the qualities (trust, ego, action, and method) you have in depth and which might still be incomplete? To help you ferret out the answers to this last question, take the T.E.A.M. Test.

T.E.A.M. TEST

Please read the following statements and mark a "1" if it sounds somewhat like you, a "2" if it sounds just like you, or a "0" if it doesn't sound like you.

_____   1. When asked to explain my work to someone else, I worry about sharing my know-how with a possible competitor.

_____   2. I have many good ideas that I never feel are quite ready to present to others.

_____   3. I am often persuaded by people who are glib, super-friendly, out of the ordinary, or intriguing.

_____   4. I readily accept other people's excuses for being late.

_____   5. I ignore negative feedback from most people because they're critics not qualified to judge my work.

_____   6. I can barely tolerate participating in team projects and committee assignments because I know I'm more effective alone.

_____   7. I would resist a transfer, no matter how promising, because I have such strong ties to this area.

_____   8. I am the kind of person who'd turn down a dynamite job if I thought others would envy or resent my success.

_____   9. I take on every task that comes my way.

_____   10. Although I enjoy novels and mysteries, most of my reading is work-related or for self-improvement.

_____   11. I don't ask for raises, promotions, or public recognition.

_____ 12. When I see signs that point to cutbacks, layoffs, and firings, I think to myself, "I'll cross that bridge when I get to it."

_____ 13. I refuse to alter my plans or schedules for so-called emergencies.

_____ 14. When I face a problem, I use the same standard procedure for coping with it that has worked for me in the past.

_____ 15. I have trouble explaining or teaching in my field of expertise.

_____ 16. Each new step in life seems more difficult for me.

*   *   *

You probably noticed that the statements in the T.E.A.M. Test are grouped in fours. Each group represents one of the four skills to be mastered if you are to be able to handle change. The statements in the first group relate to trust; the second, to ego-identity; the third, to action skills; and the fourth, to method.

Please enter the number (1, 2, or 0) you marked for each statement on the score lines as in this example.

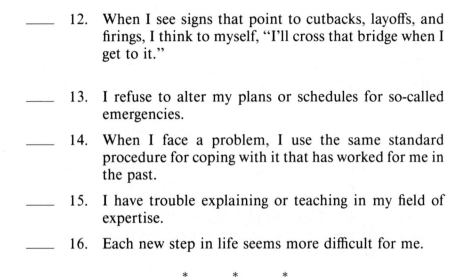

Statement	1	2		3	4	
Distrust	2	2	TRUST	1	0	Overtrust

If you scored more than two points at either end of the continuum, you may have some work to do in that particular area. In the example above, the score indicates that the individual may have a propensity to _distrust_ since he has four total points on the distrust side. Since these statements all focus on extreme points of view, a "0" usually indicates a balanced attitude on that task. Entering all "0"s on a given line indicates a fair mastery of the skill or someone who has not yet been tested in this area.

Keep in mind that four questions per task merely samples your feelings. Therefore, the results might reflect the kind of day you're having or a recent traumatic experience.

Score Sheet

Group 1—Trust

Statement	1	2		3	4	
Distrust			TRUST			Overtrust

If you are close to mastering trust, you will have no numbers on this line. If you have 2 points on the left side, you may have some slight discomfort with trusting others and at times yourself.

Four points indicates a much stronger *distrust* of your world. A 4 on the right side shows a tendency to *overtrust*. If you have totals of 4 on both ends of this continuum, you are frequently ambivalent about undertaking new projects and friendships.

But don't despair. It's good to know what is inhibiting you most in everyday life. The techniques in this book will help you develop this and other qualities which affect your ability to change.

Group 2—Ego-identity

Statement	5	6		7	8	
Independence			EGO-IDENTITY			Dependence

If you have 4 points on either side, you may have some strong feelings about your *independence.* On the left side, you might have a tendency to be a loner. At the opposite end, you may need a lot of support from others to handle change. If your numbers are less than 4, then you have less discomfort with independence and dependence and have a stronger sense of identity.

Group 3—Action

Statement	9	10		11	12	
Aggression			ACTION			Passivity

High numbers on the left side of this continuum are often scored by energetic people who feel they must always take action. This activity is sometimes considered manipulative by their peers. At the other extreme is the rather laid-back person who waits for others to lead or hopes problems will solve themselves (as they sometimes do). If you score high on both ends you may have a tendency to over-commit yourself, then get burned out and give up. Developing a proper balance between these two end points leads to action skills that enable you to act positively, yet with restraint, when making change.

Group 4—Method
Statement   *13*   *14*   *15*   *16*
Perfectionism ___|___| METHOD |___|___ Incompetence

If your numbers are high on the left side of this scoreline, you may tend to be over-systematic and a *perfectionist.* While organization and schedules are valuable, at times you may be too dependent on them and too rigid when confronting change. With high numbers at the other extreme, *incompetence,* you often find yourself in a panic because your life is so hectic. Here a little more organization and attention to details will make life easier. Those with low numbers know how to make sense out of most situations.

Getting Another Viewpoint

It is very difficult to evaluate your own behavior and attitudes —especially in such subtle areas as the four life skills. To help overcome this difficulty, we have designed another version of the test you have just taken. It parallels the first, but it is to be completed by someone who knows you quite well—your spouse, best friend, or business associate. It is also informative to compare the scores of individuals from your private and professional life. If you decide to do this, you will want to make several copies of the T.E.A.M. Test-2. Later, you will learn how to correlate the results of the two, fine-tuning this picture of your way of handling change.

T.E.A.M. Test-2

You have been asked to complete this survey by a person you know quite well. Throughout the T.E.A.M. Test, this person will be referred to as "X." Please read the following statements and mark each with a "1" if it sounds somewhat like X, a "2" if it sounds just like X, or a "0" if it doesn't sound like X.

_____ 1. When asked to explain his work to someone else, X worries about sharing his know-how with a possible competitor.

_____ 2. X has many good ideas that he feels are never quite ready to present to others.

_____ 3. X is often persuaded by people who are glib, super-friendly, out of the ordinary, or intriguing.

_____ 4. X readily accepts other people's excuses for being late.

_____ 5. X ignores negative feedback from most people because they're critics not qualified to judge his work.

_____ 6. X barely tolerates participating in team projects and committee assignments because he believes he's more effective alone.

_____ 7. X would resist a transfer, no matter how promising, because of strong ties to this area.

_____ 8. X is the kind of person who'd turn down a dynamite job if he thought others would envy or resent his success.

_____ 9. X takes on every task that comes his way.

_____ 10. Although X enjoys novels and mysteries, most of his reading is work-related or for self-improvement.

_____ 11. X doesn't ask for raises, promotions, or public recognition.

_____ 12. Even when all signs point to cutbacks, layoffs, and firings, X takes no steps for retraining or finding other work.

_____ 13. X rarely will alter his plans or schedules for emergencies.

_____ 14. When X faces a problem, he always uses the same standard procedure for coping with it that has worked for him in the past.

_____ 15. X has trouble explaining or teaching in his area of expertise.

_____ 16. Each new step in life seems more difficult for X.

*   *   *

As you compare the results of the self-scored survey and the one completed by your close associate, do they seem to agree? If so, you can feel comfortable focusing on the area with the highest score. Obviously, if your gut feelings and the opinion of your significant other both homed in on the same skill, that is the place to begin.

The following form enables you to see at a glance how these scores relate.

TRUST

	Distrust		Overtrust	
Self Score				
Colleague				
Other				

EGO

	Independence		Dependence	
Self Score				
Colleague				
Other				

ACTION

	Aggression		Passivity	
Self Score				
Colleague				
Other				

METHOD

	Perfectionism		Incompetence	
Self Score				
Colleague				
Other				

If you sometimes agree and sometimes disagree, you might want to discuss the responses with your survey partner. Find out what you do that prompted your partner to agree with a particular statement that you would not have thought applied to you.

When there is total disagreement about which skills need work, you may want to ask someone else to complete the survey.

Because we often behave in completely different ways at home and at work, you may want another point of view. If you have a work colleague complete the T.E.A.M. Test-2, don't be surprised if the score is more closely aligned with your self-score than that of your roommate or family member. After all, most of us spend more time and effort communicating with those at work than at home.

From the two surveys in this chapter, you have clues to which of the four skills you have mastered completely and those still to be worked on. If it seems that you have only begun developing trust, ego-identity, action skills, and method, keep in mind that you have countless opportunities throughout your life to continue to develop them. Each period of life offers you a new chance to refine these qualities that are so essential to becoming a successful changemaker.

The next chapter describes how the childhood experiences of four individuals affected their ability to manage change as adults and illustrates how we sometimes develop barriers to change because of the incomplete mastery of the four T.E.A.M. tasks.

Step 5: Your attitude toward change is evident in your behavior and is the outcome of your mastery or nonmastery of the four life skills: trust, ego-identity, action, and method (T.E.A.M.). You now know which of these qualities you have refined and which require more work. Review now your T.E.A.M. test scores and think about the skill that causes you the most problems.

6

How Barriers to Flexibility Develop

As we worked with hundreds of people in our workshops and seminars over the past three years, we began to detect a pattern in those who were having problems coping with the changes they were experiencing at work. As we got to know some of them quite well, we found that their work problems seemed to parallel difficult phases in their early lives.

We began to research the field of adult psychology to see if we could identify specific barriers to change and indeed found there are unconscious ways of resisting change that clearly match the first four stages of childhood as described by various psychologists. Perhaps Erik H. Erikson is the best-known of these for his lifetime of study and writing. He was one of the first psychoanalysts to study the way *healthy* persons behave.

Further interviews with clients confirmed that individuals who had positive experiences with trust, ego-identification, action, and method at the appropriate stages in childhood were relatively free from resistance to necessary change throughout life. But when they had insufficient or negative experiences at any level, they were troubled in adulthood by changes directly related to the unmastered task.

This chapter contains four stories that illustrate this correlation particularly well, as well as showing how individuals were able to make progress in their development as a result of changes and disturbances they experienced. The chapter concludes with a fifth stage, a new chance to get it together.

Each of the four developmental steps to be mastered is displayed on a continuum. The ideal state is in the middle, and the unsuccessful extremes are at each end. This seesaw arrangement graphically shows how you can slip out of balance in either direction—usually because of childhood traumas or inadequate experience. For example, the first stage is to achieve a proper level of trust—to avoid the extremes of over- and undertrust.

In these four stories, watch for the clues that tell you how barriers to change develop. Notice, too, whether you can identify any parallels to the way you face change.

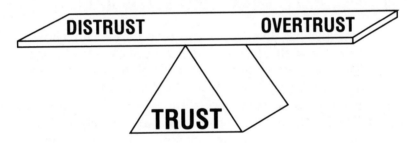

First Skill—Trust

Seth Goldstein, a product design consultant with Video Pac Systems in Cincinnati, Ohio, was born two months premature with a physical condition that required that he spend his first ninety days of life in an incubator. Neither his parents nor anyone could touch him directly. He was fed, bathed, and cared for in his plastic tent by a pair of antiseptic gloves.

Seth survived, thanks to state-of-the-art medical care. Actually, he thrived throughout his childhood in large part because of enlightened parents who did everything possible to compensate for his "untouchable" status both during the period that is so crucial to proper bonding of infant to parents.

Now a successful, well-adjusted adult, Seth thinks of the effects of that early experience in this way: "Even with all that great care, I think there's still some fallout; I consistently have this strange uneasiness with the most benign kind of change. It takes me a long time to settle in, and when I find a place where I'm comfortable, I really don't want to leave.

"As far as work is concerned, I think it has affected the way I make major career decisions. For example, I worked for this small company in California that really wasn't going anywhere. I had an exciting offer from another firm and almost turned it down because I was so comfortable with the people I was working for. I'm basically an energetic, ambitious person, but I have difficulty changing my commitments and trusting new people. In this case though, my reluctance to change worked for me. The company wanting to hire me upped the ante. They admired my commitment to my company and felt they really needed someone like me on board.

"In relationships, I've had really good luck in my choices—I seem to be able to feel a person's intentions. When I get bad vibes, I check them out. I am careful about the commitments I make. I take my time making friends, but then it's for life."

Seth has learned to trust others, though the effects of his early months linger. Unlike Seth, those who have not learned to trust often have a pessimistic and uneasy view of life. Like houses with shaky foundations, they may look solid but are easily toppled. They are without security and have little basic trust in themselves or others.

To compensate, they may try to manipulate their environment unfairly: stack the deck so they can get a fair shake, load the interview team so they can win the job, gain inside information so they can survive in what they consider a dog-eat-dog world. When a coworker calls in to explain why she's late, this distrustful person can't believe that the car broke down. When a peer gets a promotion, someone who has not mastered trust thinks there's chicanery afoot.

This pessimism presents a tremendous barrier to change of any kind. Such "distrusters" in our workshops felt better once they realized why they felt so anxious and suspicious about even small changes. One said, "It was a relief to realize that I'm not petty and mean-spirited. Knowing that my resistance to change stems from some things that happened a long time ago has really given me a lift."

Overtrust can also develop during this first stage of development if children have little contact with the outside world, or if parents are not frank with them about realistic dangers. For instance, the child who is always urged to "put on a happy face" or "see the bright side" of everything may continue to avoid reality as an adult.

Also, children who are not allowed to express anger or criticism often become adults who do not trust their own intuition. And so, they float trustingly into adverse situations because they have kept down anger and criticism so long that they no longer recognize its hidden, accurate messages.

People who reach adulthood without trusting themselves can be gullible, deny harsh realities, avoid confrontation, and be easily manipulated.

If your seesaw leans too much in either direction, the next skill, ego-identity, might be more difficult for you. Trusting your world enables you to trust yourself, which is part and parcel of self-worth, identity, and the ability to be independent. See how they all intermingle in Bill's story.

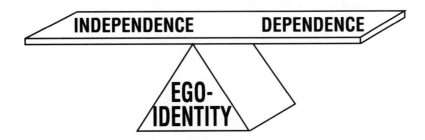

Second Skill—Ego-identity

Bill Ford, manager of quality control at a San Jose computer facility, spent the first two years of his life in Washington, D.C. where his parents were politically active at the national level and enjoyed a wide social circle. They were eager to establish themselves as perfect parents and wanted a perfect child. They had limited parenting skills, however, and were not aware of the symptoms of the normal struggle for autonomy that occurs during "the terrible twos." Bill could be charming and confident one minute, then sulky and thumb-sucking the next. He'd gladden his mother's heart with a cute remark to the checkout clerk, then humiliate her by throwing a temper tantrum. In the middle of all this, they moved to San Jose.

There, his parents failed to notice his widening interest in the neighborhood and never established boundaries for his roving. To their surprise, several weeks after the move, he wandered away from home and was lost. When, screaming hysterically, he was returned to his parents by neighbors several blocks away, his parents chided him for being such a crybaby.

Now that he is a parent himself, Bill understands how difficult it is to set limits for children that age while still allowing them to establish autonomy. Nevertheless, there is latent resentment that his parents did not properly supervise him and then humiliated him when he was in dire need of their sympathy.

However, he does partially credit this unpleasant experience for his self-discipline and will power. He remembers telling himself that "no one would ever call me a crybaby again." Even though he was small for his age, he persevered in sports and excelled in soccer, track, and tennis.

Today, Bill is successful in his career, community, and home life. He notices only two remnants of those early experiences: his strict exercise regimen and a tendency to overplan even social occasions.

PERFECT PARENTS

One of the interesting insights Milton Rokeach discovered in his research on dogmatism related to the effects of parenting styles on an individual's flexibility in adulthood. He found that the more adult children idealized their parents and approved of their parenting practices, the more likely they were to be rigid in their thinking. On the other hand, adults who were ambivalent about how their moms and dads had parented them were the least dogmatic and most flexible.*

The sudden wish to make choices and be autonomous emerges at about two years of age. The child who learns to trust his environment during the first year becomes confident enough to venture forth and make decisions on his own.

Each time such a venture produces success, the child's confidence and competence is reinforced. His behavior becomes very assertive, and he ventures out in ever-widening circles of exploration. Sometimes the child is uneasy about this freedom and fears that he is getting out of control. Limits are therefore necessary to assure that she will feel safe in making these forays into independence.

While the child learns from both the successes and failures of his free-wheeling experience, if he is not protected by parental limits from meaningless, painful mistakes, a sense of shame and self-doubt usually results. Too many of these failures lead to a desire for obsessive and minute control of the environment in later years. Parents often feel "damned if they do, damned if they don't" at this stage of their child's development. But their ambivalence may be the approach needed to produce flexibility in their child. (See Perfect Parents box). This crucial second task of developing your own ego-identity, then, is accomplished by learning to separate from parents and operate autonomously. When we have a good balance of limits and freedom, we are fortified with both independence and strength for a lifetime.

If, however, we don't, we will resist change in a variety of ways. If we feel uncertain about our independence, we may recklessly jump from one scheme, job, or interest to another, resisting advice to be patient or slow down.

*Rokeach, Milton, *The Open and Closed Mind* (N.Y.: Basic Books, 1960).

At the other end of the spectrum, we may engage in planning and overplanning, preparing and researching to the *n*th degree. We sabotage speedy resolution by seeking a predictable, secure environment.

A sense of independence is essential to all of us. We must know we are worthwhile as individuals and that we are not defined by the presence or absence of a spouse, children, job, family name, or organization.

Likewise, we must have a healthy sense of our *dependence* because there are times when we need the skills and help of others. We must recognize when and where we really do need help and when it is best to operate solo. In the workplace, being overly independent can keep you isolated, unable to network with others, and unable to accept the help or opinion of others.

Achieving equilibrium between dependence and independence helps you establish a clear and positive sense of self.

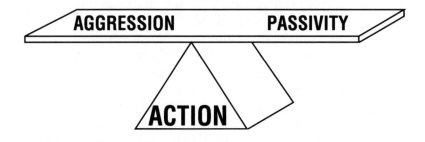

Third Skill—Action

Marilyn Owens, now the owner of a Boston travel agency, was keenly aware of problems with her parents' marriage. At four, she sensed a decline in affection and respect between the two adults who were her whole life. "Merry" saw her father as charming and loving; she did not understand that he was slipping rapidly into alcoholism. She unconsciously interpreted his loss of interest in her mother as her mother's failure to be sexually attractive. And she felt his lack of interest in her as something she was not doing or doing wrong. Marilyn stopped imitating her mother's behavior and began trying to connect with her father in a variety of ways. During her teen years, as her father's alcoholism became more serious, Merry, her sister, and mother formed a "what to do about Daddy" alliance. Merry could at last understand what triggered her mother's loss of strength and spirit and made her so passive. She could understand but not forgive her mother's "allowing" Daddy to ruin his health, their family life, and Merry's cheery perception of love, life, and marriage.

Merry later became a strong, energetic adult who, for some reason unknown to her, had difficulty enjoying her considerable success.

"I'm always driven to do more, better. I must have people admire me; I can't rest unless I have more—but then I feel badly that others regard me as driven and manipulative," she confesses.

"The conflicts I suffered over my father's alcoholism made me very sensitive to people's feelings and eager to achieve. Resentment of my mother's passivity made me determined to be strong. In a way, these problems have helped me in the business world, and now that I have financial security I'm working to get my personal life in order. I understand now why I resented Mom, so I don't feel so guilty and fearful around her." As she nears fifty, Merry has made a lot of progress in overcoming the inner conflicts that stem from those preschool years.

The initiative stage in which one learns to take action is the one in which the child "falls in love" with the parent of the opposite sex. The child strongly models himself after the same-sex parent in hopes of winning the heart of the other parent. After all, "She married him, didn't she?" Boys become rather aggressive in seeking the affection and admiration of their mothers; girls focus on their appearance and sometimes act seductively in front of their fathers.

The irony of this conflict is that the child actually doesn't want to win the battle with this opposite-sex parent because he or she fears losing the parental love of the same-sex parent that is so crucial to all of us.

Typically, children "win" when parents divorce or are not close during this stage. If the mother allows the boy to be "her little man," confiding in him and relying on him for adult companionship, she has tacitly invited her son to replace Daddy. The son has won the father-son battle but lost his male role model. He's lost a father he can look up to.

The father who takes his daughter everywhere in lieu of his wife or who depends on her for advice and affection is allowing his daughter to replace his wife.

In both instances, the child is defeating the same-sex parent and often struggles in adulthood with passivity or compulsive action. When passive behavior is the outcome, the son will fail in school or in a career so as not to outdo Daddy again. The daughter will marry a clod or continually fail in relationships to get her "just deserts" for defeating her mother. Compulsive action is seen in the restless person who competes continually, whether in the boardroom or on the tennis court, but gets little satisfaction from winning. This person can never get enough support, money, or recognition.

In a healthier situation, the child wages this battle with the opposite-sex parent and loses. The outcome is usually admiration for both parents. The child then has a good model. Later in life, males who have negotiated this stage successfully can be sensitive without feeling wimpy, strong without acting like Rambo. The female can be assertive without aggression and vulnerable without taking abuse.

The ability to initiate action is vital to all of us. It involves recognizing the part of us that likes to act on our own, to do things, to strike out, to produce. But there is also a part of us that enjoys idleness, likes the status quo, does not want to spend the energy, or is afraid to take action to do something new. Recognizing and getting comfortable with both sides is essential for mastering the action skill. We have learned that taking action in this world is not bad. It is not defeating Mommy or Daddy; it is freeing us to become competent, industrious people at the next level of development.

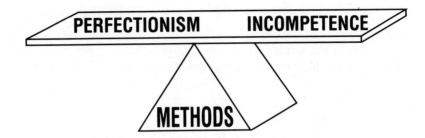

Fourth Skill—Method

Harriet Gordon's happy small-town life was shattered when her family moved from Louisiana to New Jersey during her thirteenth year.

"I remember feeling on the spot constantly. I didn't look, talk, or act like the kids in New Jersey. They seemed so hard and sophisticated. They knew all the latest songs and sins, and they called me 'Harriet the Hick.'

"We moved in the summer, so I started school in the fall just like everyone else, but I stood out like a sore thumb. My clothes were different—I supposed that everyone thought they were tacky, and I thought so too. Here I was in pastels with white shoes and jewelry, and they were covered from head to foot in Reeboks and dark cords. Of course, theirs carried designer labels, while mine had 'made by Mom' written all over them."

Harriet's early life had been a Norman Rockwell scene of rural domesticity and simple pleasures. She had lived on a small farm at the very edge of town, which gave her access to friendships and activities yet allowed her to develop an affection for solitude.

Harriet was poor but didn't know it because there was always plenty of food and warm fuzzies. Her father worked part time in the town's only factory, a manufacturer of paper containers. Her mother tended the garden and other field crops when the workload was too heavy for Mr. Gordon to do it all. They all canned and preserved food and did farm chores. Harriet took on several complex tasks that earned her admiration and praise. She gathered, counted, graded, and packed eggs that the family sold to the

local markets. In fact, at ten, she designed a remarkably sophisticated method for recording the transactions of their egg business.
She felt good about her importance to the family's survival. They
would not have had money for going to movies and taking music
lessons without her.

The guitar lessons were for her sister, but Harriet profited most
from the movies. When she'd return from the local movie house,
the entire family would listen to Harriet's blow-by-blow description of the plot, its heroes and heroines, the clothes and costumes.
No one realized that these oral accounts were stretching her
vocabulary and speech skills. But they would serve her well at her
new school.

As the plight of small farms worsened, Harriet's parents
decided to move to an area where jobs and high wages were
plentiful. Mr. Gordon got a transfer to his company's headquarters in New Jersey. The Gordons were pleased and excited with the
home they found in a beautiful green setting reminiscent of
Louisiana—but when school started, the tranquillity was over for
Harriet.

"I'd been a good student *and* popular back home. It was a real
shock to be a nobody. I guess I just withdrew—from everyone and
everything. I was grumpy at home. I cried and sulked and
threatened to run away. If anyone had asked, I'd probably have
tried drugs or anything else to get into a clique. Then one day in
my senior speech class, we had to give a five-minute talk about our
own personal life history. I started off my speech with some funny
things about my hometown—that it had a population of 703 until
we moved, and now it has 699. That the town's only industry was
destroyed in 1976 when Tummy's Noodle Factory burned down.
Then I told them about myself, all the things we did on the farm,
all the responsibilities I'd had.

"By the time I finished, they were all interested—and im-
pressed. From that time on, I was comfortable and accepted. I
suddenly felt a sense of freedom and an urge to try new things.
That's when I found and fell in love with computers. They seemed
so easy to me . . . programming is just the kind of common sense
you use on the farm. I'm finishing my degree in computer science
this year, and I'm going to design computer software in the field of

agriculture. Who knows, maybe I can help save the family farm!" Harriet concluded with a grin.

If Harriet's early life had not offered so many opportunities for mastering the first three developmental skills, she might have failed the fourth one—finding a system for learning how to learn and generalizing it. Harriet knew how to get things done in her rural setting, but she floundered temporarily with the move to New Jersey. Then, with the success of her speech, she realized that she could use what she'd learned on the farm to achieve in the city.

When we have mastered the first three developmental skills that are basic for emotional health, the stage is set for the fourth, a method for learning.

Such positive early experiences as building a birdhouse without supervision, planting a garden, sewing a skirt, and interacting with others give us a feeling of competency and a strategy for getting things done.

Once the first learning strategy is established, a child generalizes to such useful abilities as finding names in the phone book, making change, and figuring out who's in charge of specific situations. These skills become more and more sophisticated with each experience. Individuals who do not develop a method for learning and doing skills during childhood face each new job as though it were the first they ever had. Their resistance to change becomes a pattern. They may be intelligent and attractive people who can get jobs, but they have not figured out how to apply what they know. The result is that every change is traumatic to them, and they see change in a negative light.

During this stage of development, if too much is expected of children or if they are complimented solely for working, they are apt to become adults who feel good *only* about their work skills. They are uncomfortable with leisure time and feel uneasy about "wasting" time with personal relationships. They are often workaholic adults who make a task out of everything. They are practitioners of the working vacation and the seven-day week. And their way of dealing with change is to work longer and harder.

Taking the Fifth

If you reach your teen years with these four skills fairly well mastered, you will most likely negotiate the fifth stage easily. It is one of reorganization, review, renewal, and generally getting it all together. In cases where experiences with the four skills have been incomplete or unsuccessful, adolescence is usually the first opportunity to catch up. The earlier this occurs, the more easily it is accomplished. We saw how a radical change disrupted Harriet during adolescence, and she negotiated the fifth stage rather easily. On the other hand, Marilyn's major moment for renewal came during middle age, another prime time for reorganization that is very similar to that of the teen years.

It is ironic that at the same time of your life when you are most disorganized, most beset by conflict, and most confused, you are also most able to redo, rethink, and make up for all the incompleted tasks of the past.

This opportunity to get it right occurs because we are in such a fluid state. One day we feel like grown-ups, the next like babies. One day we feel confident of our abilities, the next we despair of our looks, intelligence, and general worth. One moment we love someone, the next we hate that person. One moment we want help, the next it's "Please, Mother, I'd rather do it myself."

Being in this flexible state, then, is actually a second chance to get on the path to developing good change skills. While this is an ideal time to catch up, there are always other opportunities to do this work. Gail Sheehy points out in *Passages** that the kinds of inner conflict we suffer during the time of the "midlife crisis" are similar to those we experienced during the teen years. We might feel glad to be responsible, but burdened because everyone depends on us. We might be happy about our peaceful, committed associations, yet yearn for the intense, exciting relationships of youth. On the physical side we might enjoy a slower pace and activities that allow for reflection, but at other times we worry that we're losing our energy and drive.

*Sheehy, Gail, *Passages, Predictable Crises of Adult Life* (New York: Bantam Books, 1977).

One of the most disturbing inner scenarios at midlife is that in spite of our skills and experience, time is running out. We feel we can't risk mistakes. We may want to start a new business or lifestyle, but decisions must be made too soon for comfort.

There are other times of life when we are in flux and are therefore able to catch up. Interestingly enough, they almost always accompany a great disturbance—the emotional disturbance of a divorce at any age, the challenge of a transfer, the need for completely new job skills. In other words, if we did not completely master the first four tasks of life as children and then failed in the teen years to redo them, there is still time and opportunity to develop these skills.

The more you skipped a particular stage, the more you may find your options limited there. For some, the later in life they work through them, the more difficult their mastery is. And some individuals just seem prone to a "hardening of attitudes" and so become resistant to change. But such resistance also has a price. If the payoff for staying the same is greater than the price, there is little motivation to change.

But if you want to, if you need to, if your old behavior is no longer valuable to you, it is always possible to complete these tasks. There are three ways this happens: (1) Radical changes make you open to change; (2) you go through a stage of life during which you are naturally flexible; and (3) you consciously take steps to overcome your barriers to change.

In Chapter 3, you learned how four successful changemakers found kairos in situations created by radical forces from outside. In Chapter 4, you saw examples of change for change's sake. And in the surveys of Chapter 5, you discovered your change strengths and weaknesses. From this chapter, you have an idea of how your barriers to change might have developed.

In the next chapter, you will discover the physical process your brain goes through as you encounter and deal with changes.

STEP 6:   Now that you understand how barriers to change develop, select one skill to work on. Then, to help determine when you will be most malleable, review in your mind how you have made successful changes in the past.

7

Your Flexible Brain

Scientific evidence suggests that change in your life provokes physical changes in your brain. In this chapter, you'll learn the physical effect of what you allow yourself to think and do.

SMILE AND CHANGE YOUR BRAIN

Not only does the expression on your face influence the mood of those around you, it changes the temperature of your brain, thereby altering your mood. Robert B. Zajonc, professor of psychology and social science at the University of Michigan, reports that facial expressions reflect and regulate the brain's climate. Furrowing your forehead when you concentrate "puts a tourniquet" on carotid and facial veins, thus sending more blood to your brain—a much-needed strategy when you're balancing your checkbook or learning new software—and it may also send a leave-me-alone message to those around you.

What about consciously "putting on a happy face"? Does this falsification of a mood effect real changes? Yes, says Zajonc, assuming certain expressions change heart rate and blood flow (both of which greatly influence the brain). Perhaps this accounts for the mercurial personalities of actors. Their brains change in reaction to the expressions they create for different roles. They devise a strategy to help them really "be" their characters. So when they shift from one role to another, they are not only changing parts but also developing and changing their brains.*

*Ziegler, S. "Facial Expressions May Regulate Brain's Climate," *Rocky Mountain News,* May 4, 1985.

Furthermore, we will give you some experiences that will help you get the feel of change. Knowing that change is real and that you can be in charge of it will make change easier and more exciting for you.

To get a feeling for how your brain operates, go through the steps of the following mental exercise.

The first step is to add these two numbers:

```
1000
  40
```

Say the total aloud:

The second step is to add these numbers:

```
1000
  40
1000
```

And say the total aloud:

Continue this process with each of these problems:

```
1000
  40
1000
  30
```

Remember . . . say it aloud

```
1000
  40
1000
  30
1000
```

```
1000
  40
1000
```

```
     30
   1000
     20
   ----

   1000
     40
   1000
     30
   1000
     20
   1000
   ----

   1000
     40
   1000
     30
   1000
     20
   1000
     10
   ----
```

What was your final answer? If it was five thousand, you answered as most people do, and you were wrong. The correct answer is four thousand, one hundred. If you erred, check back for a moment to see if you can discover where you went astray.

If you add only the numbers in the last problem, it is easy to get the correct total. When you go through the steps saying each total aloud, you are lulled into a rhythm of making increments of one thousand, and almost always, you will say "five thousand."

As you mentally processed this problem, a specific physical reaction was occurring in your brain. Explained in a simplified way, when you thought and said "one thousand and forty," certain neurons in your brain connected. When you said "two thousand and forty," the same connections were made again, but a few more were added onto the same train.

By the time you had gone through this routine a few more times, the beginning connections were quite strong, so there developed a natural impetus for the new bit of thinking to follow the established path. A thought pattern had formed. Your approach to thinking about that problem became set and inflexible. This is how we establish habits—by forming stronger and stronger thought patterns.

Most of us solve most problems in this one-step-at-a-time way, merely extending previous thoughts a tiny bit in the same direction. It saves time and energy to perform routine tasks in this automatic way. However, by following well-established thought patterns, we often err when confronted with something new, or we do not use the best approach available to us. We sometimes become as fixed in our responses to change as some animals.

The Graylag Goose and the Earthworm

The dangers of this kind of thinking are apparent in the Konrad Lorenz and Nikolaas Tinbergen's classic studies of the Graylag goose, which are described in their book *Studies in Human and Animal Behavior.*† Both the male and female goose have a fixed response engrained in their simple brains to the large red eggs the female produces. Her automatic reaction is to sit on them until they hatch. The gander's response is to bring food to her during her period of confinement, which is approximately ten days.

Researchers who followed Lorenz and Tinbergen wondered if the geese could be deceived by an artificial egg, and, if so, how long these fixed responses would persist. They placed several red wooden eggs in the nest. They found that the goose would sit on this ersatz egg until it hatched or she died, while the gander would continue to feed her for the obligatory ten-day period and then abandon her.

---

†Lorenz, Konrad, and Nikolaas Tinbergen, *Studies in Human and Animal Behavior* (Cambridge, Mass.: Harvard University Press, 1970).

Because Graylag geese have programmed brains, they are not able to change in accord with deviations from their usual experience.

Even more limited is the lowly earthworm. Its brain is isomorphic—"we may point to a particular individual cell in a particular earthworm, and then identify the same cell, the corresponding cell in another earthworm of the same species," according to David Hubel, a neurophysiologist quoted in *The Amazing Brain*.‡ He is saying that when you've seen one earthworm brain, you've seen them all.

It is not so with the human brain. Robert Ornstein, a professor at Stanford, has looked at a hundred or more human brains and says each one looks as different as the faces we wear. He theorizes that the topography of your brain is a record of the thinking you've done throughout your life, and therefore looks completely different from any other brain. When you make a decision or think a particular thought, your brain's structure actually changes. In other words, what you do with your brain determines how it will look. Your experiences "grow" the bumps and wrinkles that produce your brain's distinctive look—which thus reflects your own distinctive way of thinking.

The brain you're born with has about 100 billion cells called "neurons" all tucked neatly into a skull about the size of a grapefruit. This skull is soft and pliant at birth, not only to ease your entry into this world through the birth canal, but also to accommodate the rapid increase in the size of your brain's outer layer during the first two years of life.

This increase derives not from the addition of neurons but from the development of many connections between brain cells. As you take in information, more and more of these connections are made, thus increasing the surface area of your brain, the cerebral cortex. By the time you're an adult, this expanding layer would be two and one-half feet square if you were to spread it out like a tablecloth.

---

‡Ornstein, Robert, and Richard F. Thompson, *The Amazing Brain* (Boston: Houghton Mifflin, 1984).

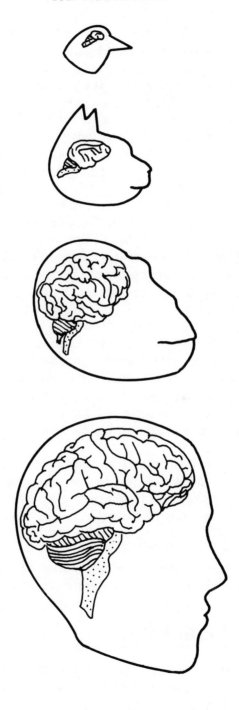

How is all that continually expanding "gray matter" stored in a skull that is as hard as a coconut by the time you're six years old? Simply by becoming more and more folded, eventually developing the wrinkled surface that gives it the look of a walnut kernel. Only mammals have wrinkled brains, with primates having more wrinkles than lower species. Your pet cat and dog have brains with lumps and bumps on the surface but your parakeet or fish does not. Compared to humans, a chimpanzee has the next most wrinkled brain, as shown in the brain drawings.

The convoluted exterior is one reason that humans have many more responses to the environment than earthworms and graylag geese. Because our brains are much more complex, we can change ourselves and our environment. Not only can we alter conditions at home and work to increase our Change-Friendly Quotients, but we are also capable of increasing our personal flexibility scores by learning new ways of doing things and by meeting new challenges. We have an incredible array of abilities not only to manipulate our environment but also to control what we think and do.

Our capabilities cause us to be curious, excitable, gregarious animals who simply must tinker with the environment. In turn, the altered environment sends back stimulating experiences. Thus, we perpetuate and thrive on constant stimulation and change. The more we observe and are aware of, the more mental connections we make that can result in new and perhaps helpful ideas.

All of us feel this urge to excite our brains' cortex but find ways of doing it that are suited to our tastes and personalities. Some people love to learn from books or in classrooms, others through travel, sports, the business world, or the arts. Even the inert "couch potato" thirsts for stimulation and finds it in beer, chips, and television.

How this universal urge for stimulation affects and is affected by the brain is the subject of much recent research.

How the Brain Works

Over the last three decades, the interdisciplinary branch of science that studies the brain, cognitive science, has developed several models of how the brain works. We're going to look more closely at the most popular models because they explain how the brain changes physically as it absorbs new ideas—and why such stimulation actually develops your brainpower.

The technology of the neurosciences now makes it possible to track minute occurrences in the human brain. As Dr. Gary Lynch, a University of California researcher in neuroscience says, "We have proven that new learning physically alters the brain: all learning leaves a biological trail, whether it's learning a new word or the conceptualization of an idea."[*]

The electrochemical model explains how the neurons, the basic cells of the brain, communicate. The messages pass between the neurons over nerve fibers called "axons" and "dendrites." A neuron has many short dendrites which *receive* signals from other neurons, and one long axon, sometimes as long as three feet, which *sends* signals. But between one cell's axon and another's dendrite is a gap. When thought occurs, as in the addition problem that began this chapter, a tiny electrical spark forces the chemicals sodium and potassium into the void between the neurons. They travel at a speed of at least five hundred miles per hour. The bridge

---

EXERCISE TENSION AWAY

If you carefully read and performed the problem at the beginning of the chapter, you might now feel slightly tense. Research shows that when you focus intently for 20 to 30 minutes, the sodium and potassium accumulate in your body and brain at levels that produce water retention. If you had exercised enough to perspire immediately after reading, you'd have experienced little or no tension. You can see why exercise breaks can actually enhance learning and ward off tension.[†]

---

[*]Restak, Richard, M.D. *The Brain* (New York: Bantam Books, 1984).
[†]UPI wire service, "Exercise Releases Tension Through Brain Chemicals," *Chicago Tribune,* February 15, 1985.

HOW BRAIN CELLS TALK

One of the world's foremost theoreticians on the structure of the brain, Dr. Donald Hebb, holds that a memory or thought process results from the formation of "associative cell assemblies" in which cells are connected in specific circuits.‡ Normally, these cells activate each other, rather like talking to each other on a party line. Forgetting is a direct result of a failure in communication between nerve assemblies. It's as if there's static on the line—the information is there, but the parties are not connecting. To maintain memory, we need to strengthen the "party line equipment"; to develop larger circuitry, we must provide new stimulation. This is why we need varied experiences—to continually provoke broadening of the pathways through lots of talk within those associative cell assemblies. Change and challenge do the job.

---

they form is called a synapse. With every message sent on its way, a slight trace of these chemicals is left. With repeated crossings, the thought becomes established and easy to slide into but difficult to alter.

The Specialization of the Brain

Surely the survival of mankind is the greatest success story of all time. And we got there the old-fashioned way—we earned it! We had no armor plates like the triceratops to ward off a hostile environment. We didn't have the bulk or speed or sharp teeth of the saber-toothed tiger to hunt down our daily bread. We didn't have the tails and nimble ways of the monkey to avoid our enemies. We survived because of our brains and the work we put them to.

‡Ibid.

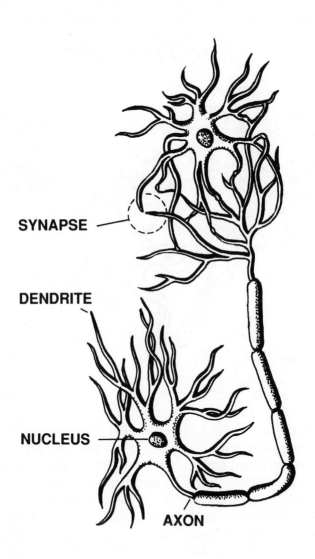

How this happened is explained by Dr. Paul MacClean's Triune Brain Theory, which says that, to meet the challenges of the environment, over time our brain formed separate but related layers that made different contributions to our thinking abilities.

The Triune Brain

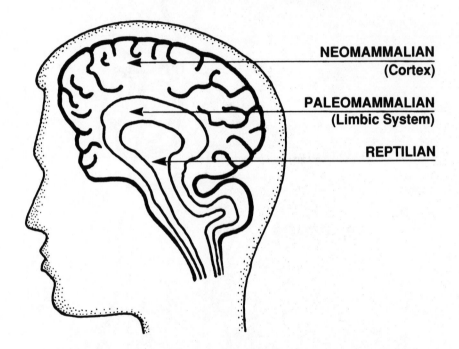

NEOMAMMALIAN
(Cortex)

PALEOMAMMALIAN
(Limbic System)

REPTILIAN

The earliest of these layers is nestled deep within our skull and rests on top of the brain stem. Called the "reptilian brain," it controls respiration, perspiration and other such automatic functions. When you are anxious, this primitive part of your brain sends messages to speed up blood flow, brain waves, heart rate, and muscle tension—the "fight or flight" response. This layer and its response lead modern men and women to suffer stress disorders when dealing with the dangers of the workplace jungle. When we're verbally attacked or feel an enemy surveying our weak points, the reptilian response to hit or run overwhelms us. Neither response is appropriate, and so we swallow hard and stifle it.

Repeated episodes lead to tension, heartburn, and kicking the cat when we get home.

The reptilian brain has no memory; it is instinctual and reflexive. But the middle layer is much more sophisticated. This limbic brain enables you to make the fine distinctions that help you recognize what is yours exclusively: your baby, your cave, or your 280Z. Your present memory system owes much to the limbic brain. This more discriminating limbic layer also equips you to devise ingenious survival techniques—witness the intern who mysteriously loses every game to his boss even though the intern is a scratch golfer. A contrasting survival strategy of the reptilian brain is that urge to strike out automatically when you feel threatened.

Both of these remnants of the primitive brain are covered by the new mammalian brain, variously known as the "cerebral cortex," the "neocortex," or just plain "cortex." This layer is limited to mammals and is most highly developed in humans. It is the area where new learning takes place, where *you* process your *own* view of your environment and invent ways of dealing with it.

As the brain developed, the cortex became clearly divided into two hemispheres with special functions. And thus was born the highly sophisticated brain we enjoy today, the right/left brain.

Dr. Roger Sperry is a neuroscientist who won the Nobel Prize for medicine in 1981 for proposing and researching the Split Brain Model. Sperry and his colleagues studied patients with life-threatening epilepsy who'd undergone surgery to sever the corpus callosum, the tissue that connects the brain's hemispheres. The intent of this operation, a commissurotomy, is to stop the misfiring of electrical charges between the hemispheres that sometimes causes epilepsy.*

They determined that the two sides of the brain perform special and different functions. In most right-handers, the right side of the brain controls the left side of the body and processes information in a general, emotional way, while the left side of the brain controls the right side of the body and is more specific and

*Russell, Peter, *The Brain Book* (New York: Hawthorn Books, 1979).

logical in its processing. The situation is sometimes reversed in left-handed individuals.†

LEFT	RIGHT
LOGIC	**RECOGNITION**
Reason	Patterns
Mathematics	Metaphors
Analysis	Analogies
LANGUAGE	**VISUAL**
Reading	Images
Writing	Spatial
Verbalizing	**FEELINGS**
LINEAR	Revelation
Listing	Emotional
Prioritizing	Intuitive

Later, related research showed that most of us tend to use one side of the brain more than the other and that therefore we have a "cerebral dominance," a specialized way of working, communicating, playing, and behaving.

This division of labor between the two halves of the brain allows us to become very good at what we do. We can write letters and repair circuits because we have specialized skills. In most of us, the dexterity required for writing rests in the right side of our brains, but we use the left brain to select the most appropriate words. Circuit repairing requires an accumulation of skills that may have started millions of years ago when someone struck out in fear with a stick and felled an animal, thereby discovering a hunting tool. The concept of using a stick for a tool sprung from the reptilian and limbic layers of the brain, but the many refinements the tool concept underwent to become a circuit board were

†In a study of 262 left-handed and ambidextrous persons, researchers using the Wada test found that 15 percent had speech in the right hemisphere and 15 percent had speech on both sides of the brain. Blakeslee, Thomas, *The Right Brain* (New York: Anchor Press/Doubleday, 1980).

accomplished in the cortex. By the time we got to repairing circuits, this outer layer of the brain had divided and the specialization of skills looked like this:

Left Brain	*Right Brain*
verbalizing the problem	mental picture of circuit board
computations	concept of electricity
detecting differences	manual dexterity
analysis of problem	feeling where the trouble is

Instead of relying on the reptilian and limbic brains to merely survive, humans developed the new outer layer of the brain and began to remember, to plan, to invent, and to communicate ideas. The new brain divided in half, and each half developed special abilities that we refined each time we responded to the changes and challenges around us. We found the kairos in change even in those early days.

Today, we use this specialized brain with greater sophistication to accomplish much more complex tasks. Rather than planning the bison hunt, we develop a business plan. Instead of chipping a new scraping tool, we devise a new piece of software. We have replaced cave drawings and monosyllabic grunts with satellite television and hundreds of languages.

Humans survived and improved because they developed more than one way of responding to changes they faced. This resulted in four distinct differences that make us mentally superior to other living creatures:

- It has the most convoluted surface, indicating higher levels of memory and learning.

- It has the most clearly divided hemispheres, showing the highest level of specialization and sophistication.

- It has the greatest body weight to brain weight ratio, signifying the importance of thinking to our survival.

- It has the most complex set of frontal lobes of all this world's creatures, a possible indication that we are even now "growing" more tissue in this area where planning, social sensitivity, and invention are located.

But how does this state-of-the-art brain look in action? What happens to the brain when it is stimulated? When you hear a beautiful musical score, certain responses are provoked. When you hear a lecture or load the dishwasher, other parts of your brain are affected. So the circuitry of the brain constantly rewires itself in response to changes in the environment.

Listing the thousands of studies that identify what turns your brain on and off would most likely leave your brain unstimulated. So, to illustrate just a few of the varied stimuli that cause changes in your brain and behavior, imagine yourself having this kind of a day:

The Wickersham Dilemma

You awaken at 6:29 A.M., one minute before the alarm goes off. You hate the sound of the alarm, and your brain seems to accommodate this aversion by awakening you in time to turn the alarm off before it rings.

You press the button down, then lie quietly for a few moments trying to pull together the wispy thoughts floating through your mind. You dreamed about something and awoke with the distinct feeling that the dream had a valuable insight . . . for . . . what was it about . . . oh, yes . . . the Fred Wickersham problem.

You hired him to work for you part-time six months ago, and it's just not working out. You are self-employed and needed someone to do research, organize files, and cover the phones when you're out of town. But he is slow with the research projects and doesn't do files. He stretches out projects so that he is there about thirty hours a week. You feel as if you're working half of your time to support him. You never promised him full-time work, but he seems very dependent upon you and the job. Now you have a deadline for a major proposal approaching quickly and he seems more trouble than help.

As you lie there trying to connect the dream to the problem, your thoughts wander to the day's activities, and you recall that it was supposed to snow last night. "The streets will be icy this morning. . . . I'd better get going or I'll be late for my 8:30 appointment," you think.

You leap out of bed, slip your workout tape in the video tape recorder and do twenty minutes of brisk exercises. At first you glance at the clock on the mantle several times to see how much longer you have to go, but once you get into the rhythm, you feel as if you're in another time and place. You see Wickersham writing at your word processor and wonder if he knows how to write proposals. Suddenly the twenty minutes is up and you are back in the present, feeling energetic, righteous, and positive.

You put the coffee on and jump into the shower. Once again you seem to forget where you are. The sound and feel of the water release your thoughts, and you see your desk piled high with papers. All the words are indecipherable except the date, February 21, which glows like an orange neon light. "How many days do I have?" you wonder, and then you begin to compute the number of hours left to complete the project.

DREAM ALERT

EEG (electroencephalograph) tests show that most of us exhibit our highest levels of right hemisphere brainwave activity during sleep, particularly during dream cycles. "Deep sleep" is usually experienced midway through the night when the least left-brain activity occurs. If you are awakened during a dream cycle, your recall is about 20 percent because your verbal left side is "on hold." As morning draws near, right-side activity declines and left-side increases; your recall of dreams increases to about 80 percent. This shift to the left increases your awareness of time, your day's schedule, and your wish to avoid the jolt of your alarm clock.

Recall also depends on your thinking style. At the University of Edinburgh, cognitive, convergent, left-brained thinkers could recall only 65 percent of their dreams, while the less logical, divergent right-brain thinkers recalled 95 percent of their dreams.‡

THETA THOUGHTS

When you are falling asleep and waking, you are normally in a brainwave state called theta. These pleasant times allow you to recover fleeting daytime thoughts and assemble them in patterns that are sometimes full-blown solutions to a problem or gorgeous creative concepts. To preserve these fragile images and insights, allow yourself to slide into sleep peacefully and to awaken slowly without blaring radio or TV sounds.*

‡Ibid.
*Wonder, Jacquelyn, and Priscilla Donovan, *Whole-Brain Thinking* (New York: William Morrow, 1984).

You take your new suit out of the closet, but in a forward flash see yourself at your first appointment. "No, Daniel's too conservative for that one." You put the new suit back and take out your standard navy blue.

As you dress, you have a mental dialogue with Daniel, rehearsing all the points you intend to make. As you conclude, you look straight in the mirror and say, "Daniel, I'm not paying a dollar more than $300 for that software. Take it or leave it."

You become aware of the aroma of the coffee that is brewing in the kitchen. The image of your breakfast (a croissant and a banana) appears, and you salivate. You skim the headlines of the morning paper as you eat, finally settling on a story about the homeless woman found frozen to death under a bridge fifteen blocks from your office. Breakfast rests uneasily on your stomach. As you drive to work, you wonder if Wickersham has any savings. You notice a number of poorly dressed, cold-looking people at bus stops and in doorways and feel guilty about your warm, jazzy car. You think about offering a ride to the next down-and-out person you see. Unfortunately, that happens to be an ominous-looking hitchhiker who thumbs his nose at the car in front of you. You quickly reconsider and avert your eyes as you pass him. In your peripheral vision you see him shake his fist at you. Your heart skips a beat, your foot presses the accelerater, and you take a deep breath.

EXERCISE GOOD FOR BRAWN AND BRAIN

Not only does exercise help you look better, it seems to improve your mental abilities. In a study at Scripps College, psychologists Louise Clarkson-Smith and Alan A. Hartley found that individuals, age fifty-five to eighty-nine, who exercised vigorously at least seventy-five minutes each week had better memory, reasoning ability, and reaction time than cohorts who exercised less than ten minutes. Although the researchers admit that the high-exercise group may have been healthier and more astute to begin with than those who exercised less, they believe this comparative study shows a connection between maintaining physical vigor and mental abilities.†

CAFFEINE ALERT

How your thinking is affected by the caffeine you drink in the morning depends on what sort of person you are, according to William Revelle, a psychology professor at Northwestern University. He has studied seven hundred people over seven years and found that impulsive extroverts work better on complex reasoning tasks such as proofreading for grammatical errors after ingesting caffeine. More thoughtful introverts, who like to take their time in making decisions, were hindered by caffeine. Both types perform better on extremely simple tasks when they have taken caffeine in some form.‡

†Cross Talk, *Psychology Today,* Jan. 1988 (report on American Psychological Association annual meeting, 1987).
‡AP wire service, "Caffeine Can Hurt or Help Reasoning," *Rocky Mountain News,* Denver, Aug. 21, 1987.

After the elevator ride up to your office, your mood and your step are lighter. Perhaps it was the cheerful, peppy music that's playing in the elevator.

You put your key in the door and realize it is not locked. "Damn, Fred left the door unlocked last night. What's wrong with him anyway? I suppose he forgot to turn off the word processor again," you think. You feel anger in the pit of your stomach, right where the doctor said you were working on an ulcer.

Sure enough, the desk light is on and you can hear the hum of the machines. But your anger turns to fear, then guilt, as you see Wickersham slumped over the desk. "He's dead. I've worked him to death. Oh God, please don't let him be dead."

As you move quickly to his side, you notice for the first time how much he looks like your father—the same thinning brown hair and the thick, unruly eyebrows. Your fears are abated by the loud snore, which also reminds you of your father. In a flash, you see your father as he was one Sunday afternoon when you were eight, snoring loudly on the couch, the newspaper collapsed over his face and rattling with each snort. You and your brother are convulsed with laughter. This scene plays out in your mind in an instant, but it is long enough to bring a chuckle to your throat.

You relax and your stomach feels better. You also feel more kindly toward Wickersham. Just as you are about to awaken him, the phone rings, and he reaches out automatically to answer. "Hullo . . . this is . . . uh . . . ," Wickersham mumbles. He looks around helplessly and hands the phone to you with obvious relief.

On the phone is fast-and-furious, get-to-the point Daniel, your nine o'clock appointment. "Who was that Neanderthal? Why don't you hire employees with IQs that have at least reached room temperature?" he jabs. Dan talks faster than the speed of light—which makes him an interesting speaker but an impatient listener.

DEEP BREATHING

Taking a deep breath to relieve anxiety is a survival-smart reaction since it makes more oxygen available to the brain, thereby improving thinking. The brain uses 90 percent of the blood's oxygen, and so oxygen is truly the food of the brain. Yawning and laughter are other ways the body increases the intake of air. This may be why we laugh nervously and even occasionally yawn or sigh in stressful situations.*

MUSIC AND YOU

Music's effects on the brain can help you change. For example, music therapists use it to calm coronary patients, to break through the psychological isolation of autistic children, to raise the spirits and antibodies in the physically ill, to reach deaf children, and to treat drug and alcohol abusers. Slow music sells more groceries. Receipts in supermarkets were 38.2 percent higher with slow, "easy-listening" music than with faster versions. Muzak, "elevator music," is programmed in fifteen-minute segments, alternating tempos and instruments to increase "stimulus value." Violins and flutes are less stimulating than trumpets; slow beats less stimulating than fast ones. Such musical programming has been used to offset the midmorning or afternoon slump, to increase alertness, to raise productivity, and to reduce staff turnover.†

*Padus, Emrika, *The Complete Guide to Your Emotions & Your Health* (Emmaus, Pa: Rodale Press, 1986).
†Rosenfeld, Anne H., "Music, the Beautiful Disturber," *Psychology Today,* Dec. 1985.

He asks you to bring the spec file to the meeting, and you are off the phone in forty-five seconds.

Wickersham still seems slightly dazed, and in a rush of emotion, he tells you a rambling tale that explains his behavior for the past six months. You are stunned by how poorly you have understood him, yet relieved by the revelation. It seems that Wickersham has another job offer but felt you were so dependent on him that he couldn't bring himself to quit. He worked through the night to finish his current project so he could resign with a clear conscience. You accept his resignation in the same serious spirit it was offered, but inwardly you are jumping with joy.

In this slice-of-life drama, you experienced at least ten kinds of stimulation that provoked changes in you. Even if you had not reached a happy resolution of the Wickersham problem, you would be better off because of the variety of stimuli you had experienced. The more stimulation your brain receives, the healthier it is and the more vigorous your thinking process is.

During this two-hour period of your life, you responded to and initiated changes that caused specific physical reactions in your brain and body. You were challenged by a variety of situations, and you dealt with them using automatic responses or newly devised ones. As the parallel studies showed, these activities had a physical impact on your brain.

The Wickersham story is also useful in clarifying the way we are pushed and pulled between our brains' hemispheres and layers. When you were awakening, recalling the image of your dream about Wickersham, you were pulled right (if you have the brain organization of the typical right-hander). When you stepped on the gas at the sight of the angry hitchhiker, you were pushed to your reptilian brain. When your anger with Wickersham ebbed and turned to affection because he reminded you of your father,

FAST TALK

Because listeners generally find fast talkers to be more interesting and credible, an entire industry has developed for speeding up video and audio tapes. Studies show that compressed TV ads can increase viewers' recall by as much as 40 percent and that attention is much more focused on fast-paced messages. In recent years compressed tapes have become an accepted tool in television, radio, sales training, college instruction, talking books for the blind, and reviews of hospital emergency calls. Many of the movies you see on television have been compressed to save time and make them seem more interesting. Radio stations have been speeding up Top 40 songs for years to create excitement.‡

One outcome of this and other aspects of our high tech world may be an increase in impatience. In his book *Time Wars,* Jeremy Rifkin cites psychological studies that show that "computer compulsives," individuals who spend a great deal of time working with computers, put a high premium on efficient communication. They avoid or ignore people who talk slowly or in general terms.*

‡Leo, John, et al., "As Time Goes Bye-Bye," *Time,* July 19, 1982.
*Rifkin, Jeremy, *Time Wars* (New York: Henry Holt, 1987).

your limbic brain was in action. And your left brain? It analyzed Wickersham's rambling resignation and quickly recognized it for what it was—a solution to the Wickersham Dilemma.

You're Never Too Old

Over your entire lifetime, stimulation is the key to a growing brain. Some people feel that when they reach middle age, their brains start to "go"—that they become too old to learn new tricks. But cognitive science and its models have shown that consciously seeking new stimulation can lead to greater brainpower at any age.

From birth to two years of age, your brain develops connections among its cells more rapidly than at any other time in your life. But the refinement of your thinking skills continues throughout your entire life in direct proportion to how fully you use your brain. Around five years of age, a pruning process begins and continues as you mature! The connections that are used frequently become stronger; those used less are stripped away. As you grow into an adult, your maturing brain loses about 40 percent of the hairy fibers of the synapses, those all-important connections between your brain's neurons.

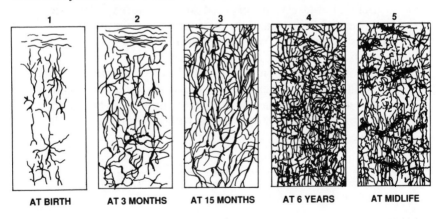

AT BIRTH   AT 3 MONTHS   AT 15 MONTHS   AT 6 YEARS   AT MIDLIFE

But do not despair—your brain is getting smarter, not just smaller. This loss represents a streamlining of your brain and its powers. The neural connections that you use most grow stronger, and those used least are stripped away. This process, called "synaptic pruning," is analogous to the beneficial pruning of branches of trees. This pruning allows us to make quick, strong, efficient responses and decisions. It also may help to explain why memories of early childhood are so sparse.

Moreover, the dendritic nerve cells that receive impulses are stimulated by use. "Dendrites in a healthy older person's brain get bigger with age, showing plasticity of the brain," according to Carl Cotman, a professor at the University of California at Irvine.† Not only that, Cotman says that the brain is like a self-repairing

---

SLICED BRAINS

Dr. Marian Diamond, a professor of neuro-anatomy at the University of California-Berkeley who has studied a slice of Einstein's brain, reports that it has 73 percent more glial cells for every neuron than in the average brain. Glials are the hairy extrusions surrounding neurons that feed and nourish them.

Perhaps this abundance of glials stems from the wide variety of interests he enjoyed and the turns in life he experienced. We usually think of him as a scientist, but he was also a musician. We think of him in the laboratory, but he also was a teacher and a civil servant.

Dr. Diamond's study of glials indicates that stimulation *is* a factor. She spent years studying the neuron-glial relationship in rats and found that those who are given treadmills and other toys to play with develop more glials for every neuron.‡

---

†*AARP News Bulletin,* "How We Age." Washington, D.C., Vol. 28, No. 8, Sept. 1987.
‡Krieger, Lisa, Scripps-Howard News Service, "Age-Old Theories," *Rocky Mountain News,* Aug. 16, 1987.

computer that constantly reprograms itself to let healthy cells "take up the slack and sprout new connections."

With experience, you also refine your brain skills: wisdom really does seem to come only with age. Two researchers, Karen Strohm Kitchener, from University of Denver, and Patricia King, from Bowling Green State University, are on the cutting edge of the study of "reflective judgment," an ability they theorize begins to develop in preteen years and flowers in midlife.* They describe reflective judgment as the ability to balance reality with personal bias. Those who remain open in their attitudes throughout their lives are those who reach the highest levels of reflective judgment. They are the tribal chieftain, the wise grandmother, or the elder statesmen on whom we rely for wisdom. Their varied activities are the stimulants that keep them functioning and flexible.

So if you want to be healthy and wise, change the kinds of stimulation your brain receives. The techniques offered in this book can help you do so. They are designed to engage different parts of your brain in order to activate it more fully.

Very Varied

Now it's time to try some mind-stretchers that will get many parts of your brain going.

- Let's start with some two-liners:

Question: How many psychiatrists does it take to change a light bulb?
Answer: Only one, but he has to really want to change.

Or try this:

Question: How many team owners does it take to change Billy Martin?

---

*Bowen, Ezra, et al. "Can Colleges Teach Thinking?" *Time,* Feb. 16, 1987.

Answer: Five, but they've all got to be named George Steinbrenner.

To make such a leap in logic is good for you. Here are some other mind-stretchers.

- Look around you and identify one aroma you find pleasant right where you are. Whether at your desk, at your kitchen table, in the airport, on the subway, or wherever, find one smell that you like: the fragrance of a bouquet of flowers, a whiff of buttered popcorn or pizza, the scent of lotion or perfume on the back of your hand, the smell of the printed page of this book, or the slightly dank odor of wet wool that reminds you of an embrace under an umbrella. Allow yourself to breathe that aroma and enjoy it.

- Now, moving to another sense, choose one of these songs to hum:

    "Twinkle, twinkle, little star,"
    "The Sounds of Silence,"
    "Born in the U.S.A.,"
    or one of your own choosing.

- Shift your posture around till you feel comfortable, take a deep breath, lean back in your chair, momentarily let your eyes return to the page, and then read this limerick:

An indolent vicar of Bray
His roses allowed to decay.
    His wife, more alert,
    Bought a powerful squirt
And said to her spouse, "Let us spray."

Here's another:

There was a dull man from La Grange
Who said, "This is all very strange.
    I've written her twice,

Sent her three dozen mice,
But her attitude still doesn't change."

Now, fill in the blanks of this topical limerick:

There was an executive strong
With credits exceedingly long
   Said she to the _____
"You'll think I'm a hoard
But more money is mine or I'm _____."

Our version fills in the blanks with *board* and *gone*.

If you'd like, you can add other verses. However, if your muse is fully used, move on to the next flight of fancy.

• Look at the cartoon below and fill in the balloon:

Did all this talk about change inspire a related concept in your balloon's message?

Since you have just flexed different senses, you can use them as you draw your own picture starting with the line that follows:

TITLE

Now, give it a title—and sign it please, because you are so proud of it!

The exercises you just went through are designed to address your sense of smell, your sense of rhyming and humor, and finally your ability to connect visual images with language. You used different parts of your brain in each one.

In the first one, an aroma in the present provoked a feeling about or mental picture of something previously experienced or imagined. Both usually stimulate activity in the visual areas of your brain. If the picture is a memory, the impulse will travel over previously traveled neural pathways. If the picture is a new one, it usually begins with an old pathway, then makes detours. A similar process is followed in the other exercises:

- Humming a familiar song, as you were asked to do in the second exercise, might provoke a visual memory of a person you were with when you first heard the song. A trained musician might "see" the musical score for that song. A composer might soar off into new areas, hearing a melody and seeing its score.

- If you read limericks a lot, you have a set of those associative cells described by Dr. Hebb that are activated when you read a new one. Even though your brain has never experienced that particular limerick before, the lilting cadence of its rhyme helps you anticipate how to fill in the blanks. Furthermore, you expect humor and absurdities in a limerick and thus have other clues to how to complete it. Humor also stimulates the output of endorphins into your brain and makes you more relaxed and open to new ideas.

- In the previous activity, you were asked to add two words to a limerick, and you had several hints to help. Adding words to the caterpillar cartoon asks you to go a step further and connect someone else's picture to language. While the artwork of others can stimulate memories and excite new ideas, translating these memories and ideas into words complicates the process and makes this exercise more difficult than the last. But when you come up with a clever caption, the payoff is a mental high.

- Because most of us don't draw or paint after early school years, we have little experience with transferring our mental pictures to paper and, so, are often stymied by the final activity, drawing. Although you had a line to get you started, the process can be challenging if your neural pathways for drawing have rarely been traveled or have been lost in the synaptic pruning process. Restoring your comfort with drawing may be the most difficult of all but also the most rewarding, because you are accessing untapped powers of your brain.

These exercises resemble the kinds of activities used in our creativity workshops. Participants are led from the familiar and comfortable activities with mental pictures and language, singing, and rhyming to finally creating a picture with a title. They go from using old, well-established thought paths to new and scattered ones. Stimulating their brains in a variety of ways (aroma, music, visual images, rhyme, and humor) makes it easier for them to draw—even if they had no particular experience or skill with art. We also noticed that when they were rushed or worried, this final exercise was less productive and creative. The point, as we see it, is that the freer and more comfortable you are to use more parts of your brain, the more apt you are to be creative and productive.

Another lesson learned: Varying the mental stimulation you are exposed to improves the quality of your thinking. The more varied your experiences, the more options you have, and the flexibility of your thinking thereby increases. With each experience, excitement builds, and soon you find yourself full of energy, enthusiasm, and new ideas. All the while, another awareness is developing, of other innate and subtle skills—skills essential for anticipating change, the subject of the next chapter.

Step 7: Commit yourself to spending a few minutes each day being aware of the aromas, sights, and sounds around you—and to playing with words and drawing each day.

PART THREE

Techniques for Managing Change

8
Anticipating: The Avalanche and Other Techniques

The Harmonic Convergence, on August 16, 1987, celebrated an astronomical phenomenon that occurs every 23,000 years, when certain planets and stars are in a special configuration. Mystics, students of the Mayan and Aztec calendars, and longtime members of the peace movement had eagerly anticipated this date. They believed that it marked the beginning of a new age, when the universe would be ready for change, when worldwide peace and harmony would be possible.

Participants in the Harmonic Convergence relied on two ancient calendars and modern astronomy to forecast a time that would be ripe for positive change. These are a few of the many ways we employ to predict changes that affect our lives.

Other methods abound. The sections of your daily newspaper with highest readership are those that seem to offer help in anticipating change. The business pages help you predict where the stock market will go; the sports pages predict the trade of your favorite player; biorhythms and astrology predict what sort of day you'll have. Even the editorial pages are designed to help us anticipate social and political changes. Yes, we read all of these for information, but whether we're aware of it or not, we are mainly interested in improving our ability to anticipate change and perhaps gain from it.

We often have the feeling that, if we have enough data about a situation, we can ward off the bad effects of a change or perhaps avoid it altogether. And so we search the media and poll our friends and colleagues to gather all the information available.

Some of us gather this data in a less deliberate way: we unconsciously assemble bits and pieces of information from the body language of those around us, their tone of voice, and mysterious "vibrations" in the air. The data compiled in this intuitive way is then converted into hunches, guesses, and gut feelings.

Both kinds of information gathering are helpful in anticipating and preparing for change. Even though you don't know exactly what will happen, just having an inkling about the kind of change that is coming often enables you to make the best of an opportunity or to minimize the losses from an unfavorable change.

Preparedness and Pain

The value of knowing what to expect has even a physical impact. For example, research done by Irving Janis, from the University of California at Berkeley, shows that surgery patients who make the quickest recovery with fewest complications are those who have been forewarned about the kind and degree of pain they'll experience.*

The vast changes in childbirth methods show the value of preparation for medical procedures. At one time, virtually no one was privy to the birth process but doctors and nurses. The mother was either terrified by the whole process or anesthetized. With the advent of Bradley natural childbirth in the fifties and LaMaze and other embellishments in the sixties, each stage of delivery became well known to the mother, the father, and anyone else interested enough to participate. These days the mother knows exactly what to expect—and normally suffers discomfort or mild pain rather than agony.

*Padus, Emrika, *The Complete Guide to Your Emotions & Your Health* (Emmaus, Pa.: Rodale Press, 1986).

Have you ever experienced an operation for which you have been fully prepared? Have you also ever experienced emergency surgery? If so, you can appreciate the value of being prepared mentally. When fully prepared, you still experience pain and discomfort, but it is more bearable and less frightening.

We have found that the same principle applies in organizations: The ones that recover most quickly and fully from such "radical surgery" as mergers and layoffs are those that kept employees informed about upcoming changes. The more information employees got, the less stress they experienced and the more realistic their expectations were. Consequently, their companies were "healthier"—that is, more successful throughout all stages of the change.

Most changes seem to arrive unannounced. They come hurtling over the doorjamb like an unruly, unexpected guest, or they sneak through the window like a burglar. But in truth, you do get hints that they're coming. The uncouth guest might have said "I'll drop by soon" the last time you encountered him on the street. You might have read about the burglar's activities just two blocks away the previous week. The signals were there but went unnoticed.

Gradual change is even more difficult to anticipate. Management consultant Larry Wilson makes this observation: If you had two frogs and put one in a bucket of hot water, it would jump around and make quite a fuss. If you put the other frog in a bucket of cold water and placed it over a low flame, the frog would just sit there. Eventually you'd have cooked frog. Because the change happened gradually to the second frog, it did not notice what was happening to it, and so it died.

Wilson says that too many managers are like the second frog. They simply do not sense change until it is too late.

Staying One Jump Ahead

To help you avoid a similar fate, this chapter will offer you some ways to increase your awareness of gradual change and even of change that seems to come without warning. The chapter will close with the Avalanche Technique, a method for mitigating the effects of a change that you know is on its way. But first, you need to understand that change has identifiable characteristics.

The Harmonic Convergence, the horoscopes, and the newspaper columns described earlier all have a common thread running through them: They show a desire, a need to get a handle on change—to define and quantify it. This urge is so strong in all of us because we subconsciously feel that defining and quantifying change will make it more predictable and thus more manageable. Perhaps, too, the scientist in all of us demands a rational explanation for our experiences. We are trying to answer the age-old question "What's it all about?"

Indeed, science has done its share of explaining change: Mathematicians and physicists have studied it and produced an array of laws and mathematical theorums, such as the Laws of Conservation, that help explain how change occurs. Here are nine laws of change and what they mean for us.

The Physics of Change

Beside each concept is an inference that can be made and applied to the change you experience daily:

Law	*So What?*
Change is a natural mechanism for maintaining balance between two extremes.	CHANGE IS NORMAL AND A SIGN OF HEALTH.
The first natural response to change is inertia.	RESISTANCE TO CHANGE IS ALSO NORMAL AND A SIGN OF HEALTH.
Without disturbances, the status quo deteriorates.	CHANGE IS AN OPPORTUNITY TO AVOID DECAY.
Once deterioration begins, the rate of negative change increases.	BETTER TO ACT BEFORE YOU'RE ACTED UPON.

Tension is created between an urge to conserve and an urge to change. When this tension is broken, energy is released.	BECOMING RESOLVED ABOUT CHANGE RELEASES ENERGY.
Altering an established pattern requires more energy than initiating a new one.	IT'S EASIER TO START ANEW THAN MODIFY AN OLD HABIT.
Once the barrier is broken, the change-energy gathers momentum.	ONCE YOU INITIATE CHANGE, IT BECOMES INCREASINGLY EASIER TO CHANGE.
Each attempt to make a breakthrough weakens resistance and increases the likelihood that change will occur.	EACH TIME YOU TRY TO CHANGE, YOU ARE ONE STEP NEARER TO SUCCESS.
In any seemingly random series of events a coherent pattern can be discerned.	THERE IS ORDER IN CHANGE AND YOUR ABILITY TO MANAGE CHANGE CAN BE IMPROVED.

Discovering patterns in your world will help you anticipate the future. Knowing that you have the innate ability to detect them is a major step toward doing so.

Vibes in the Air

Have you ever said, when a calamity occurred to you, "I had a feeling something was wrong, but I just couldn't put my finger on what it was"? And have you also said, "If only I'd paid more attention to that funny feeling I had"? Whether the feeling was based on concrete information or whether there really are vibrations floating in the air, you can improve your ability to anticipate change and thereby to prepare for it. The key to anticipation is awareness. Often you do get signals that a change is coming, but you overlook them or discount them.

That's what happened to Melissa Baker, manager of human resources for a large telecommunications company. Here's her story:

"For several months before I was let go, I had an odd, uneasy feeling . . . something seemed wrong. There wasn't the same camaraderie between me and the other managers that there had been. I didn't get feedback about my performance, good or bad.

"I knew that some of the employee training courses I developed got poor ratings and that some of the people I'd hired for key jobs didn't work out. But I rationalized that many of my hires *had* worked out. Besides, one of my career-track programs had the highest enrollments and ratings of any in the company.

"I kept telling myself I would ask for a brainstorming session with all the divisional vice presidents to see what improvements they might suggest. I kept meaning to take care of several complaints that course materials were poorly organized. But I never did either one.

"Months went by, the courses I designed filled up regularly, and I told myself it was crazy to bother them. Then, in July, the divisionals for personnel and marketing scheduled a meeting with me. I prepared a list of resources I needed and some brand new courses I wanted to schedule.

"At the meeting, I immediately launched into my agenda, but Nora, the divisional for personnel, stopped me. Without mincing words, she said, 'We've decided to let you go. You have six weeks.'

"I felt like I'd been punched in the stomach, but I also felt oddly detached, and I thought, 'So this is what I've been feeling uneasy about.' I thought back to the vague feelings I'd had for the last six months and wished I'd paid closer attention to them. During the next few weeks, I vacillated between anger and despair. Then, about the fifth week, as I started getting interviews for other jobs, I felt glad to be leaving . . . glad to make a fresh start. And apprehensive but excited to be off in a new direction.

"Now that I've had time to put it all into perspective, I can see that the big plus for me in this experience is that I'm paying more attention to my gut feelings and learning to use them to head off problems."

Just like Melissa, most of us overlook the signals that a change is coming. Think back now to sudden changes you have experienced in the past six months. In reality, didn't you have some inkling of most of them? Rarely do changes sneak up on us without some warning. Reviewing the hunches and flashes of intuition you've had will strengthen the abilities you already have to foresee change. And this is a skill to be valued.

One of the clearest differences we have noted between those who handle change well and those who don't is this ability to anticipate change. The literature of business management is full of stories about the intuitive skills of successful entrepreneurs and leaders.

For instance, T. Boone Pickens's success with takeovers has more to do with his intuitive grasp of how American business really works than with market analysis.

Richard Thalheimer's Sharper Image stores and catalogs were founded on the hunch that successful young people, primarily men, would spend lots of money for such "grown-up toys" as an $8,400 Wurlitzer jukebox, a duck decoy telephone that quacks instead of rings, and a ten-foot suit of armor.

Merv Griffin's show biz sense of timing helped him outguess the legendary real estate developer, Donald Trump, in a bid for Atlantic City casino holdings.

The gambler's instinct of John Kluge, who has been called "the last great entrepreneur" by fellow billionaire Armand Hammer, dates back to college days when he supplemented his scholarship to Columbia University with poker winnings. He built a single radio station near Washington, D.C., into Metromedia early in his career, then in the eighties became a high roller by being one of the first to use the leveraged buyout and parlayed Metromedia into control of Orion Pictures and major cellular phone interests.

And perhaps "women's intuition" has helped female entrepreneurs quickly become a factor in the economy. They now head 3.7 million of the more than 13 million sole proprietorships in America.

Similar stories occur throughout history in all fields, from the military to medical. It is little wonder. Seeing obstacles and opportunities before they actually confront you gives you a decided advantage.

Ten Trend Tips

To help you further develop your ability to anticipate change, we have compiled the following list from our own experiences and from conversations with clients.

1. *Listen.* Like a pro. Recognize that listening is an efficient use of your time. Listen at parties, on the phone, in the restroom, at meetings, on the train. Listen to your boss, the mailman, children, store clerks, and the radio. (To help you get more from your listening, see the box.)

LISTEN LIKE A PRO

"Professional listeners," such as judges, counselors, therapists, and psychics, develop special abilities to gather information. Even if you are already considered a good listener, try these techniques. They can help you sharpen your ability to gather information and ultimately your intuition:

- Tell people *what* you're listening for and *why*. If they know what they're saying is important to you, they'll be more forthcoming. They're more likely to be helpful and provide other sources of information.

- Listen for what's *not* said. What does it mean when a client doesn't return your phone calls? What can you learn when a competitor makes a speech and doesn't mention the latest development in your field?

- Listen to *how* your questions are answered: angrily, reluctantly, enthusiastically, stupidly. Nonverbal clues and voice tone often say more than words.

- Listen sincerely. Be interested in the person you're listening to—or at the very least the topic. Your encouraging words and body language help the speaker feel comfortable and confident.

- Listen actively. When you restate and rephrase what has been said, you are actually helping the speaker clarify his or her thoughts. Furthermore, you are acknowledging that the message has been heard and understood.

- Do something with the information you've heard as soon as possible. Tell it to someone, write it down, apply it in a conversation. You'll remember more of it longer and have a better understanding of it.

2. *Watch the competition.* Through journals, speeches, classes, and meetings, discover all you can about the competition to see if you can detect trends. Hospital administrators noticed how well the one-stop shopping concept worked for retailers and added their own array of related services. Now, when you visit a hospital, you can get your cholesterol level checked and information on lipsosuction and hair transplants—while you wait.

3. *Look to the past to predict the future.* To anticipate what might happen in 1998, look back to 1978. What was being invented then that affects us now—and what effect will that same invention have ten years down the road? For example, the Walkman personal stereo changed our listening habits and paved the way to learning with books on tape. This comfort with listening eventually made the car a sales office, complete with phone.

4. *Look at what's popular.* The hottest cartoonist, musician, presidential candidate, kind of food. Are there trends in movie themes, TV series, book topics, and college courses that tell you anything about the future? Analyze what values and interests, needs and wants are being expressed in the popular culture. For example, the popularity of video tape players might cause a decline in the sale of running shoes but an increase in the sales of popcorn.

5. *Adopt the methods of professional trend watchers such as pollsters and intelligence agents.* During World War II, a Swiss intelligence team was able to predict where German troops would mass by reading the social pages of small-town German newspapers and noting which generals were in what towns. You, too, can detect trends by scanning newspapers, magazines, books, and news digests, by reading junk mail, billboards, and advertisements.

6. *Watch the activities of the businesses and institutions associated with your profession.* Watch the regulators, the unions, the suppliers. What happens to them inevitably brings change to you.

For example, when federal import regulations were relaxed, the resulting flood of foreign goods told U.S. manufacturers they needed to control costs to compete. Union leaders might have realized this would eventually affect labor policies.

7. *Search for solutions to negative trends.* Think about what could be done about pollution, oil spills, and child abuse. You may discover some useful solutions, and, at the very least, you will be aware of the growing concerns of many other people.

An example? For many years creosote has been applied to wood to preserve it. When it was learned that creosote residue washes off and pollutes the soil with PCB, builders began to burn the soil to clean up building sites. Recently, researchers discovered that this practice pollutes the air. Whoever comes up with a solution to this double bind will no doubt earn a fortune *and* the gratitude of environmentalists.

8. *Look at the trends in your activities, beliefs, and interests.* How have your attitudes and behaviors changed in the past five years? Do any changes in your life reflect more general trends? If you are atypical, (for example, you'd wear dark brown and black clothes in Florida) and want to discover trends, just notice which ones you are not involved in.

9. *Give credence to your hunches.* Remind yourself of the times your predictions have been right, and delight in them. When

you feel you'll find a parking space in the next block, take note. If you are correct, crow about it.

10. *Analyze the nature of the trends you perceive and the factors that drive them.* What events start new trends or interrupt old ones? Are the trends cyclical or structural, moving quickly or slowly?

Both kinds of trends are illustrated by the Vietnam War. Over history, the structure of wars has gone from small to large, with this growth finally culminating in World War II. The atom bomb provoked a reverse in this structure—from worldwide, heroic struggles, to small skirmishes—"police actions" in which war is never officially declared.

To offset the demoralizing effects of this new kind of warfare, soldiers were assigned individually to Vietnam on a random basis and for one year only. Unfortunately, this change hindered more than it helped. Most soldiers entered and exited the war singly and quickly, and so the normal cycle of orientation and debriefing was interrupted and the Vietnam veteran was denied a gradual transition back into society.

Compounding their re-entry problem was the antiwar sentiment at home. Although there have always been waves of discontent with other wars, seeing the Vietnam War close-up on television every day intensified the emotional swing toward antipathy—a cyclical change.

Currently, the mood is swinging back and there is a great wave of sympathy for veterans. It is interesting to note that, structurally, wars have gotten even smaller since Vietnam. Some feel that terrorism, although awful, is a scaled down version of war. Perhaps this new way of looking at war and its soldiers presages a trend that will extinguish war altogether.

Three Questions for Change

These ten tips will help you gather information for detecting trends. But how can you apply your knowledge to your worklife? How can you use that information to help you make a career or other decision? Ask yourself:

1. *What do I really enjoy doing?*   How can you make a living doing what to you is fun, challenging, and never boring?

Apply your answers to this question to the trends you've noticed. Does anything fit? If you love making French pastries and sense that French restaurants are becoming increasingly popular, start your own bakery or apply for a job in a French restaurant.

2. *One year from now, what will I wish I had done today?* Do you see yourself with a stress-related ulcer and wish you'd followed doctors' orders? Do you look twenty pounds heavier and wish you'd curbed your appetite? Does your Mastercard bill look like the national debt and do you wish you'd curbed spending? Do you see stains on your oriental rug and wish you'd taken your dog to obedience school?

3. *What needed service or product is not currently being offered in the field I'd like to be in?*   Perhaps the job has not yet been invented. By looking for voids to fill, you are using your prescience in a practical way. You have accomplished more than the most accurate psychics, weather forecasters, and prophets who merely predict the future. You have done something about it in the same way that experts do something about avalanches.

The Avalanche Technique

In many ways, changes in your daily life can be similar to avalanches. Avalanches pose a great threat to life in the high country. They can bury ski runs, highways, and entire villages in a few moments. Likewise, changes in your life can build to danger-ous proportions, sweep over you, suffocate you with their weight and momentum. Knowing when and where avalanches might occur is a great help in avoiding loss of life. Professionals who predict and control avalanches use techniques that suggest ways we can anticipate change:

- These experts know the terrain. They know that certain areas are "snow pathways" where avalanches are likely to build. They determine the degree of the incline, realizing that the steeper the grade, the less stable the snow buildup —and the more likely an avalanche will occur at that site.

- They watch for gradual erosion of bonding of snow layers. To do this, they constantly review weather patterns since avalanches build during cycles that go from new snow to a melting period to another new snow. During the melting period the snowflakes lose their sharp points, and so the bond weakens between the layers of snow. And then just one five-minute downfall of new snow can sometimes provoke an avalanche.

- They watch for conditions that provoke sudden shifts in snow. Rain, heavy snowfall, and strong winds can precipitate slippage and movement, especially in areas where faults already exist.

- They also constantly take the broad view of potential sites. They eyeball snow accumulations which take on a blue tinge when the snow bonds weaken. They are familiar with the look of change in avalanche areas.

- They insist that detection must be ongoing, not last-minute or one-time. Constant vigilance in the long and short view is the foundation of their profession.

- They focus on spreading awareness of information on avalanches. Since they realize that victims often set off the avalanches that trap them, avalanche professionals alert skiers, travelers, and residents to prevailing conditions through signs, media, and word of mouth.

- But the most intriguing service they render is to set off small avalanches before devastating ones happen. They set off small dynamite explosions or fire bazookas in specific areas to get the snow moving under controlled conditions.

Does this say anything to you about changes you see ahead? Think what Melissa might have done to avoid losing her job. What if she had listened to her feelings that things were not going well?

It might have been uncomfortable to insist on feedback about her job performance, but she could have used it to revise her way of doing things. She might have had some unpleasant moments if she had asked the divisional vice presidents for ways to improve, but she might also have detonated the resentment that was building. She might have avoided her avalanche entirely or at least diminished its impact. Here's a technique that may have helped Melissa anticipate and avoid her avalanche:

When you sense that a change is coming, try some strategies extrapolated from avalanche detection.

- *Make small changes* that will either correct the situation or provoke a confrontation. It is better to be knee-deep in trouble than in over your head. It is better to have short, productive confrontations with your manager than one ferocious argument that ends in a blowup.

- *Spread these detonations* out over the entire field. If you are accumulating small irritations in a number of people in your workplace, they may compound into one group complaint that snowballs into a gigantic problem. So settle the individual problems one at a time and as soon as possible.

- *Develop an awareness of your own tension level.* Sometimes we suffer small losses and hurts over a period of months or years and fail to recognize them. We often neglect grieving for these losses. We fail to acknowledge the damage that fear is doing to us physically and emotionally. This stiffling blocks access to intuition. Finally, the pressure becomes too great, and an avalanche of emotions comes hurdling down upon us and others around us.

- *If the worst comes,* and you find yourself in the middle of a snowslide, *remember these avalanche survival guidelines:*

1. Call out so your friends can help.

2. Try swimming with the tide so you can stay on top.

3. Discard items with you for maximum freedom and flexibility.

4. Leave a trail of markers to help others help you.

5. Avoid panic; stay confident.

6. If you find yourself becoming buried, hold your body in a circle so that you can trap enough air to keep you alive until help arrives (in other words, keep your space, your integrity about you until you can get out).

Of course, the key to surviving the ultimate disaster is to have *anticipated the change and prepared for it.* In this chapter you have learned to recognize your innate capacity for *anticipating* change, and you've gotten some tools for fine-tuning those predictive skills.

Preparing for the changes you anticipate requires other skills. In the next chapter, you'll learn and practice specific techniques to use when sudden changes are thrust upon you.

9

Responding: Four Options

The historic surgery Sunday that successfully separated seven-month-old Siamese twins joined at the head actually began in West Germany five months ago. Last spring, a team of physicians from Johns Hopkins Hospital visited the infants and devised a unique plan that they thought could divide them without causing lasting brain damage.

Daniel Stillwell, the deputy sheriff shot and killed Sunday by a hospitalized convict trying to escape, expressed concern in June to his supervisor about the safety of deputies guarding inmates at Denver General Hospital, authorities confirmed Monday. In a memo, Stillwell said deputies who work at DGH should have bulletproof vests or more personnel to lessen personal risk. He died from two bullet wounds in the chest and back.

These two stories ran above the fold on the front page of a large metropolitan newspaper on Tuesday, September 8, 1987. In awful contrast, they illustrate the value of anticipation and planning.

Both the surgeons and the policeman had to respond to circumstances beyond their control. The first response was planned and practiced; the second, reactive and desperate. Granted, the surgeons had five months to devise their strategy for correcting the twins' problem, but Officer Stillwell's intuition had warned him of the dangers he faced. He had suggested several solutions but, tragically, was unable to get them implemented. And so his death occurred, a terrible imposed change.

We all face imposed change in the form of emergencies every day: a blown tire on the highway, a power outage, or an unexpected visitor who disrupts the day's schedule. Likewise, we all face opportunities daily: meeting an interesting stranger, discovering a stimulating book, or getting a new client.

The emergencies and opportunities might be one and the same:

a blown tire could produce the interesting stranger who helped you get off the highway; the power outage could have forced you to read on the patio instead of watching TV; and the office drop-in could be a troubled but rich client. You can determine whether the experience is positive or negative and whether it produces more options for you or more restrictions.

Many of the changes imposed upon us seem to be bad luck over which we have no control. This feeling of powerlessness is probably why we so often dread change—because we feel that we can only react or respond to outside forces. As the story of the twins' surgery shows, you do have power when you develop a method and persevere in using it.

In this chapter, you will learn four strategies to help you respond to change that is imposed upon you. Each of these major change techniques has a related Quick Changemaker. These long-form and short-form versions will give you some control over the changes that are visited upon you. They come from our workshops that have helped people successfully handle such circumstances as demotions, mergers, bankruptcies, transfers, promotions, and the loss of a valued account or colleague.

As we experimented with a variety of change strategies, we noticed that some people preferred and were more successful with certain techniques, while others got nowhere with them yet made great gains with entirely different methods. As we studied this phenomenon, we realized that the Change-Friendly Quotient Survey test predicted which technique they would prefer. Reasoners, Refocusers, Relaters, and Riskers were each drawn to one of the approaches for responding to change.

As you read through these four techniques and their matching Quick Changemakers, you may well feel much more in sync with the one that relates to your change style. However, don't tune out the other techniques. Learning other approaches will expand your personal flexibility.

The Loss Technique

Whether it is the breakup of a friendship, a financial setback, or a mislaid briefcase, all of us experience losses often. Most of the time, it's easier to deal with the lost briefcases in life because they can be replaced. But even then, look what you might go through:

"Oh no . . . it can't be lost! The Hastings report is in there. I'll bet it's in the back seat of Jim's car." So you proceed to look everywhere for it, feeling certain that it will turn up. When all efforts are fruitless, *you begin to feel anger and guilt:* "Dammit. How could I be so stupid? I must have left it on the train *before* I got into Jim's car. Yeah . . . now I remember . . . Ann asked me to run all those errands, I set my briefcase down . . . but where? She's always loading me down with those tasks that 'will just take a minute' and 'it's on your way.' It's her fault . . . and I'm going to let her know it." And pretty soon you're in a real snit about it.

Then sometimes you'll petition the gods and promise to reform: *"If only I could find it, I'd never let her get me overloaded again.* That would help—I should just be real careful not to get too much on my mind. If I get out of this one, I'll make sure this never happens again."

Next, you assess the loss and what it means to your future. And you usually get depressed: "What a bummer. *That calendar is going to be impossible to recreate.* I'll be missing appointments for the rest of the year. Next week, I'm supposed to meet with Meg Jennings but at what time? Nuts, I can't even remember where. I suppose I'll have to call her secretary to find out and he's such a pill. Some days it just doesn't pay to get up."

But finally you begin to go through all the lost items and analyze their importance: "The Hastings report is on the word processor, and the pen is easily replaced. The idea file had some good stuff in it, but the ideas will come around again if they were really useful. It's the calendar that's going to hurt. Actually, I'm better off without the pen—it always leaked at crucial moments. And the briefcase had a loose handle and a broken zipper. I should have replaced it years ago. Maybe Sam has some of these appointments on his calendar—we've been working pretty closely—he'll remember a lot of them. So I miss a few appointments. *It's not the end of the world."*

You went through a chain of emotions in reacting to the loss: first, *denial* or disbelief that the briefcase was really lost; then *anger* with yourself and Ann; next a *bargaining* period in which you promised to change your ways if the loss isn't final; next *depression* when the full impact of your loss hit you; and finally *acceptance.*

These five steps parallel the stages of grief that psychiatrist Elisabeth Kübler-Ross found we go through when a loved one dies. Many psychotherapists have developed "grief" therapies and workshops to help individuals experience the stages of grief fully and thereby regain control over their lives. Further, fully experiencing the five stages of grief frees you to take action and make progress.

One of the most valuable discoveries of grief research and therapy is that there is an optimal time for each of us to begin the process of restructuring our lives after suffering a loss. If you can find the "right time" for you and the situation, the action you take will be positive and fruitful, and you will experience that surge of energy that enables you to move on.

The optimal moment for action in the example of the lost briefcase came soon because the loss had little emotional value; if you'd lost your engagement ring, your time for acting would have been later. If your fiancé had broken your engagement, the ideal moment to begin restructuring your life would have been even later.

Rushing through the grief process is often seen in the actions of the widow who sells the family home within months of her husband's death and then lapses into a depression soon after. Her pain is so strong at the moment of loss, she feels she must do *something* to get relief. So she involves herself in disposing of her husband's clothes, cleaning out the house to make it salable, engaging a realtor, and finding another place to live. In her fever to act, she might sell her house below market value and dispose of articles she can never replace.

Widows once did not make hasty decisions because they were expected to withdraw from society for months. Although the purpose was to show respect for the dead, the mourning period gave them time to grieve. Likewise, in the business world, severance pay is a financial bridge to the next job, but it also allows time to get beyond the disorientation, anger, or grief felt over losing the old job.

Experiencing the five stages of grief is a normal and necessary process, but our society often denies this redress for loss—particularly job losses. We are told to "keep a stiff upper lip" or "try a little harder" when we lose face or fortune at work. Corporations also deny themselves the mourning process. When Kodak laid off people for the first time in thirty years, when AT&T reduced its work force by 20 percent in 1987, or when the local department store sells out to a national chain, all departments of the organization feel grief. This is not surprising when you consider how strongly we identify with our work. Even a small or positive change on the job can provoke a sense of loss. Ted moves up to supervisor and no longer jokes at lunch with coworkers; Jennifer becomes secretary to the dean and relinquishes the right to goof off.

Rosemary Chang, a senior partner in a medium-sized accounting firm, recalls the gloom she felt as she concluded a deal to merge with one of the Big Eight firms. "Even though I was moving in a direction I wanted to," Rosemary sighed, "with ample support staff and the opportunity to work on large, interesting corporate accounts, I was incredibly sad about the merger. We weren't able to take everyone with us, my name would no longer be on the wall above the receptionist, and perhaps I'd never know all the employees intimately again."

If positive moves provoke a sense of loss, you can imagine the impact when you lose your job due to circumstances beyond your control. It can be a devastating experience, especially if you try to suppress the natural emotions that result and move immediately to action.

When you take action before you have fully experienced the five stages of loss, you place a debilitating drain on your energies. Take the case of John C., who lost his engineering job with Martin-Marietta on a Tuesday. Two weeks later, he was working for another firm. He had spent the intervening period frantically searching for a job and had taken the first decent offer he got. He did not even stop to recognize his feelings. He was too busy job hunting to get out his anger, guilt, or blame.

John said later, "That first morning, driving to the new job, I was congratulating myself on finding another position so quickly when a wave of despair washed over me.

"I felt sad and exhausted. I'd have to start all over again, making friends, getting the feel of the operation, carving out my niche. I almost turned around and went home. I had an awful time those first few months, forcing myself to act positive, interested, and energetic at work. I'd drag myself out of bed every morning and then drink coffee all day long to keep myself moving. I just couldn't get excited about my job. I was sarcastic whenever other employees talked about our glowing future, and I held myself aloof from them. Why commit my enthusiasm and energy? I had given my all to Martin and for what? The first cut that came, I was gone. I felt like a disposable food tray—discarded without a thought.

"I talked to my wife about this—my feeling of being discarded and the isolation and disinterest that went with it—and then even discussed it with friends.

"Then at work, they began asking me for ideas and really listened to them. I grew to trust the department head and others. I began to have faith in my new company's future. That's when I began to leave the other job behind and feel good about my new position."

If John had allowed himself to experience denial, anger, bargaining, depression, and acceptance over the loss of his job initially, he could have begun his new job with enthusiasm.

Below is an exercise to help you go through a grief experience. Choose a loss you've suffered recently at work and go through these steps:

Step 1   (to overcome denial). Fill in the blank:

I lost _____.

You may have lost face, love, ground, admiration, opportunity, or something tangible—but be specific. It is important to identify exactly what you've lost. If your company moved to another location, you might believe you feel bad because you can't look out over the park anymore. While that *is* a loss, if your new view is even better, then your feeling of loss is related to something else: Will you miss the comfort of knowing the restaurants, resources, and people in the area? Is your supervisor farther away in your new quarters? Does the new location mean a loss of easy access to convenient transportation or parking areas? Will you now be stuck in bumper-to-bumper traffic going to and from work each day?

The process of analyzing exactly what has been lost helps you accept the reality of the loss and therefore overcome the denial stage. It also helps you know exactly where the problem lies and thus tells you where to begin. So, to overcome denial, Step 1 asks you to describe what you've lost.

Step 2   (to experience anger). Fill in the blanks:

I am angry with _____
about this loss because _____.

You may be angry with several people—including yourself. Identifying who's involved helps dispel the anger, but understanding why is even more helpful. For example, sometimes you think you're angry with one person but another is the real culprit, in which case you are focusing your energies in the wrong place.

Step 3   (to experience bargaining). Fill in the blanks:

If I could have _____ **back, I would promise to** ____
_____.

Once you've filled in these blanks, go out for a brisk walk, mop the floor, hit tennis balls against the backboard, or involve yourself in some other vigorous, solo activity . . . all the while picturing your bargaining scene.

This step allows you to think of ways to recover your loss without just compounding your problems. You are vulnerable to unwise actions because the anxiety over your loss drives you to want to take action. Obviously flawed and hopelessly complex strategies may seem attractive because you are so eager to bargain away your suffering.

By mentally rehearsing the bargaining, you make three gains.

You can convert this natural tendency to bargain into a search for positive alternatives; you can expend your anxiety-driven energies in a helpful way; and you can accomplish both of these without taking an action you'll regret later.

Step 4   (experiencing depression). Fill in the blanks:

Regarding the loss of my _____, I feel (now list in the left column below four separate adjectives that describe how you feel about your loss:

_____	_____
_____	_____
_____	_____
_____	_____

Now, look up the four adjectives you've listed in the dictionary and write a definition on the line opposite the word. Analyze and compare these words and definitions. Do they really express fully how you feel? Do they give you any insights into why you feel so badly about your loss?

This step has two purposes. Pushing yourself to come up with four different adjectives ensures that you will more fully recognize the depression that accompanies grief. When you go beyond first reactions, you get under the surface of your feelings and touch on the deeper despair.

Also, taking action on your depression helps dispel it. Therapists who work with depressed patients get them moving physically and mentally. Step 3 got you into a physical action. Looking up words in this step gets you moving mentally. Now you're ready for the final phase.

Step 5   (accepting your loss). Fill in the blanks:

I have really and truly lost _____
_____ but gained _____.

This last step helps you recognize the reality of your loss while realizing that you have benefited in some way. Even in the most difficult emotional losses, some gain is made: The widow loses her husband but gains free time and the challenge to her survival abilities; John lost his job but discovered how valuable communication with his wife and friends could be.

Throughout this exercise, you have been asked to focus and define your feelings. The purpose is to force you into left-brained kinds of thinking. As you learned in the chapter about the brain, analyzing and defining are tasks done most of the time on the left side of the brain. When you are overwhelmed by emotions, your impulsive, intuitive, right side is in control. Therefore, to get control over yourself and the situation, you need to move to the left, which is just what this exercise does for you.

There is a final step in the grief process, and that is to take action, to perform some act that is a direct outcome of your experience with loss. During the grieving, you have had to control and divert your energy lest you pass through your grief too quickly or become involved in ill-advised projects or actions. Now that you have dealt with your grief, you can forge ahead, making positive changes in your life that will help diminish the grief. Without this final step the energy from the emotion may be lost. If it's a job you've lost, start surveying newspapers and magazines— try to skim the employment situation. Then prepare a list of all the places you'd like to work and perhaps update your resume. And take a good look at yourself. Do you like what you see? Get in good shape physically; maybe get a haircut or spruce up your clothes. Then take your list of employers and set a goal to arrange interviews with one a day or two a week. Plan your goals and methods carefully and write them down (in twenty-five words or less)—then get started!

You have now walked through the loss exercise and are prepared to use it the next time you experience a loss. A form is provided to help you through it. Each time you use it you may want to refer to these pages to be sure you are working through your grief fully. When you have used this technique a number of times, you will find yourself able to use it much more quickly and without referring to the text. It will become an automatic and comfortable part of your change repertoire.

THE LOSS TECHNIQUE

Fill in the blanks.

Step 1   (to overcome denial):

I lost _____

Step 2   (to experience anger):

I am angry with _____
because _____

Step 3   (to experience bargaining):

When I talk to _____ about this, I will
say:

_____

_____

Step 4   (experiencing depression):

Adjectives: Dictionary definitions:

_____   _____

_____   _____

_____   _____

_____   _____

Step 5   (accepting your loss):

I have really and truly lost _____
but gained _____

Now, in 25 words or less define the action you'll take to deal
with your loss.
I will _____

_____

_____

*   *   *

For the Reasoner, this comfort will come quickly because the Loss Technique is so logical, analytical, and rational. The technique is also comfortable for the Relater, because it fits naturally with a style of sharing emotions and seeking the opinions of others. The Refocuser and Risker may need to work with the technique a little longer, but in the end, they'll find it worth the effort. Because loss is such a common problem, all four styles will use the technique frequently. And so you'll see the loss technique recurring throughout the book.

When you are comfortable with the technique, you might try this shorter version for less significant losses.

The Quick Changemaker for Loss In 25 Words or Less

To clarify the actual loss involved and experience all aspects of the grief process quickly, fill in the blank spaces in the box. There's room for twenty-five words altogether; you may use more in one place and fewer in another, but for best results, think within the limits of a twenty-five-word total.

Here's how it works. If you've ever lost a piece of jewelry with sentimental value, you can understand Candy's grief over the loss of a silver butterfly brooch:

I have lost my silver butterfly brooch and feel angry with myself because I am careless with jewelry. If I could recover it, I'd be more careful. I feel sad, guilty and will probably feel that way for several months. But, I can live without it and have learned a valuable lesson from my loss. This lesson is: rushing through life takes its toll

Once you have worked your way through this quick form of grieving, you are prepared to take action. Now think what that action will be and write it below, restricting your statement to twenty-five words that should answer the five W's: Who? What? When? Where? Why? (And sometimes how?) The five W's are well-known to journalism students who are required to cover all five, sometimes in fewer than twenty-five words, when learning to write the lead paragraph of a news story.

Newswriters must learn this discipline to save space and to ensure that even when readers do not go beyond the first paragraph, they will have the essence of the story. This consolidation is helpful to the changemaker because it helps you identify the first action you need to take in response to your loss. Here's how Candy expressed her action plan in twenty-five words or less:

To be sure my jewelry is secure, I'll put it on and remove it
      (why)   **(who)**   **(what)**

in front of the same mirror each day.
  (where)   **(when)**

This statement went through several rewrites to boil it down to twenty-one words. The rewriting spurred Candy to mentally go through the details of her way of wearing jewelry. She discovered that it had been her habit to put on jewelry as she walked out the door or while driving to work in the morning. She realized that if she placed her jewelry box in front of a mirror, she could do a visual check of each piece to make sure it was securely fastened. She committed herself to spending at least thirty seconds in front of the mirror each time she put jewelry on or took it off. She thereby increased the chances that she'd remember what she had worn that day and would also be more likely to return it to its proper place. She promised herself that if she felt she couldn't make this thirty-second check at each end, she just wouldn't wear jewelry that day.

Here again, the Quick Changemaker for Loss will initially come more naturally to the Reasoner, but it can easily become an effective tool for the other three change styles. Anyone can do it comfortably and automatically with practice. Your goal should be to complete the Loss Analysis in one minute, then write and rewrite your Action Statement in one minute. Eventually you'll be able to complete both in one minute. Use the Quick Changemaker form the next time you experience a minor loss and want to get over it quickly.

In 25 Words or Less

Fill in the blanks—use no more than 25 words total:

I have lost _____ _____ _____ and feel angry with _____
         (overcoming denial)
_____ _____ because _____ _____ _____ _____ If I could
         (experiencing anger)
recover it, I'd _____ _____ _____. I feel _____ _____ and
         (bargaining)
will probably feel that way for _____ _____. But, I can live

without it and have learned a valuable lesson from my loss. This

lesson is: _____ _____ _____ _____ _____ _____ _____
         (acceptance)
_____ _____.

Then, in 25 words or less, state what action you'll take to mitigate your loss. This statement should say who, what, when, where, and why the action will be taken

_____ _____ _____ _____ _____ _____ _____ _____

_____ _____ _____ _____ _____ _____ _____ _____

_____ _____ _____ _____ _____ _____ _____ _____

_____.

When you first begin using this Quick Changemaker, apply it to the loss of a file folder or a telephone message slip. Later, you'll find you can use it in more serious situations, such as the loss of a client or of a promotion. However, truly significant losses, such as the loss of a job or of a loved one, can never be grieved over in such a short span. To do so would simply be glossing over your loss and could have serious consequences later.

You'll discover other applications for the Loss Technique in Chapter 13 on organization change. Now, on to the second approach, The Immersion Technique.

The Immersion Technique

The Immersion Technique is designed for situations in which you have tried other solutions and failed or when you are suddenly confronted with a major change. It can help you gather momentum as you battle your way towards success.

The Immersion Technique is not a paper exercise. You must actually do it, practice it. To begin, all you need to do is totally submerge yourself in the topic of the change you are trying to make—but this sometimes takes some doing. Perhaps this explanation of the process will help:

When you surround yourself with the subject of the change you'd like to make, your awareness level rises and your attitude becomes more open to change. Soon you find your behavior changing—not without effort, but certainly more easily than otherwise.

The Immersion Technique is particularly well suited to the Refocuser because it requires total involvement in a situation. As you know, the Refocuser has the ability to concentrate intently on the task at hand, excluding other thoughts. This characteristic is a disadvantage when it keeps the Refocuser from discovering options and opportunities, but it is a real help in dealing with a drastic change.

Paris Rogers, a young architect, just couldn't get his life together. He had a degree but hadn't passed the state boards for architects; consequently, no firm would hire him. Paris floated from one temporary job in construction to another for several years, enjoying all the delights of bachelorhood but never having enough money to pay bills, buy a dependable car, or acquire more than basic carpentry tools. Then, he met Emily at a party and ten months later had a wife, a baby girl, and a home mortgage.

"What will happen to them? They don't have insurance. He doesn't have a regular job. How can they survive?" his relatives worried.

Paris more than survived. He made great gains and completely overcame his family's fears. He had to respond to these new responsibilities by becoming more productive and disciplined. Paris plunged headlong into every construction job he could get: He painted, he roofed, he laid tile and carpeting, he built window boxes. Being involved in so many activities earned him a reputation as a jack-of-all trades. Within a year, he had a steady stream of work, some of which he could subcontract and earn a percentage from. They saved the money Emily earned from her part-time job and added it to a small loan. These three tactics enabled them to keep up the mortgage payments and comfortably furnish and landscape their home.

Both their families were amazed by such progress. But the admiration turned to horror when Emily became pregnant again, four months after their first child was born. "Paris is going to crack under the pressure; he's never had to be responsible" was the new concern.

Immersion is how Paris did it. He immersed himself in providing for his family. He involved himself in the day-to-day care of both babies, diapering, feeding, and bathing them on the nights Emily worked. By day and on weekends, he pursued every lead he got for his new business and studied professional magazines and seminars to refine his knowledge of architecture. Finally, he enrolled in a four-week evening class to prepare for the architecture examination.

He earned one of the highest scores ever made on the examination. Because of this and on the basis of his handyman business clientele, he was able to negotiate a partnership in a small but established architectural firm. In three years' time Paris changed his style from scattered to focused, from irresponsible to responsible, by immersing himself totally in a way of life he wanted.

Granted, the time was right. He had the youth and energy to accomplish a great deal. He had raw talent, the natural intensity of a Refocuser, and a support system.

But then, he had had all that before. By immersing himself in obligations, he was able to focus his mind and energies on achieving what had seemed impossible before.

The Immersion Technique applied to most work problems does not require such sacrificial abandon. Paris's achievements merely illustrate that you can accomplish a great deal simply by channeling your attention and resources in one direction.

Smaller gains require smaller efforts. Take the case of Arnold Jacobs. For six years, he'd worked in a small branch of a national advertising agency. His office was cheery and comfortable, with the coffeepot always brewing, doughnuts and marketing plans on the desks, and schedules evolving with each new idea or circumstance. Although individuals were often late for appointments and deadlines were usually met by a whisker, the happy, creative staff worked as a team and always managed to get the job done.

Then the unimaginable happened. The main office sent out a new branch manager, Paul, who was a stickler for details, schedules, and deadlines. The first time he walked in the office with his daytimer in hand, Arnold suspected that the idyll was over. When Paul devised a flow chart of the next six months' projects with weekly deadlines for each, Arnold was *sure* of it. This flow chart wrapped around two walls of the conference room and was the focus of each morning's eight o'clock meeting.

Arnold had not thought much about time for years and had developed a disregard for punctuality. But Paul sent out this edict: "Beginning immediately, work hours will be from 8 A.M. to 5 P.M., a schedule for staggered lunch hours will be posted each week, and all employees will be expected to be on time for appointments, meetings, and deadlines."

What a change. How could Arnold possibly overcome his habitual tardiness? He did—by Immersion—and here's how you can do it too:

To break the "lateness habit" using the Immersion Technique, completely surround yourself with reminders of time: calendars, clocks, kitchen timers, and metronomes. Put colored markers on your clocks to remind you to look at them—even your car clock and the one on the coffeemaker.

As you drive or ride to work, make a mental note of every clock you see along the way on banks, churches, and public buildings. Cross-check them to determine whether they are all in sync.

Take a course in time management. Read books and articles on the topic, then leave them lying around or fastened on your bulletin board. Buy a large, book-sized desk diary to carry with you.

Visit a clock shop and experience the ticking of hundreds of clocks. Breath in the aroma of the oiled wood of the grandfather clock. Notice the details of the bird in the cuckoo clock. Feel the cold, hard plastic of the modern quartz clocks.

Think about how important time is to mankind. Stonehenge and many other archeological sites were designed primarily to keep track of time so that the changing seasons could be anticipated. Think how important an awareness of time has been in producing the high state of technology we enjoy today. Think of prisoners who "do time": they no longer enjoy the privilege of controlling their own time.

As you become more aware of the importance of time and the devices that help you track it, you develop a greater respect for your time and others'. In these few steps (see box) you have experienced time with several of your senses, along with your mind and even your emotions. The more completely you immerse yourself, the more easily you will overcome your habit of being late and missing deadlines.

Immersion Technique

1. Surround yourself with the subject of the change you'd like to make:

   a. raises awareness level
   b. attitude towards the change softens

2. Behavior automatically begins to adapt to the imposed change.

As you consider applying this changemaker technique, realize that it can be used in many kinds of "need to respond" situations. It helped Arnold become more prompt to accommodate his new time-oriented boss. It can help you learn French in six weeks when you're given an overseas assignment or speak with clarity when your CEO is taken ill and you must present his speech to the board of directors.

When time does not seem important, it is difficult to be prompt for appointments and deadlines. If you have no use for your high school French, you will not expend the effort to practice it. If your boss makes all the speeches, you won't ever collect your thoughts on the company's status. But when circumstances change and you do need to be prompt, learn French, or make a speech, if you immerse yourself in the desired behavior, you are likely to respond successfully.

Immersion is usually easy for Refocusers because of the intense attention they give to any situation. They also periodically step back from what they are doing and refocus on new areas even without an imposed change, so it is fairly comfortable for them to make a shift when change requires it.

Reasoners do not naturally make such periodic shifts. It usually takes a strong shock for them to pull away from the present project or way of doing things and refocus. But once the change is truly imposed, Reasoners will focus anew just as intently as Refocusers because they are able to coolly assess the value of concentrating and learning all they can about the new situation.

Relaters also find Immersion easy to move into because they have a network of people who can help them. Relaters probably already know three people who can speak French and would be happy to practice with them. Riskers, too, are quite comfortable with the Immersion Technique because of their penchant for spontaneous action. They will immerse themselves totally and effectively as long as the period required is brief.

You can see that Immersion is useful to all four changemakers in many situations, but it is especially helpful when the imposed change requires you to alter long-standing attitudes. A shorter version, the Engineering Strategy that follows, addresses less complex situations.

The Quick Changemaker by Immersion
The Engineering Strategy

The Engineering Strategy is a surprisingly simple way to effect change, but discovering how and where to apply it requires ingenuity. The technique involves altering an element in your environment to cause a change in behavior and/or attitude.

This approach is based on the premise that an external change begets a change in behavior which eventually begets a change in attitude. Graphologists have long used similar methods to help clients. For example, if you're attending a meeting in which you need to be open to ideas then focus on a plan of action, you would first produce large, flowing circles as below.

When the time comes to complete an action plan, shift to making tall and precisely retraced *t*s with the crossing firm and high on the bar:

Try this a few times, and you'll find that altering your actions changes your attitude.

To begin applying the Engineering Strategy, first get a broad view of the problem, then focus on remedying one detail at a time. Once you start looking in this way at a change you must make, you'll have fun teasing out one part that can be altered by a simple manipulation of the environment.

For example: If your CEO has dictated a more formal, businesslike ambience in your office, focus on one change that would help to effect his wishes. You might notice that most staff members don't wear coats or jackets. One simple change in the environment will work: Turn down the heat in winter and turn up the air conditioner in the summer. You'll find jackets in place all day long. This chart illustrates the process:

Unwanted Situation	A Related Factor	The Strategy	Desired Behavior/ Attitude
(sloppy appearance)	(room temperature)	(lower the temperature)	(dress more formally)

Now, look for some other single factor that needs altering by skillful engineering. In a profession where dignity and tradition are important, do staff members project an attitude of professionalism? If not, try installing brass nameplates on office doors or desks, each one engraved with "Ms." or "Mr." before the employees' names and a prestigious title following it. Just seeing their names presented so properly each day causes them to take themselves more seriously and quickly affects behavior. This second phase looks like this:

Unwanted Situation	A Related Factor	The Strategy	Desired Behavior/ Attitude
(unprofessional behavior)	(office ambience)	(install brass nameplates)	(more professional attitude)

You can apply this Quick Changemaker as many times as you wish to any situation. The secret to success is focusing on one element each time. Use the form provided to use the Engineering Strategy the next time you must respond quickly to change. Now you are ready for another technique.

The Engineering Strategy

As you look at the change you must respond to, identify the unwanted situation and then find one factor that influences this situation. Now devise a strategy to alter this factor in a way that will produce the desired situation.

Unwanted Situation	A Related Factor	The Strategy	Desired Behavior

The Poll-taking Technique

The third technique for responding to change is ideal for the Relater, the changemaker who gathers opinions and information from a variety of people when making a change, then synthesizes all this data into an overall plan. Poll-taking requires you to do just that—get four viewpoints on the imposed change.

Pretend you have been a real estate agent in a small town where business has been steadily declining for five years. In fact, the market has gone so low that nothing is selling. Real estate is what you know, but the depressed economy has imposed a "nothing's for sale" sign on the town. As you wonder how to survive, you come across a large old house that's attractive on the outside but a real wreck inside. It can be purchased for a small price—about the same amount of money you have in the townhouse you own (and owe on). Should you or shouldn't you? Get the views of persons in four parts of your life:

1. **Family—your eldest son, Christopher, who is sixteen.**
   "Yeah, that's a cool place. A lot of college guys rent apartments in that neighborhood. They hold great rock parties—with live music—all the time."

2. **Social—president of the local women's press club.**
   "It's a lovely old house. I believe it would qualify as an historic landmark. There's lots of low-interest money available to renovate it if someone wanted to take the time. I've always fantasized holding my daughter's wedding there—that graceful winding stairwell and the leaded glass windows! What a perfect setting."

3. **Work—another salesperson.**
   "That place is a bomb. I wouldn't touch it with a ten-foot pole. The roof is bad and the porch looks like it might have termites."

4. **Fantasy—Cher** (imagined conversation).
   "Go for it. A little fixing up and it would be a real draw. You could hold concerts on the lawn in summer and make

a bundle. Have a music 'salon' the rest of the year. You could attract artists from all over—let them stay in that third floor apartment."

Now on to *synthesizing* these viewpoints in the true Relater fashion. Break out the comments into two groups—ones that make you feel good and ones that you out-and-out dislike or that send up red warning flags. The realtor made the following lists:

Positives	Red Flags
beautiful exterior	campus parties nearby
reasonable price	real estate decline
winding stairwell	termites?
gracious setting	making the payments
salon and music	bad roof?
low-interest loan	

The four points of view reveal more options than the realtor had originally thought possible. For this reason, in making a diagnosis, medical students are taught to cite at least four possible causes for the symptoms noted. Pushing the possibilities to at least four dislodges routine thinking and helps them go beyond the obvious.

The Poll-taking Technique requires that you seek opinions and data from four individuals in your life, but not just any four persons. To ensure that you find and stretch many options, the interviewees should be from four separate categories: work, social, family, and celebrity.

Here's how the technique works. As in other change techniques, the first step is to define or clarify the change that's been forced on you. Think it through and be as specific as possible. Then describe this change to someone from each of the categories and listen to the response.

Category 1. A member of your family. Family members may not have first-hand knowledge of your work problems, but they *do* have background information about you. Even though this intimacy may color their views, they *are* able to give you perceptions you'll find nowhere else.

If you have already discussed this change with a close family member, you might want to break through to a less traditional view. Solicit or imagine the thoughts of a small child, a deceased grandparent, or the family black sheep. You're sure to get a unique response.

Category 2. Someone from your social life. Even if you're not a Relater, you probably have a best friend you always go to when facing an imposed change. You might find that your hiking buddy and fellow birdwatcher can offer valuable insights about work or family changes. You can ask directly or say to yourself: "What would Pam suggest I do?" Asking a friend who is outside the problem can produce a fresh viewpoint.

Category 3. Someone from your work life. Here again, be flexible in selecting your opinion source. Rather than always asking the most authoritative person in your work life, consult (mentally or actually) with the receptionist, the computer programmer, or the supervisor of the secretarial pool. If you work alone, talk to the mail carrier, the stationery sales rep, or the bank loan officer.

Category 4. A celebrity you really admire. In this instance, you'll want to go to the top—to the smartest, richest, or most highly acclaimed individual. Whose thinking or philosophy do you value most? What person, living or dead, would you consider the wisest and most in tune with your own attitudes and feelings? Ask yourself: What would Winston Churchill, Sarah Bernhardt, Bryant Gumbel, or Jeane Kirkpatrick say about this change? You can see that it doesn't cost you any extra to go for the top person, so get the best.

THE POLL-TAKING TECHNIQUE

Describe the change imposed upon you. Then solicit the opinion, comments, or advice of four individuals from these separate categories of your life:

Category 1: Family member: _____

_____.

Category 2. Social life: _____

_____.

Category 3. Work life: _____

_____.

Category 4. A celebrity you really admire: _____

_____.

Positives: **Red Flags:**

Synthesis and Action:

   Poll-taking helps you understand and clarify what it is about the change that worries or frightens you. It is useful in developing alternative responses. The shorter version, Inner-viewing, also broadens self-understanding.

The Quick Inner-viewing Changemaker by Poll-taking

Inner-viewing also involves poll-taking, but you conduct interviews with all parts of yourself. Instead of asking four people how to handle a change, poll your senses: your feelings, visual perception, and even the smell, touch, and taste of the change. Asking the following questions will help put you in touch with your inner feelings.

   1.   Does this situation have a smell? Is it aromatic and exotic, or is it bland and stultifying?

2. What color is this change? Is it bold and exciting, or is it dull and depressing?

3. What was my first emotional response to this change? Anger, fear, joy, curiosity, confusion?

4. If I could touch this change, what would it feel like? Resilient and inviting, cold and inflexible, warm and fuzzy, strong and overpowering?

Inner-Viewing

Poll yourself with these questions:

1. Does the change have a smell?

2. What color is the change?

3. What emotion did I first experience when I encountered the change?

4. How does it feel to the touch?

Now put them all together in a consensus of your Inner-view.

Don't restrict yourself to the words suggested here. They only demonstrate the kinds of descriptions that might occur to you. Once you have identified these inner responses, put them all together and get the consensus of all the players in your Innerview. One warning: Since your Inner-viewing information comes from only one source—you—the data are limited. Therefore, apply it in less serious situations or in balance with other techniques. Still, Inner-viewing is a valuable experience because it provides a system for investigating and clarifying feelings and thoughts that are sometimes buried. And you will feel less frightened and overwhelmed by the change once you know your true feelings about it.

So far, you've experienced three techniques to handle imposed change. The fourth and final approach is the Replacement Technique.

The Replacement Technique

The Replacement Technique for responding to change is favored by Riskers, the action-oriented people who thrive on newness and excitement. They respond much better to learning a new technique and to hearing positive instructions than to correcting an old one.

For example, a Risker who needed to change his body stance for downhill skiing would love this challenge: "Between here and the crest of the hill, see if you can make twenty short turns." The coach actually wants this Risker to stop leaning so heavily at each turn because it slows him down and distorts his turns. But rather than tell the Risker what *not* to do in the changed conditions, the coach gives him something *new* to concentrate on.

While this kind of guidance is especially appealing to the Risker, it works well with all change styles. Reasoners applying the Replacement Technique are so interested in the whys, in data and instruction, that they may appreciate such introductory information and gentle feedback as "Notice how you are overturning? This causes you to make only a few, wide turns and then you lose control." Relaters love to tell their skiing buddies about the new method they're learning. Refocusers find it easy to concentrate on the new way because it is different from the old way.

Part of us (the right brain in most of us), is highly susceptible to positive suggestions, so telling us what we *can* do, rather than what we *can't,* is much more effective than criticism. Criticism can be internal, too, and the Replacement Technique circumvents the self-scoldings we all have experienced when we wish to respond to an imposed change with grace.

To face an imposed change with a positive attitude, perform a "habit-bypass":

1. Stop thinking about the old way you've done things.

2. Focus on and enjoy the new way; feel the excitement and challenge of the new.

3. Pretend you've never had any experience with this situation. To get into this mode, think of yourself as a child, singing, skipping, laughing as you perform some exciting task for the first time.

4. Once you're in this free-wheeling mood, you'll be making the change you desire because you have a new attitude.

On the job, abandoning the old and embracing the new can work like this: After practicing law for twenty-six years, the bloom was definitely off the rose for Rand H. In law school, he'd dreamed of reaching eminence in this prestigious and financially rewarding field. Besides, he passionately believed in our justice system and wanted to be a human rights advocate.

Rand worked for a small law firm for several years after graduation, but then was tempted into corporate law. He joined an old and respected firm to represent some of their largest corporate clients. He fell into a comfortable routine. He lunched each day at the University Club, talking to the partners. He tried nothing new and indulged in no courtroom theatrics or spontaneous pleasures.

Early in his career with the law firm, Rand was excited by the magnitude of the issues he handled: labor disputes, consumer controversies, and anti-trust law. But ultimately, he became disillusioned. It became clear to him that the company policies he was defending were often wrong or in opposition to his own altruistic leanings. But he also saw clearly that many of the complaints filed against his firm's clients were unfair. "It's just Greed versus Greed," he said.

At the same time, Rand felt the entire legal profession was losing its dignity. Many of his associates hired marketing representatives. Rand was particularly disgusted when one of his colleagues taped a television commercial to increase his practice . . . and it worked. The TV spot was a tasteless pitch for personal injury cases, "which made all lawyers look like ambulance chasers," Rand complained. While lawyers have often been the butt of jokes, Rand felt there was a new, ugly edge to the derision heaped on them, and he could understand why. Rand realized the profession he had chosen had changed into a cutthroat marketplace. He was bored and discouraged with his work.

Some might say Rand had simply burned out. But actually, his energies and expectations were still high. He still valued his knowledge and justice and the law in general. What he did not like was the antagonistic mentality of corporate law. The change in society's attitude toward the law profession fed his growing disillusionment, and he felt he simply had to make some changes in his life or else he'd turn sour on everything.

Rand still jogged and worked out, but he shifted most of his after-work pursuits to altruistic and mentally challenging activities. He volunteered for the boards of the local mental health association and a children's home; he joined a "Great Books" discussion group and the art museum. These were interests he'd always wanted to pursue but had never found time for before.

Not only did he learn stimulating things in each of these activities, he found himself associating with a variety of new, interesting people. One of these, the executive director of a charitable foundation, was leaving her position and recommended Rand as her replacement. He accepted and today feels fulfilled by his new position. Replacing elements of his private life with new ones led to a new, more satisfying career.

Rand's example shows how a Reasoner would use the Replacement Technique—by careful analysis and measured steps. Rand's original intention was not to change careers, but merely to have his private life compensate for discontent in his work life.

Riskers will jump on the Replacement strategy for change because of their love of the new; it may take the other styles a little while to work up to it. But the principle is the same: Stop fussing with the things you don't like about the changes imposed upon you and focus on some new action that is interesting, challenging, and pleasant. The focus on the new, as in Rand's case, often produces serendipitous benefits. It is almost as though you are creating your own auspicious moment for change rather than just having change imposed on you. When you make your own replacement, you can use the form provided.

The Replacement Technique Checklist

1. Stop thinking about the old way you've done things. (Example: Close your eyes tightly and squeeze those thoughts out of your head)

2. Focus on and enjoy the new way; feel the excitement and challenge of the new. (Example: See the new way, smile, think of the pleasure the new way will bring)

3. Pretend you've never had any experience with this situation.

4. Once you're in this free-wheeling mood, begin to act in the new way, fortifying your new attitude.

To get warmed up, try the following Quick Changemaker a few times:

The Paper Throw Checklist
(The Quick Changemaker)

1. Fold a piece of paper lengthwise.

2. On the left half, write down the new behavior you must adopt because of a change imposed upon you.

3. Think about the one element of this change that is most irksome. Feel your resentment fully.

4. On the right side of the sheet, write one good outcome of the change—no matter how small.

5. Tear the sheet in half along the fold line.

6. Crumple the left half with the old, negative feeling on it, and throw it as far as you can.

7. Feel the tension leaving your body as you rid yourself of resentment.

8. Think about the positive outcome this change brings you.

The Quick Changemaker by Replacement:
The Paper Throw

Write on the left side of a piece of paper a new behavior you must adopt because of a change that has been forced upon you. (For example, your company relinquished its on-site parking facilities to save money. You must now park six blocks away and pay the parking fee besides.)

Think about the one element of this change that is most irksome. Feel the full force of your resentment. ("I hate the inconvenience and expense of the new parking arrangement.")

On the right side of the same sheet, write one good result of the change, no matter how small. ("Parking six blocks away causes me to get more exercise.")

Now fold the sheet lengthwise and tear it in half, crumple the left half (with that old, negative feeling on it) and throw it as far as you can. There. Doesn't that feel good? Just throwing the paper releases some of the physical tension brought upon you by imposed, unwanted change. And it opens you to the new. Now that you are free of the old resentment, think about other benefits from the change. ("I don't have the hassle of renewing my company parking sticker every quarter. I can park wherever I like. I may take the bus to save money and find that the ride is more relaxing than driving.")

Something about forcefully disposing of the old, even if it is only symbolically, makes room for the new. Card sharks use a similar strategy for remembering which cards have been played: as each card is played, they visualize it disappearing from the deck. So, as the game proceeds, their new perception of the deck has fewer and fewer cards and is therefore easy to recall.

Even if your style is that of the Reasoner, Refocuser, or Relater, you might discover the hidden Risker within you that this strategy appeals to. Use the Paper Throw Checklist that is provided to help you become familiar with this method. The more times you experiment with it, the more open you will be to the new.

The Four Techniques

This chapter gave you four major techniques for handling imposed change and four matching quick changemakers:

THE LOSS TECHNIQUE (most comfortable for the Reasoner) and its Quick Changemaker, *In 25 Words or Less*

THE IMMERSION TECHNIQUE (most comfortable for the Refocuser) and its Quick Changemaker, *The Engineering Strategy*

THE POLL-TAKING TECHNIQUE (most comfortable for the Relater) and its Quick Changemaker, *Inner-viewing*

THE REPLACEMENT TECHNIQUE (most comfortable for the Risker) and its Quick Changemaker, *The Paper Throw*

Though your change style may influence how comfortable you are initially with these techniques, rest assured you will find all of them useful. With repeated experience you will be able to implement any or all of them effectively, and you will greatly extend your flexibility.

Here's how individuals applied this chapter's techniques when change was imposed upon them.

Loss and Replacement Techniques

Skip Terell, a Houston developer, posed this problem to us:

"I was a successful developer of office complexes in the Houston area until a few years ago, when the bottom fell out of the oil market. I had been going at a hectic pace for years, surrounded by a growing staff of bright young people. When there was no need for more office space and my operation, I closed the doors. I hated to let all those people go—but none of us was needed anymore. Money is not a problem. It's just the way I feel: antsy and impatient."

Skip tested out as a strong Risker, so we knew he needed action and mental stimulation! Since he had considerable savings and many productive investments, we asked him to think of the one thing he'd always wanted to do but had never had time for. His eyes sparkled then turned dreamy, and he said:

"I've always wanted to sail the South Seas, exploring primitive cultures, being master of my own ship."

While this is a romantic notion many people harbor, we knew that Skip had the resources to fulfill the dreams and needed only to deal with his strong resistance to such a drastic change.

First, we took him through the Loss Technique. He protested at first that he hadn't lost anything. We pointed out that he had lost the companionship of his staff and the authority and responsibility for a demanding business. He reluctantly agreed and went through the Loss Technique with us. He was genuinely surprised to find that much of his discomfort was due to the grief he felt about closing his business.

Then, when we suggested that he replace his sorrow with his dream and allow himself to buy a sailboat, he was ready to jump. Even though he had no experience or training with boating or navigation, he bought a LaFitte forty-four-foot sloop.

"In those first few months, I learned a lot about mechanics and electronics, celestial navigation and weather predicting," he said later. "I've never been happier in my life."

You guessed it: Skip completely worked through his irritability during the year he and his wife Kari sailed. Skip is now back in the development business in Silver Springs, Maryland, partly through a contact they met while docked in the Virgin Islands. He replaced the old with new mental and physical challenges—and found opportunity in change.

Immersion Technique

While we were conducting a Change Workshop at a dude ranch near Cody, Wyoming, the owner, Nan T., overheard us describing the Immersion Technique. She remarked, "That sounds like what I did four years ago when Hudson died." Here's how she described it:

"Hudson's expertise in environmental issues and knowledge of birds and their habits had long attracted guests to our dude ranch. With his death and the subsequent loss of reservations, I faced the possibility of losing the ranch. There was just not enough income from his insurance to keep us going without guest fees.

"One day, feeling particularly overwhelmed and helpless, I went into the huge storage area of the ranch, sat down in an old, dusty, stuffed chair, stared into space, and contemplated what to do. As I looked around at all the memorabilia—framed photographs, citations, awards, trophies, and mounted animal heads— the solution hit me! I would change the emphasis for guests from ecology and bird-watching to bird-hunting.

"It had formerly been a hunting ranch—that was clear from the photos and trappings . . . and though Hudson detested shooting of any kind, I didn't have those same feelings. Besides, I wanted to survive."

She was soon buying birds, setting up shooting blinds and screens, and promoting a new sort of dude ranch. And the new approach was successful. She had come upon the Immersion Technique quite naturally—and it had worked.

Poll-taking Technique

Mike Wilfley is the fourth generation of a family that owns Wilfley Motors, a company that manufactures specialty pumps and motors. His question was this:

"I am the president of a small but unique company. We have long been known as the Cadillac of the industry and have earned a niche by producing mining pumps and motors tailored to our customers' needs. As more and more government regulations are imposed on these products and as the big boys like General Motors enter this line, I'm faced with a shrinking market share. What can I do, other than go public, to combat this change in my industry?"

The strategy: Mike had been to our creativity and communication seminars, and so we knew he was particularly comfortable with brainstorming and also that he valued getting ideas from others. So we suggested he try the Poll-taking Technique. He did, and here are some of the opinions he got:

- **Family member** He polled his dead grandfather, and was reminded of his grandfather's fascination with China.

- **Work colleague** About the same time, the Chinese mining industry sent a form letter requesting a meeting. A colleague said, "Geez, if you could work out a deal selling your knowledge and technology to China, I could help you develop your product for other, third world countries.

- **Social** He discussed his situation with an artist friend. She recalled how refreshed and full of new ideas she felt after two recent trips abroad.

- **President of the United States** "If you can sell your expertise to China, you'll help our balance-of-payments problem."

The result of these four opinions: Wilfley Motors is presently expanding its market with sales to Chinese mining companies.

Now that you've learned techniques for productively responding to imposed changes, make sure you practice them so you can feel how exciting it is to be prepared for and in control of imposed change. You're now ready to move to methods for dealing with more subtle, adaptive change. In the next chapter, you'll discover two techniques that are particularly helpful in dealing with changes that occur gradually.

10
Adapting: Using Your Whole Brain

Scene: Lyle and Robert are partners in an insurance firm in a small Southern town. A noisy old air conditioner, hidden behind the louvered doors of a closet just to the right of a bay window, is laboring against the late August heat without much success. Suddenly, a new sound emerges from the closet. Lyle and Robert look up and say in unison, "We've got to do something about the air conditioner."

The following dialogue ensues:

LYLE: I'll call a repair service and get this air conditioner fixed.

ROBERT: That old thing is so ugly and noisy, I wish it would break down totally so we could get a new one.

LYLE: Do you have any idea how much that would cost? Air conditioners are expensive.

ROBERT: Money isn't everything. I just hate the smell of that piece of junk. And the noise drives me up the wall.

LYLE: I should get three estimates on the repair. I wonder if it would be cheaper to replace it?

ROBERT: You know, we need a refrigerator in here too . . . so we could have cool soft drinks. Wouldn't it be great to have a microwave too?

LYLE: If it costs more than one third of the new price to fix it, it should probably be replaced. But it's too soon to invest in anything as major as air conditioning. We're fully rented now, because the rates are low, I think. We'd better not mess with the overhead here.

ROBERT: I wonder why someone doesn't invent an air conditioner with a refrigerator built in—just for small offices. They must have the same kind of mechanism involved. Sort of like those vending machines that . . . hmmmmmm . . . A pop-vending machine with a microwave unit . . . that's also an air conditioner . . . what a great idea!

LYLE: I'm going to write down the numbers of three repair services.

Lyle and Robert have two entirely different ways of confronting a problem and making change. It is particularly difficult for them to notice gradual change because of their extreme change styles. The air conditioner obviously has been deteriorating for some time, but neither has dealt with it. Lyle was probably insensitive to its failings, and Robert attends to such matters only when they become emergencies. That moment has arrived, and the partners continue thinking in their usual ways and using their favorite change styles: Lyle prefers a logical, step-by-step method, while Robert lurches and lunges in many directions but always with a grand design in mind.

You might wonder why two people with such different ways of doing things became business partners. But if you think about it, you'll realize that such "odd couples" occur repeatedly in marriages and romances, partnerships and collaborations, mergers and alliances. Perhaps some underlying dynamic favors such pairings.

We are attracted to our opposites because what is difficult for us seems so easy for them. And their different abilities fill in our gaps. We may become uncomfortable and at times irritated by this different point of view, but more growth occurs when the opposites have worked on each other. The constant pull and push of opinion doesn't allow us to become stagnant.

You have a similar dichotomy within you. The left and right hemispheres of your brain have different points of view—both valuable. The left brain is good at reasoning and is specific. Your right synthesizes, looks for patterns, and is intuitive.

These differences between your two thinking styles create the same dynamic tension that so often occurs in a productive partnership of two people. Suppose you are trying to decide between completing your budget and going to your regular exercise class and meeting your friend for lunch. The left side of your brain says, "You should finish your budget"; the right brain feels the need for exercise and companionship. The "correct" answer is up to you, but by recognizing that *both* goals are valid and

---

A's and B's, Lefts and Rights

Opposites really *do* attract and apparently for good reasons. Certainly, Type A's and B's do. They are the behavioral types identified in the sixties by cardiologist Meyer Friedman for their differences in handling stress. He noted that A's are always in a hurry, do many things at one time, and are goal-oriented, while B's are more laid-back and handle life with less physical symptoms of stress. Later, Dr. Friedman related the behavior of Type A's to left brain thinking characteristics and Type B's to right brain thinking.*

Recent studies by Michael Strube and his students at Washington University in St. Louis describe how A and B behaviors affect relationships. There is an immediate attraction between the two types and conflicts soon arise, particularly if the Type A is a nontraditional female. However, these "mixed matches" seem to work through their differences and enjoy the advantages of having a balance between them.

You might have assumed that two B's would have the most peaceful relationship because of their calm attitudes. To the contrary, they had the most conflict, with the Type A's just behind them. The rising conflict between B's indicates that they are emotional and think in a right-brained way. Type A's may be just as irritated by their own kind but develop a logical way of handling the discord.†

---

*Friedman, Myer, M.D., and Diane Ulmer, R.N., M.S. *Treating Type A Behavior and Your Heart* (New York: Alfred A. Knopf, 1984).

†Cross Talk, "Type A: Affairs of the Heart," *Psychology Today,* May 1, 1987.

important, you open yourself up to alternatives. When you have a partner with the opposite style, that person provides the other point of view, thus ensuring that you see several options. You are more likely to find the best resolution, which would somehow meet both needs.

Just as each partner makes some special contribution to a business, each side of your brain provides a skill essential to a given task. For example, in speaking, it is your *left* brain that helps you use the right word at the right time and puts your thoughts in a logical sequence. And it is your *right* that adds tone, passion, and color to the way you deliver those thoughts. Both are necessary to speaking effectively, just as the special skills of partners are essential to the success of a business.

If you had to speak without your left brain, you'd sound like Daffy Duck—talkative, enthusiastic, and nonsensical. Without your right brain, you'd sound more like Henry Kissinger—logical, correct, and monotonous.

In the previous scene, Lyle represents an extreme left-dominant thinker who is sharp and focused. He is interested in dollars and cents, the concrete and practical. Robert is an extreme right-dominant who is sensitive to the emotions of a situation and given to flights of fancy. If you've ever been party to an exchange between extreme thinkers, you know how difficult it is for each to really listen to the other's ideas. To the left-dominant, the right seems flaky and disorganized. And to the right-dominant, the left seems boring and slow.

We often fall in love with our own style and fail to recognize other options. Or we discount nudges and murmurings within us that might lead to new but uncomfortable conclusions. Eventually, we may become mired in reasons *not* to alter our thinking or course of action. To see how Lyle and Robert got "unstuck" from such a situation, let's return to their office.

As we left them, Lyle was about to call three businesses to get estimates on repairs. Robert was dreaming of a yet-to-be-invented air conditioner that would solve all the problems of the world. At this point, Ramona enters the picture. She is a sales rep who is one of their tenants. She walks in fanning herself with an advertising brochure.

RAMONA: Phew! My office is like a blast furnace. Even my cactus plants are wilting. Everybody at my end of the hall is sweltering too.

LYLE: Yes, it's bad in here too. I'm calling some air conditioning people to fix the unit or replace it.

ROBERT: Replace it. Replace it with a new one. That's what we ought to do.

LYLE: (*irritably*) Not so fast. We've got to think this through . . . We ought to prorate the cost of a new one over the next seven years versus the likelihood of more repairs, and then decide whether to fix it or—

ROBERT: (*interrupting*) But fixing it is just temporary. We should think long-term. Insulate the walls! Plant shade trees in front! Put in awnings! And maybe some of those vertical blinds they have in the first national . . .

LYLE: (*interrupting and glaring at Robert*) Hold on . . . our business plan doesn't call for another capital investment for two years.

RAMONA: Well, it sounds like the two of you have given this a lot of thought and have some interesting solutions. I'm glad to have landlords right here. It sure helps when emergencies occur.

Lyle and Robert look at each other in surprise as they realize they've not been listening to each other. Each says to the other at the same time:
"What was that you were saying about the air conditioner?"
At this moment Lawrence enters. He is an independent precious-metal assayer, whose office is at the opposite end of the building from Ramona's.

LAWRENCE: Say, I'm not getting any cool air at all. I know the air conditioner is here in your closet—mind if I look at it?

LYLE: Be my guest.

LAWRENCE: (*looks in, fiddles with some parts*) I think the fan belt slipped off. Give me a hand here, and I think I can get it back in place.

Lyle hands him some gloves and a wrench from his bottom drawer. Robert holds the wheel.

LAWRENCE: It's fixed for now, but I can't guarantee how long it will last. See those little metal filings? You can tell the gears have been wearing down. I'm afraid there'll be more problems from this unit before too long.

RAMONA: Before you arrived, Lyle and Robert were thinking about some ways to make this building more comfortable year-round. Have you talked to any of the other tenants about it? Maybe we could get some ideas on how to . . .

As the scene fades, all four are engaged in a brainstorming session: Lawrence drawing diagrams, Lyle at the calculator, Robert staring out the window, and Ramona guiding the conversation from one person to another.

You have just witnessed the birth of a plan to adapt to the gradual breakdown of an air conditioner. The first half of the scene involves a dialogue between partners who own the building.

The brain dominance of a person relates to the four changemaker styles, as this dialogue shows. Left-brained Lyle is a reasoner—Robert a Risker.

The second half of the scene shows how two people with other and different change styles might behave in such a situation and how their unique viewpoints helped bridge the gap between the extreme positions represented by Lyle and Robert.

Ramona shows right-brained characteristics in her intuitive grasp of the strife between Lyle and Robert and her openness to variety. Both these attributes are present in the Relater. Notice that Ramona sought many opinions about the air conditioning and helped the two extremes, Robert and Lyle, communicate. Relaters are usually right-dominants, but to a lesser degree than Riskers. Typically, they are ideal go-betweens for people of all change styles because of their left-brained goal orientation and their right-brained empathy.

Lawrence is the Refocuser in the scene. Refocusers are left-brained but not to the same extreme as the Reasoner. Lawrence gathers facts carefully as does Reasoner; but unlike Reasoner, he reasseses the situation regularly and revises his opinion or approach. Lawrence first focused on solving the immediate problem with the air conditioner but then wanted to make changes with more long-lasting benefits.

A continuum would look like this:

Left Dominants		Right Dominants	
Reasoner (Lyle)	Refocuser (Lawrence)	Relater (Ramona)	Risker (Robert)

Many of us do not have such clear-cut change styles, nor do we behave in solely right- or left-brained ways as do the players in this scene. Nor are the people with whom we interact so patently left- or right-brained or so clearly Reasoners, Refocusers, Relaters, or Riskers. We have used extreme examples to make these differences clear. Understanding the distinctions between left- and right-brain characteristics and relating them to the four change styles is the first step toward learning to use *all* the styles and *both* sides of your brain. You will be better able to adapt to a change because you will be more flexible.

The dynamic tension in a left- and right-brained partnership nurtures adaptability in an individual or a relationship. So, too, the push and pull of four change styles increases the ability to make changes.

For example, in the scene Ramona effectively mediated the differences between Lyle and Robert by validating both approaches. Poll-takers have this knack for seeking opinions and gaining consensus. But it is also easier for an extreme left (Lyle) to listen to a moderate right (Ramona) than an extreme right (Robert). Likewise, the extreme right-dominant person is more open to the ideas of a more moderate left (Lawrence) than the extreme left (Lyle).

In the same way, when you are adding more options to the way you think about a change, it is often easier to move across the continuum one step at a time than to jump between the two endpoints. *Gradually adapting to a different changestyle is less stressful than making great leaps from one approach to another.*

This chapter is designed to help you broaden your ability to adapt to change by showing you how you can become aware of this movement between the extreme ways of approaching change. The techniques offered shift you between left and right ways of thinking and can thereby help you become comfortable with and skilled in adapting to change. Because the activities of the left and right are so intermingled and because brain preference is both inborn and environmentally produced, you usually cannot make changes overnight. Nor would you want to give up the specialized skills of your brain's hemispheres. But you do need to experience both left and right styles. Two changemakers, Internal Brainstorming (I.B.S.) and Inside Outs, will let you do this.

Shifting Between Hemispheres on the Job

Below are some examples of shifts between hemispheres you typically experience all day long on the job. While they happen automatically, you can influence your own shifts and others' by purposeful employing of the activities list.

Left-to-Right Shifts	Situation	Right-to-Left Shifts
visualize, daydream	sitting at your desk	organize, make to-do list
discover the big picture, pattern	reading reports	outline, take notes, mark key words
open up to irrelevancies, respond to body language and voice, lean forward, smile, nod, say "hmmmmm"	listening	evaluate, eliminate, conclude, analyze body language, logic, syntax words

talk to yourself in a supportive, care-free way	preparing to speak	practice exact words and comments before a speech or meeting
shift phone to your left ear (controlled by right brain) to be empathic	phoning	shift phone to your right ear (controlled by left brain) to gather gather facts
doodle, draw, print, hum, reminisce, joke, tease, horse around	relaxing	do crossword puzzle, pun, recite wise quotations, talk shop, bet
carry a clipboard, notes, and other comfort symbols	gaining confidence	use pointer, cite statistics to make you authoritative
take a mini-vacation at your desk; lean back, relax, close your eyes, let go	reducing stress	go off alone, write a memo describing your anger or problem, clarify your position
make eye contact with adversary, feel out his or her problem, walk to the water cooler	solving "people" problems	report details to your boss or spouse, check the facts, ask adversaries factual questions
be aware of colors, space, aromas; sounds; see the whole situation, how each person and element relates	solving "big" problems	estimate money-value of your precision, economies, foresight; break problem into parts and revise until consistency prevails

move, exercise, get a drink, enjoy the plants and pictures in your office	taking a body break	work out at nearby gym, organize intra-office sports competition

As you practice the two changemakers, be aware of the shifts they provoke, as described on the chart. You may be experiencing the feelings, reactions, and approaches of the right and left. Each time you go from analyzing to creating, you are also moving from one change style to another: from Reasoner to Refocuser to Relater to Risker, or from Risker to Relater to Refocuser to Reasoner.

These changemakers are designed to help you expand your own approach to change by experiencing and using both right- and left-brain skills. They can help you make the most of your two minds and the four change styles available to you.

Both of the following techniques were first described in our book *Whole-Brain Thinking.* They have been helpful to individual clients and workshop participants in both short-term problemsolving and long-term development of creativity. As we analyzed this success, we realized that these two techniques provoke several shifts between the hemispheres rather than just one. What seems to happen, then, is the use of more change and thinking styles. So be prepared to give your brain a workout.

Internal Brainstorming

Internal Brainstorming uses the same principles that make *group* brainstorming so helpful in problemsolving. It is a creative device that is a favorite in advertising, script writing, research and development, and other "think tank" operations. In group brainstorming, the first step is to *clearly define the problem* that the group will work on. Then the group selects a recorder who keeps track of all the wonderful solutions suggested. Then comes the fun! In the *idea-gathering* stage, everyone spontaneously offers solutions to the problem, following these guidelines:

1. **Defer judgment**—each idea suggested is accepted without

comment, negative or positive. Even praise or laughter is not allowed because they cause you to evaluate the worth of the idea (which shifts you to a left-brained way of thinking, away from the free-wheeling right).

2. **Be outrageous**—say anything that comes to mind, the wilder the better. Outrageous ideas seem to push you past mental blocks and provoke a flood of useful ideas.

3. **Go for quantity**—the more ideas the better. Listen to all of your inner voices. In our experience we've noticed that the most productive ideas come after the fourth one. So keep pushing.

4. **Hitchhike**—plagiarize and improve! Take the ideas others mention and put them in slightly different terms. Building on another's idea often improves it or leads to another idea.

In Internal Brainstorming, you follow the same process as in group brainstorming, only *you* are the entire group. The chart illustrates how all these stages work in Internal Brainstorming. This is your guide for brainstorming alone—a process that can be productive for you but that also helps you be a better brainstormer in groups.

Executive Ventures, Inc., management consultants who specialize in developing corporate teamwork and who are themselves a group of creative people, found that when individuals first practiced Internal Brainstorming, any *group* brainstorming efforts that followed were markedly more productive. Here's how we explained the phenomenon to them:

As you become more practiced in shifting hemispheres through Internal Brainstorming, you also become more accepting of your ability to create. This change within you then builds self-confidence and enables you to express your ideas more spontaneously in group brainstorming sessions. Furthermore, because you are hosting more viewpoints, you find it's easier to understand and hitchhike on the ideas of others. Now that's flexibility.

Internal Brainstorming Analysis

Steps	Process	Feelings
I. Writing out the problem or need (LEFT-BRAINED)	listing defining verbalizing delineating	efficient controlled focused
II. Thought-wandering (RIGHT-BRAINED)	ideas, sounds, pictures, and concepts, irrelevant thoughts, and defocused, blurry ideas appear and flow	"other" controlled, relaxed, let go; time whisks by or stands still; expectancy, wonder, curiosity, and effortless thinking
III. Evaluation (LEFT-BRAINED)	eliminate, judge scoff, quantify, ask 5-W questions (who? what? when? where? why?), and apply answers to tangibles, practicalities	surprise at volume of ideas, track of thinking and value; initial waste of time on silliness
(RIGHT-BRAINED)	eliminate repugnant ideas, focus on attractive ideas	"I just couldn't"; "Sounds like fun, exciting, etc."; "I have a hunch it will work"
IV. Integration (LEFT & RIGHT)	You see the whole concept or solution and fill in the details, or they "just fall into place"	stimulated excited "aha" elated, powerful, self-confident, "It'll be fun!"
V. Implementation (LEFT-BRAINED)	devise step-by-step plan, get started, and follow it to the "T"	focused, determined

| (RIGHT-
BRAINED) | add flourishes,
embellishments;
improvise | energetic, glad to be
moving |

You can see why Internal Brainstorming will help you personally and make you a more valuable member of any team.

It certainly helped Wayne M. McDonald, a credit card company's computer technician who attended one of our Creativity Through Change workshops. An ongoing problem in his business is the detection of stolen credit cards.

"I decided to try Internal Brainstorming to see if I could find a nifty way of identifying a stolen card even before it was reported.

"As I went through the mind-wandering stage, I thought a few far-out ideas about how rich and famous I'd be if I could solve this problem.

"Then I saw myself on TV . . . which turned into a computer screen, where I saw credit-card charges filing past me. After a while, I noticed a pattern in those charges. Most legitimate ones were random, but the charges from stolen cards were all in bunches. With that an idea flashed to mind for a software program to flag these strange configurations in charges. When I get it finished, you'll probably next see me as a rich and famous person on that TV screen." A week later he presented his plan for feedback at a staff meeting.

Internal Brainstorming asks you to move from the extreme logical left (when he defined the problem), to focused left (when he concentrated on one aspect), to visual right (when he saw himself on TV), to connecting with others' right (when he presented his ideas to the staff).

Inside Outs

The second changemaker we offer for learning how to adapt to change is called Inside Outs, another technique to help you experience using both brain functions.

The first step is to begin once again by defining your problem or the situation you'd like to change. For example: "Finish the report by 5 P.M. today."

Second, reverse the objective and think of all the things you could do to make sure you do not finish the report by 5. Some people think of it as flipping the pancake or seeing the other side of the coin—whatever it takes to interfere with the primary objective of working on the report. Your list of "interferers" could include such things such as "stare out the window" and "have coffee with my office mates." Internally brainstorm a long list of the interferences at least ten to twelve of them. Write them down.

Third, *reverse* each item on the list; in other words, think what you could do to prevent the interferers from happening. You could shutter your windows to prevent you from staring out the window or dismantle the coffeemaker to prevent you from drinking coffee. List these reverses next to your original list.

INTERFERERS	REVERSES
stare out the window	shutter the window
watch TV	smash the TV
call friends	refuse to take calls
go out to lunch	skip lunch
chat with office mates	close door
read newspapers	cancel the subscriptions
drink coffee	dismantle the coffeemaker
labor over each point	don't evaluate, rush
pause between each word	write fast, automatically
go off on tangents	stay focused on outline

As you look over these interferers and their reverses, do you see a pattern? Step four asks you to do that. Can you discover a more general problem that might be interfering with your completion of the report? Look at the first seven items on the list. Only two (lunch and office chats) represent interferers from the outside. You initiated all of the others. What might that pattern indicate? A lack of commitment to your completing the report?

Perhaps you feel the report is unnecessary or impossible to complete. These are some clues to an underlying problem that you might discover by using the Inside Out technique.

On the other hand, the last three items on the interferer list indicate a different pattern: a lack of skills or at least the perception that you can't do it. You may be too meticulous in choosing words or overly critical of your writing. Going off on tangents often happens when you are working without an outline or without your main points clearly in mind.

You can see from this example that you can use Inside Outs not only to find new alternatives when change occurs, but also to discover broader problems and their solutions.

One of our European clients, Hasse Karlsson, was particularly skillful in using Inside Outs to change the stagnation of the Swedish Trade Council. He has been Director of Organizational Development for the Council since 1974. For years, he struggled with policy and personnel problems, trying to make the organization more dynamic. "Morale is low and our image is poor," he claimed in 1984, when he first learned about Inside Outs. He had thought of using a similar approach himself, and the explanation of Inside Outs at a creativity session gave him the resolve to implement the new approach. First he tried it himself, then he made it part of the training of new employees.

Today, the Council projects a sense of purpose, excitement, and energy that makes it a vital part of the Swedish economy. Karlsson generously credits his use of Inside Outs for the turn-around.

The problems he focused on were the lack of continuity between retiring and new employees and phasing in these new hires. How could the Council respond or adapt to these ongoing gradual changes? He discovered that many employees were being forced into retirement by governmental policy at the early age of fifty-two. Transition of duties to new employees was neither smooth nor complete because of the retiring employees' resistance to retirement.

Karlsson decided to reverse five procedures that related to this problem:

1. Rather than waiting until retirement to honor employees with a gold pen, new employees were given the pen their first day at work.

"It was fun to see how surprised and pleased they were," Karlsson reports. "I know it helped them feel part of the team from the very beginning."

2.   Rather than taking new employees on a tour of the plant to meet company officers, Mohammed came to the mountain. The president and other officers visited them. "Being welcomed to the Council in their own offices helped the new employees feel much more comfortable and wanted," Karlsson said.

3.   Rather than show the new employee Council procedures the first week, the supervisor, a Council officer, and Karlsson would go with the employee for a tour of the employee's former place of work.

"This helped us understand better the extent of the employee's skills and experience. Often, we found talents not on the resume."

4.   Rather than totally severing ties with retiring employees, Karlsson invited them to serve as consultants to the Council after retirement.

"This made them less reluctant to retire, because they no longer felt they'd be completely out of the work world. Consequently, they were much more forthcoming in passing on hints and information to their replacements. Furthermore, because they understand the Council operation so well, these retirees are excellent consultants."

5.   Instead of cajoling executives to attend the training sessions, Karlsson excluded management from the Inside Out training sessions from the beginning.

"It drives them mad," he smiled gleefully. "At first, there were the scoffers who thought Inside Outs were silly. So I didn't invite them. Then, when everyone had such a good time at training and we began to produce outstanding results, they wanted to join us, but I said, 'No, no, no, managers can't attend.' "

Because Karlsson is such a flexible thinker, he did relent and invited the managers. But this final reverse really worked wonders. An Inside Out is a little like putting your automobile into reverse to get better traction when you're stuck in the mud. A shift in strategy gave Karlsson better traction and helped the Swedish Trade Council adapt to necessary changes.

You might try Inside Outs on some of your personal problems before you use them on the job. First, define your goal, then think of all the things you can do to prevent yourself from achieving it. Reverse all those interferers, take a broad look at them, and then just wait for the patterns or revelations to emerge. Putting your mind through those mental reverses helps you access both sides of your brain and also gives you practice in the different change styles.

Although Internal Brainstorming and Inside Outs can be used effectively with minimal effort, they do require a little practice. However, the two one-minute Changemakers that follow are instantaneous. Cut-ups starts you left, then moves you right, while the Tongue Depressor makes the opposite shift.

Cut-ups
A Quick Changemaker

It is often difficult to adapt to a new way to do things, especially if the habitual method works well. And certainly, you don't want to change just to change. That's pseudochange. But occasionally, even the most successful strategy can use a good shaking up. So try Cut-Ups on a procedure you know well, one you feel could use an adaptation.

Wanda Rodriguez was the new editor of her company's newsletter and found it stressful and frustrating to adapt to press deadlines. "People never observe their deadlines, so I'm in a panic with every issue," she confessed. To help her adapt to the climate and people she works with, we had her try Cut-ups. In a workshop, she followed these Cut-ups guidelines:

1. To begin, write down all the steps you follow in performing this task. Phrase them as succinctly as possible, and list them in the order you currently use. Leave a little space between each.

This is the list Wanda made:

    compile list of stories
    phone contacts
    conduct interviews
    type notes from interviews
    contact printer
    contact photographer
    write stories
    edit stories
    read bench proofs
    get CEO's approval of copy

Wanda proceeded according to these instructions:

2.   Take your list and cut the steps apart. Shuffle them—move them around in front of you like the pieces of a puzzle. Try many different sequences of them. Ask someone who is unskilled in the task to arrange them in the order they think best. Close your eyes and rearrange them to see if a random order might work. Has a new organization appeared from this restructuring? If not, that's okay. At the very least, you will probably hit upon a new idea—and, of course, you will have flexed your mind muscles to the max. You have moved from your well-ordered left-brain thinking style over to the more scattered, spontaneous right.

Wanda actually *did* find a better sequence by shuffling the pieces of her puzzle. In rearranging the steps, she realized she had been contacting her CEO at the last possible moment. She had reasoned that he was too busy and important to bother with anything more than a perfunctory, last-minute "okay."

She resolved at the workshop to try contacting him *first* to see what happened. At a six-month checkup, we learned that Wanda's CEO was delighted to be in on the start of each newsletter. He brainstormed stories with her, suggested key contacts, and gave her an occasional scoop. As a spin-off benefit, she found that once the CEO was more involved, other employees were more interested in helping Wanda meet her deadlines. Big improvements can come from small changes!

The next quick changemaker starts you on your undisciplined, rambling right side and moves you back over to the left.

Tongue Depressor/Speaker-upper
A Quick Changemaker

When you want to make a change in behavior that is easily quantifiable, the Tongue Depressor is an excellent method to use. It is called "Tongue Depressor" because it *looks* like a tongue depressor, and it was originally devised to help a client who wanted to stop talking so much at business meetings and in seminars.

"I know I turn people off by always having something to say," confessed Gerry Walinski, "But I get enthusiastic about what's going on and end up doing most of the talking." So we drew a tongue depressor and divided it into four sections like this:

Then we asked him to take this to the next meeting or seminar he attended and allow himself only four turns at talking. He was to check off each turn on the Tongue Depressor as he used it. When he had checked all four, he could not initiate any more comments, suggestions, or questions. He could only speak when asked something directly.

At first, Gerry had difficulty following the rules. "Toward the second half of the meeting, I'd be sitting there with the greatest idea in the world, so I'd just blurt it out."

But after a while, he found he could pace himself and save most of his remarks for the end of the meeting. With practice, he found he no longer needed to keep track of his turns on paper; he kept a mental count of the times he spoke. Six months later, he said, "This is one of the most valuable changes I've ever made. I've found that I get so much more out of a meeting by listening to others. I'd always felt responsible for rushing in and filling gaps in conversations and responding to a lecturer. Now I don't feel the tension I used to when there was a moment of silence. I'm more apt to see the big picture than before, and I recall the meeting as a whole, rather than juct bits and pieces."

The last benefit might be because as Gerry relaxed, he shifted to his right brain, which saw the big picture.

"And maybe it's my imagination, but it seems to me that people listen to me with greater respect than they did when I was such a 'chatty Cathy,'" Gerry added.

The same procedure can be used for the opposite problem. If you don't speak up enough, you can set a goal to speak up three or four times at an upcoming meeting. Keep track of each participation on your Tongue Depressor until you are comfortable with speaking three times per meeting, then increase it to four or five. Soon you'll find yourself at ease in your participation.

The Tongue Depressor approach can work in many other situations, such as cutting back on cigarettes, reducing or increasing eating, drinking more water each day, pressing the "save" Command on your word processor at regular intervals, or complimenting and thanking others.

All you need to do is decide how many actions you'd like to take in a given time, and then work with the marker for a few times until the change becomes comfortable and automatic.

The Tongue Depressor starts with the impulsive, emotional side of you and helps you change a behavior gone astray by applying a control method to it. Essentially, this moves you from your right-brain way of behaving to the left, whereas Cut-ups moved you from your sequential left to your right. See "Practicing Right and Left" for other ways to develop right- and left-brain skills.

Practicing Right and Left

RIGHT DOMINANTS SHOULD PRACTICE LEFT-BRAINED SKILLS

Itemize all household belongings, valuable papers, etc.
Take a course in computers, bookkeeping.
Read the Wall Street *Journal* or at least the editorial and business pages of your paper.
Balance your checkbook.

Record everything—miles driven, day's activities, letters mailed.
Cost out everything—time spent driving, jogging, watching TV.
Plan and schedule—wear a watch, carry a calendar.
If you listen to country-Western or rock-and-roll on radio, switch to classical music or talk stations.
When watching TV, switch to educational or informative PBS programs; outline the plots of sitcoms if you must watch them.
Read biographies and other nonfiction books.
Join a debate team or toastmaster or become treasurer of a club.
Listen to professional information tapes on your car stereo.
Analyze everything you read, watching for typos and various inconsistencies.
Dejunk your house and office, organize your wardrobe.
On the job:
   Clear off the top of your desk each day.
   Volunteer to prepare written and oral reports
   Volunteer to investigate something (best place for company picnic).
   Take a class in or practice time management.
   Set goals and set limits for segments of your day.
   Prepare an agenda and limit time for lunches and meetings.

LEFT DOMINANTS SHOULD PRACTICE RIGHT-BRAINED SKILLS

Let your day happen, and change directions at a moment's notice.
Dress casually or flamboyantly.
Stay in your night clothes, eat popcorn, and read all day.
Surprise someone with a gift or an outrageous statement or idea.
Listen to jazz, rock-and-roll, or country-Western.
Read a romantic or adventure novel.
Turn to sports, comics, astrology *first* when reading newspapers.
Browse in an art gallery or stroll through a museum without reading the posted information.

Amble, walk, run aimlessly; forget the clock and your speed or distance.

Eat when you feel hungry, not on schedule.

Shop without a list.

Take a course in art: "Drawing on the Right Side."

Write a poem, a novel, or a children's story.

Doodle, decorating your notes and first drafts of proposals.

On the job:

Let George do it.

To deadlines say, "So what if it doesn't get done?"

For decisions, flip a coin, follow a hunch, ask a nonprofessional.

Decorate your office, hang up pictures and plants, move your furniture.

For staring, post optical illusions and puzzling art work or sculptures.

Keep clocks and calendars in your bottom drawer.

Swim during your lunch hour.

Now that you've learned the dynamics of these shifts and adaptations from right to left and left to right, you may find it easier to understand the thinking patterns of the Reasoner, the Refocuser, the Relater, and the Risker. You may even understand yourself better. But the real payoff is in the practice—that's how you raise your flexibility and your Change-Friendly Quotient.

So resolve now to use at least one of these adaptation-provoking changemakers: Inner Brainstorming, Inside Outs, Cut-ups, or Tongue Depressors. They'll help you adapt more gracefully and enthusiastically to change and also help prepare you to initiate change successfully, the topic of the next chapter.

11
Initiating: Seven Principles

Pick up a pencil right now and write your name in the usual manner. Now shift the pencil to your other hand and write your name. How did it feel that second time? A little uncomfortable? Very uncomfortable?

How did it look that second time? Shaky, unfamiliar? Most likely, your handwriting was rather poor the second time, and you felt uncomfortable. But with each succeeding effort, your writing would improve and you would feel better about it.

The first time you wrote with your nondominant hand you established new neural connections in your brain, and each subsequent time the brain impulses traveled the same pathway and became stronger and moved more quickly. Whether or not your writing improved, it nevertheless became easier for you.

This discomfort with the new is obviously one reason that few of us are adept at initiating change. It is so much easier to follow the old pathways that most of us must have special incentives for initiating a change. In the situation above, you temporarily changed your behavior to accommodate our request and, possibly, to satisfy your curiosity.

A tall, slender young electronics technician at AT&T, Mark Larsen, made just such a change entirely on his own when he was six years old. That's when Mark's eldest brother, Stafford, broke his right hand and was forced to use his left one.

"Writing with his left hand seemed to bother Staff a lot. It was a painful break, and he had to struggle with a big heavy cast for several months—and try to keep up with his schoolwork—left-handed. I remember saying to my best friend, Tommy, 'If I ever break my arm, I'm gonna be ready.'"

So Mark began writing with his left hand. He even drew his beloved Roy Rogers pictures with his left. As he looks back at a scrapbook of his drawings from preschool years through third grade, Mark notes, "I can't see much difference before and after. I never was what you'd call a gifted artist. But I'm sure glad to have the scrapbook. It's the only record I have of the switch. I'd forgotten about it until, in my twenties, Staff reminded me that I used to be a right-hander."

Now thirty-five, Mark is a confirmed left-handed writer who performs most other skills, including eating, with his right hand.

No doubt Mark was able to make this shift rather effortlessly because the human brain is much more adaptable at six than later in life. Still, the initiative Mark showed is remarkable. His brother changed in response to an accident. The same accident prompted Mark to make the same change—but he actually initiated it.

Why do people initiate change? Mark's six-year-old reasoning convinced him that switching hands would ward off future suffering. When we asked participants in our workshops what had or would propel them to initiate a change, they most often said to put an end to a painful situation or to gain some future reward. Others initiated change for the fun and excitement of it or out of curiosity. There was a pattern to their reasons for initiating change that correlated to their change styles.

Reasoners initiate change when they are dead certain it is a correct move or one that will benefit them directly. They will spend hours weighing the statistical possibility for earning a specific amount of money on the stock exchange. They'll know more about the state of the economy or interest rates than the head of the Federal Reserve. Reasoners are challenged by the task of collecting all the information necessary to make a major change. And they love to dot all the *i*'s and cross all the *t*'s.

Refocusers often initiate change because they suddenly become dissatisfied with something. They might have worked in an cold office for months but have been too absorbed to do anything about it. When they finally decide to change, they talk about nothing else until the change is completed—and then, apparently, they forget the entire episode, becoming refocused on some other activity. Whereas Reasoners might make rational decisions to postpone correcting the cold office, Refocusers initiate change as soon as they recognize the need for it.

Relaters are more likely than Reasoners and Refocusers to instigate a change because they are so aware of the possibilities that surround them. They are in regular contact with a variety of people, so they know what's current, different, improved, exciting, and helpful. It's little wonder that they want to stay in the forefront of change and keep up with their peers at work and play.

Riskers often enjoy the excitement of the change itself. They find new ideas, techniques, and products compelling. They push themselves to the limits of their abilities and resources, and they are excited by the hazards and opportunities of unexplored territory. Riskers' energy levels seem to increase with each new change they initiate.

Think back to recent changes you've made. Were your motives similar to those described for your change style? Or have you acted for reasons not even listed here? It is important that you understand your reasons for initiating change so you can properly evaluate the result and also so that you can avoid pseudochange.

Whatever the reason, initiating change *successfully* requires more sophisticated skills than responding to change. The fact is, we *must* respond to imposed change, but when we can choose between changing or keeping the status quo, most of us want at first to stay put. Understandably so—initiating change is complex. You must firmly believe that something needs to be changed; you must figure out how that change is to be accomplished; and then, you must do it. Initiating change requires commitment and drive.

How do successful initiators of change master these difficult tasks? What characteristics distinguish their way of initiating change? During the past four years we have observed that, whether they were Reasoners, Refocusers, Relaters, or Riskers, successful initiators went through seven stages to achieve their goals. While they performed these steps in varying orders and described them differently, the consistency of their experiences was remarkable. These are the steps we extrapolated from their stories:

1. They had a pronounced change style and used it to initiate the change.

2. They were excited by and committed to the change.

3. They understood who would gain and lose from the change.

4. They found the optimum starting point and time for initiating change.

5. They persuaded others to cooperate in implementing the change.

6. They persevered in spite of problems and setbacks.

7. They stayed flexible throughout the change process.

In this chapter you will learn how a half-dozen of our clients from business, government, and education experienced these steps in making big and small changes in their work lives. Then, you'll see in detail how the process worked when a forty-five-year-old, slightly-depressed developer took on a twenty-year-old, slightly-decrepit convention center.

The Process

As the pattern for initiating change became clearer to us, we began to explain the seven steps in this way:

Step 1. *Successful initiators of change have a practiced*

change style, *and they are comfortable with it.* Their self-understanding and experience bolster their confidence. Their ability to learn from past trials brings energy and drive to the change effort—enough to overcome the natural inertia of the status quo. They seem to recognize their change style immediately when they take the Change-Friendly Quotient Survey. Even the younger ones had experienced much change in their lives and were comfortable with it.

For example, when bank managers at the Allied Banks of the Netherlands needed to hold their own against competition, they looked at their Change-Friendly Quotients and saw that they were inherently Refocusers. They spotlighted their chief customers, offered additional benefits to them, and highlighted their businesses in the bank's newsletter.

When two hundred members of the Volunteers of America in Jacksonville, Florida, faced the loss of government support for many of the programs they help finance, they looked to their strengths as Relaters. Each member pledged to solicit funds from long-time school and business friends of which there were many. They set up a bank of telephones and conducted a twenty-four-hour telethon, calling friends across the country. They went over their goal—and enjoyed renewing old ties in the process.

This awareness of change style may be responsible for the next two characteristics we saw in successful initiators of change: excitement and commitment.

EXCITED AND COMMITTED

Step 2. *They are excited and **committed** to the idea of change and the particular change they are making.* With initiators, change is the norm. They take an almost parental pride in the changes they're involved in and gain strength from each small and large accomplishment.

Jonathan Crane, an MCI executive, looked elated when he described his feelings on seeing his company's logo on the public telephones at airports all over the country. The symbol showed that you could charge long-distance calls with an MCI credit card. "Of course, all the telephone services have their logos there, too, these days, but every time I see them I remember how excited our team was when we thought of the idea and got it going. We all operated on adrenalin for a couple of weeks. It was fun—we knew we had a great idea and wanted to make sure we did it first."

Responding to change successfully is no small feat, but initiating change is a loftier, more challenging and rewarding experience. It is an act of the creative inventor who lies within all of us. Then too, the emotional payoff is more intense and long-lasting.

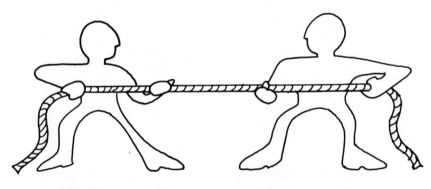

RESISTING CHANGE   SUPPORTING CHANGE

Step 3. *Successful changemakers identify **who stands to gain and lose** by the change.* What are the issues and attitudes of all the people involved? Who will support it, who will oppose it, and how strong will the support or opposition be?

When a client, Penny, wanted to open a beauty salon in a plush office building, she faced certain obstacles: the tenants who thought a beauty salon would be smelly and unprofessional; the need to get old customers to come to her new location; and possible zoning restrictions. Discovering who stood where was a great help to Penny in taking the next step forward in initiating change. Penny visited several of the most resistant tenants, showed them a sketch of her plans, and invited them to visit her current site (for a free haircut). Once they saw what a professional operation she had, their fears diminished. Zoning turned out to be no problem—and when she polled her old customers, she learned they would be delighted with the new facility because it had more convenient parking.

Crucial Point

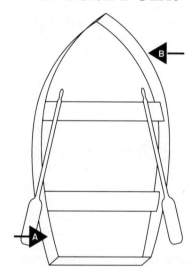

Step 4. *Successful initiators pinpoint the **crucial few** areas, individuals, or forces where the least pressure can yield the greatest results.* They seem to have an instinct for finding the one crucial area where the most effective change can be made with the least amount of effort.

Imagine that you are trying to get the boat above to turn left. Where would you exert your efforts? If you've had some boating experience or have an intuitive feel for it, you might say A, the correct answer. Most novices think that the crucial point to push is at B. Pressure there would shift the course of the boat left, but the effort required would be much greater than at A.

The more clearly you understand the structure of the organization and the attitudes of the persons you're trying to influence, the more effective you will be in determining the crucial point for initiating a change within the organization.

One way to look for a crucial point for initiating change is to apply the 80/20 rule, or "the principle of the crucial few." Around the turn of the century, an Italian economist named Pareto came to America. He noticed that roughly 80 percent of the land was owned by 20 percent of the people and that 80 percent of the wealth was amassed by 20 percent of the people. As he studied more and more situations, he discovered that this principle of the crucial few seemed to apply in many other areas. For example, 80 percent of sales generally come from 20 percent of a business's customers; 80 percent of complaints also come from 20 percent of the customers. It turns out that the majority of daily activities conform to this 80/20 ratio. You might notice that you wear 20 percent of your clothes 80 percent of the time, that 80 percent of the time you eat only 20 percent of foods available to you, and that actual play time in a sporting event is only 20 percent of the scheduled time.

Discovering the crucial product, the crucial people, even the crucial timing by applying the 80/20 rule will help you find the best spot to exert the energy necessary to begin your change. For example, in Penny's beauty shop, if 20 percent of her customers were providing 80 percent of her income, her consulting with them about the new location might be the crucial move for success.

Alignment

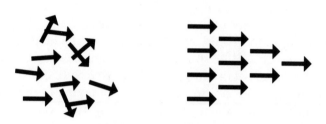

Step 5. *Successful initiators **align** all their forces (resources, people, efforts) in one clear direction.* Once they discover the forces for and against the change (Step 3) and detect the area where the greatest progress can be made most easily (Step 4), they strive to get all parties working in the same direction.

In a work situation, this effort might include aligning staff members, clients, suppliers and financial and legal resources, and other people and factors in a direction that may be needed to contribute to the change.

Alignment is achieved when your vision of what you want to accomplish is so clear and strong that others can immediately grasp where you are going. If you present them with one understandable goal, they will then want to come along too. This is what leaders are able to do. You may not think of yourself as a leader. In fact, leadership may seem too intimidating for you to even aspire to it. But think of the times in your life when you have really cared about some project, set a goal clearly in your mind, and then found others caught your enthusiasm.

Alignment is the natural outcome when people focus their energies together on one plan, one meaningful goal. The goal must be important enough to each person so that individuals will overcome differences, give up pet ways of performing a task, and work in harmony to accomplish the change.

When alignment is achieved, there is a great burst of energy, because resistance is gone and creativity is released. Everyone charges forth with enthusiasm and optimism because the goal is clear and the commitment deeply felt.

When you are an initiator, you may experience the same surge of energy when you develop your own *interior* alignment. This occurs when you've thought through the pros and cons of the changes, when you've envisioned a variety of possible outcomes, when you can see the final, perfect result, and when you've assessed the objections and have answered them. Then you have reached the point of resolution. This resolution helps successful changemakers handle the next step, keeping their goal in view when they get knocked off target.

Persevere — Keep Eye On The Goal

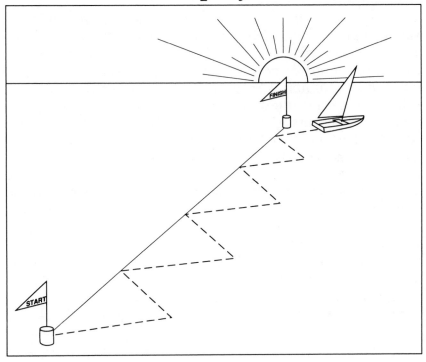

Step 6. *When knocked off track or confronted by a barrier, the successful initiator **perseveres** toward the goal from that*

point forward rather than retracing old paths and confronting the same barrier again.

This requires true focus, commitment, and perseverance. Initiators are sure to confront blocks along the way, but instead of going back to the starting point, they pick themselves up and proceed from that point forward.

Imagine yourself in a sailboat: You want to get to the far shore, but because of winds, a direct course is impossible. But by tacking and jibing, zigging and zagging, you can ultimately reach shore. The trick is to keep moving forward. You wouldn't want to dock at the first landing or go in circles.

If you retrace your steps each time you're thrown off, you'll usually waste time and energy and may confront the same barrier all over again.

For example, suppose you call someone by the wrong name. If you return to the beginning and learn the name all over again, you are likely to commit the same error again. To break the pattern, try to discover something new about the person so that you can have a different view of him. Your goal is still to use his name, but you will better reach that goal by taking a different tack.

Football runners who are pushed off route before the ball is passed to them rarely go back to their original spot. They keep the quarterback and the ball in view and readjust their run to the new circumstances. Picture a star running back weaving, jumping, and responding to other players, staying loose, staying open, ready to move when the opportunity comes. He reaches the goal of being open to receive the pass by taking new routes. Note that the key is staying flexible—the final step.

STAY FLEXIBLE

Step 7. *Successful initiators* **stay flexible** *throughout their changemaking efforts.* They keep their minds open to new methods and techniques, and they step back periodically to get an overall view of their progress. They bend without breaking.

Part of your change strength is information. The more informed you are at every step of the way, the more flexible your strategies will be. While information is plentiful today, we often understand it in a focused and sometimes narrow way. For example, look at the picture of a window on the opposite page. What do you see? Four people looking at the same window might see four different things. One notices the view outside, the second notices how well the window is constructed, a third notices the window is dirty, and a fourth notices a little spider in the corner. The ability to listen to all four points of view allows you to make use of different kinds of information, which in turn will make you a successful change-maker.

Sound decisions require more information these days than ever before. For instance, in designing a television commercial you must know more than the details of your product, the demographics of your audiences, and television production techniques. You must understand your competition, current fads and trends nationwide, and a host of other kinds of information.

It is temptating to limit our information-gathering as we become more rooted in our tasks. National and corporate leaders often seem to lose touch with their constituents as they narrow the circle of advisors around them. While politicians are campaigning and corporate leaders working their way to the top, they tend to seek advice and assistance from a wide range of people. The successful politician and leader as well as the successful initiator of change continues the search for new and better information and advisors and as a result stays vigorous and flexible.

Almost all workshop participants said staying flexible was the most challenging step of all. They described how difficult it was for them to listen to people with styles very different from theirs and to do things in different ways when "their way" worked. If they had been successful, they didn't want to change because they might jinx their success. If they had failed at something new, they were often afraid to risk again.

We suggested that our participants practice these flexers when they felt themselves digging in their heels or when they felt mired down.

How to Stay Flexible

1. Tenderize your inflexibilities. Make a list of ideas and practices you will *never* change. Underline them, print them in bold print and colors. Savor your stubbornness. Remember holding onto the edge of a swimming pool when you were a kid and shouting "no" when told to let go? Now decide to let go of the edge for a minute . . . just until you decide to grab it again. And perhaps along with that letting go, you are ready to make one small change in each of those big "no's."

2.   Identify your rock-bottom price, your absolute no-turning-back position in a financial matter. Then determine the largest change from that position that you could tolerate. One dollar, $20, $100? Then let that change rest a while. Repeat the process until you finally say, "I absolutely cannot tolerate any more." Now, when you go into your negotiations, you have parameters.

3.   Get physical with your inflexibilities. When you're in an argument, or rehearsing one, lower the tone of your voice, widen your eyes, lift your eyebrows. All these physical changes lower the intensity of your emotions and help you to be more open to the concerns of others.

4.   Risk something uncomfortable. Go slightly out of your comfort zone. Introduce yourself to a stranger at a party if you're shy. If you're opinionated, concede a minor point to someone you dislike. The discomfort in both cases might turn to comfort when you reap the rewards of knowing you can discipline yourself. You may also have changed the course of a relationship. Small concessions often lead to big gains.

5.   Out of control. Think of the things you don't need to control—in fact, can't control. The weather, the stars, the ocean. They get along fine without you, right? Now think of some areas of your life you presently try to keep under control that could really get by without you: your son's homework, your spouse's checkbook, your boss's temper. Rid yourself of the responsibility you feel for them. Doesn't that spell relief? Divesting yourself of the need to control increases the flexibility within yourself and toward others.

6.   Practice poll-taking. See a variety of views. Rather than making instantaneous decisions, take the time to expand your opinions. Pretend you're listening to a radio talk-show. By staying tuned past the first opinions given, you find an amazing assortment of views on any given topic. Some are useful, some not. But the exercise your brain gets keeps your thinking flexible.

7.   The old reliable "worst case" approach is a good mind flexer too. By imagining yourself in dire straits, you become more comfortable with anything less than the worst. You might hate the idea of working one Saturday a month. But think of working weekends all the time with only one weekday off. Worse yet: no job at all. Now, doesn't one Saturday a month seem tolerable?

8.   *Dispromise* is designed to change your attitude about how much you will do for others. In trying to accommodate others, we often make life more confusing than it needs to be. While it is important in business and friendships to be accommodating, the outcome of overpromising is a hectic, impossible schedule that makes you look disorganized and irresponsible. So when you're talking to a customer or friend and are about to agree to a request, stop yourself for a moment. If you have already agreed to several commitments that day, then change, "dispromise." Here are the words you can use: "I'd like to _____ for you, but I just can't work it in today." Your friends or customers will know that you are thoughtful enough to *want* to go by the post office or library for them, but that you just can't. Don't explain the details; just be very definite about your refusal. In such a situation, many of us ramble on defensively about our heavy burdens and finally agree to do such favors. Dispromising can change this habit.

But enough of changing you, keeping yourself flexible. What we all want in our heart of hearts is to *change other people.* Most of us think that life would be much better if other people would just change a little. Well, there are a few techniques that will help, but they won't work miracles. With that caveat, here are some techniques for becoming a quick-change artist:

How to Flex Others

1.   *Face it.* Make sure your face is relaxed and smiling when you explain or request a change. Frowning or knitting your brows sends a message: "This change is a tough one," "I'm suspicious of you," or "I'm not sure about this change myself." This may seem rather obvious and elementary, but facial expressions dramatically influence others. So watch your face in the mirror as you practice making requests.

2. Paint a picture when requesting a change. Provide a picture—on paper or in words—of the benefits of the change. For example, if you are trying to get someone to come to your office instead of meeting at hers, tell her how warm and cozy or sunny and quiet it is. Mention that you've just had four dozen red tulips delivered and tell her that "We'll have the office all to ourselves" and that there is coffee brewing. Even the most rigid thinker responds to lights, music, and action, so the livelier and more colorful, the better.

4. Their words. If they don't seem to be listening, search for a subject they're interested in. Is it money, fun, or the breeding of Shih Tzu pups? No matter how far removed it is from the change you wish them to make, plug in a few buzz words from their lexicon, and you'll grab their attention. Then you can move to the business at hand.

5. The body switch. When someone is stuck and can't see your viewpoint, try changing your behavior completely. If you've been rational, act emotional. Wring your hands, look anguished, make your lower lip quiver. If you've been warm and friendly, stiffen your spine, look serious, and speak in a monotone, citing statistics and studies. The shock may provoke a new look at you and your topic.

6. The double mirror. Mirroring another's behavior when you're trying to establish rapport is a well-known and useful technique. Imitate the expression, intensity, gestures, and stance of the person you're communicating with. When the two of you are in sync, go one step further. Lead him by altering your movements bit by bit. Usually he will unconsciously mirror *your* behavior. This works well when you're trying to soften another person's attitude towards you.

7. The leading question. Asking questions is probably the most powerful flexer of all. First of all, it displays respect for the other person, and mutual respect is a great emollient to communication. To get the most from questions, listen intently for one small area of agreement. Begin from that point in the ensuing conversation. Here again, you can start with one soft area and move on to areas of greater resistance.

After you practice several of these flexers, you'll find yourself applying them in different ways and inventing your own. That's great—flexibility is the name of the game.

Initiated change requires the most sophisticated skills of all the change you experience because *you* call all the shots, *you* determine all the whens and hows. You've come a long way since your first initiated change, which perhaps was pushing your food off the high chair tray when you were a baby. Think of the progress you've made, the complicated decisions you make, the important changes you initiate: starting up a new business, buying a house or car, moving to a foreign country, or marketing an invention.

Can you identify one such change you have recently initiated? Do you recall experiencing any of the seven steps just described? They may not have occurred in just the order given, but you probably experienced all of them. It is important to have these steps firmly in mind so that you can reach even higher levels of success in initiating change. Knowing what works for you and how it works for you makes change even more exciting and fruitful. Knowing that initiated change has identifiable characteristics of its own will make you more alert to the opportunities around you.

In the next chapter, you will read about individuals who have this awareness of the way they initiate change; they are sophisticated and successful changemakers in the business world.

12

Initiating Change in the Business World

A clear example of how the seven steps for initiating change unfolded before our eyes in Denver, when many community leaders longed for a new convention center. The current small center, Currigan Hall, was built in the early sixties, when no one anticipated the tremendous growth that would occur in Denver during the energy boom. When the energy boom burst in the early eighties, the need for a new center remained. But now, Denver needed it to prop up the economy with bigger conventions and more tourist dollars. But how to initiate this change?

Several developers and a new mayor tried. From 1983 until 1987, newly elected Mayor Federico Pena and three millionaires, Marvin Davis, Al Cohen, and Phillip Anschutz, tried to make the convention center happen. They all failed. Backed in his campaign by Marvin Davis, Mayor Pena first attempted to get voter approval for a new center next to the old Union Station in Denver's lower downtown area.

But in 1985, the voters rejected the proposal as too hastily conceived and as part of a political payoff. Davis dropped out as a contender. The state legislature got into the act with grant money. A high-stakes contest developed between contractor Al Cohen and railroad magnate Phil Anschutz, each with his own assembled parcel of land to contribute—for a tidy profit, of course. By the spring of 1987, political alliances to these developers resulted in a stalemate.

To break the impasse, the city council called in the Urban Land Institute, a reputable nonprofit organization with expertise in real estate and urban design. Given free rein by city council, the ULI developed a list of ninety-six criteria imperative for a new convention center and invited proposals, not only from Cohen and Anschutz but from any prospective developer with a good idea for bringing the new convention center to Denver.

Enter David French, a forty-five-year-old entrepreneur ready not only to bring change to the Denver skyline but also to initiate change in his own career.

In the seventies, Dave French had restored and developed the Daniels-Fisher Tower, a Venetianesque relic of old Denver. The D&F Tower, as it was called, had once stood next to the Daniels-Fisher department store, the retail center of Denver. The tower was the tallest building in five states.

When urban renewal came to Denver in 1964, the Historic Preservation Society succeeded in saving the tower, although its companion store was demolished. And for eight years, the tower, only fifty-by-fifty feet in dimension, stood alone in the urban renewal district like a lonely sentry. Finally Dave French restored it, ingeniously creating upscale condominium offices, all of them now sold to happy owners.

But with the collapse of the oil business, there was also a real estate bust, and Dave French spent the next four years running a restaurant, raising funds for political campaigns, and getting slightly bored. He was also ready to initiate some personal change.

When he heard of the ULI proposal, David French could hardly contain himself. He had earlier supported the concept of a new convention center right next to the old one on the blocks adjacent to Currigan Hall and closer to all of Denver's downtown hotels and retail shopping than the previously suggested sites.

The location was superb, but French did not control the land, and he certainly did not control the politicians. Now with the ULI in the picture, he could perhaps break the impasse, assemble an exciting convention center proposal, earn substantial fees, and bring change to his moribund career.

Dave thought about what had worked for him in the D&F Tower project and decided his own talents and experience were more important than being a wealthy landowner. "I'm a developer: That's what I do. I put the pieces all together: the architect, the builder, the land, the concept."

Indeed, Dave is a developer—one who develops relationships, patterns, ideas, and winning plans. It didn't surprise us when he tested out as a Relater. Dave continues: "When I read the ninety-six criteria in the papers, I knew it was a 'developer's dream.' I felt this ripple of excitement, and from that moment on, I didn't stop until I had a proposal ready to go.

"As I analyzed who would be for and against my proposal, who would win and who would lose if either of the two current favorites got the project, many things became clear to me.

"The current frontrunners were not popular with the public because they were considered fat cats trying to make money off land they owned. The fact that I did not own land was an advantage. It separated me in the public's perception from the other two developers who had a vested interest in their sites.

"It also helped that the ULI truly was impartial, which meant the major decisionmakers would be on my side—I knew I had the best idea. Besides, my proposal would meet most of the ninety-six criteria.

"What could be clearer? Currigan Hall was the ideal location, and adjacent land was available for expansion purposes. Now that it was a blighted area, this land was cheap and would be easy and inexpensive to acquire. Yes, forces had converged to make this the crucial site—and the time to act."

And Dave French did act. He assembled a team of professionals, worked day and night for weeks putting together a proposal that did win—much to the surprise of newspaper readers and the two established planners. "I got all my ducks in a row, and when I submitted my proposal, everybody quacked in unison. I exaggerate," he says, laughing. "Certainly, Cohen and Anschutz weren't happy, but the council, the ULI, and the public liked my plan.

"It was so exciting and energizing. I felt good about my architect and builder. We were all professionals. We knew what we were doing and worked well together.

"The excitement brought discipline. We all focused on one concept—putting that convention center in an area that would be convenient and inexpensive and one whose urban blight problems could be redressed.

"Here's an interesting thing about timing. We couldn't have made the three-week deadline that the Urban Land Institute first declared—at least not with the great proposal we finally produced. At the last minute, the ULI could not meet in July and postponed the deadline a month. That gave us enough time to prepare a polished proposal and to accommodate some last minute changes in criteria.

"Sure we took punches. There were the doubters who didn't think we or our plans were big enough to get the job done. Some of our critics said it should be the size of Pittsburgh's convention center, which accommodates large equipment, technical and commerical exhibits, and so on. It was tempting to beef up the exhibition space, but then we realized that Denver attracts a much different kind of convention than Pittsburgh. Here, we get the professional types—the nurses, dentists, educators, contractors, marketers. And our plan called for 65,000 square feet of meeting rooms—just what those folks use most.

"We hired a public relations firm to help us get the facts across to the public. They got us good press, which kept our spirits high when the bricks came flying our way.

"And throughout, we kept our ears to the ground to see what was happening, what adjustments to make in our proposal. The other developers' plans had not changed from day one, but we kept adjusting ours, right up to the final moments before we submitted it.

"And even then, we continually adapted our thinking and plans. For example, the city council suggested closing off several streets around Currigan to make it easier for pedestrians to use. "So, we said, that's fine. The city's traffic engineers have the expertise and clout to devise a transit corridor for rerouting traffic.

So we welcomed their input and help, and, by becoming involved in the actual planning, they became real friends.

"We lasted the course by listening to any criticism and acting on it. We changed tactics—but never our overall goal."

As you read Dave's story, did you identify with any of his experiences or feelings? Have you ever felt like a little David up against several Goliaths? Have you ever felt that opportunity was just barely hidden in the events around you? Have you ever felt the joy of initiating a successful change? If you have, you might relate to some or all of the feelings and actions Dave went through to initiate this change.

You might also see how clearly Dave experienced the seven steps for initiating change.

From past experience, he *knew his style* for initiating change, and the Change-Friendly Quotient Survey confirmed he was a Relater.

Remember how Dave's *excitement* about his concept was so energizing to him and his team that they all worked day and night with total *commitment* and finished the proposal in record time.

Understanding *who's where* and getting his forces in *alignment* was second nature to Dave since he understood the political and economic scene in Denver and had followed the convention center story in the daily newspapers.

Dave discovered several *crucial points and people* along the way, but probably the turn around came when he realized that he didn't need to own land to be in the competition. In fact, not owning land was a political advantage.

When criticism arose, Dave *persevered* with his plan but hired public relations professionals to keep the public informed. And throughout, Dave and his team *stayed flexible,* and in the process, improved the convention center plan and thus its potential for acceptance in the community.

In case the story of Dave French seems a little beyond you, below are a few less ambitious examples that illustrate how clients in our change workshops have experienced the seven steps of initiating change. Reviewing the experiences of others and practicing these concrete steps will bolster your skills and confidence.

Steps 1 and 2
(Self-awareness and Commitment)

Most of our clients were immediately helped simply by defining their own change style. They then understood how they work best, what their strengths are, and what kinds of changes they'd most likely have success in initiating. For example, a group of lawyers who all tested out to be Riskers had been wrestling with the problem of the public's increasingly negative attitude towards the legal profession. We had expected them to be Reasoners, but then realized that they were Bar Association presidents and as such would show high levels of leadership—a strong element in the Risker style.

At first, many of these lawyers objected to the designation "Risker" because they felt the term implied recklessness. With further clarification, they agreed that taking responsibility for a client's life or financial future requires the courage, confidence, and daring embedded in the term "Risker" as we define it. While their actions are based on the thoughtful analysis of the Reasoner, effective lawyers must be able to take risks.

With this new view of themselves and their profession, these lawyers devised a plan to improve their profession's public image by moving into new areas rather "risky" for lawyers:

- offer free "preventive law" classes (advising laypeople on measures that will help them avoid breaking the law or getting mired down in legal hassles)

- build media contacts so that news stories would carry clear explanations of legal points (and an occasional complimentary portrayal of a lawyer)

- form a discussion group on the legal ethics of such issues as AIDs, right to die, transplant banks, etc. (periodic reports on their discussions would be available to the public)

- make house calls (by serving clients in their homes, the lawyers established warmer relationships with them)

Follow-up conversations with several of these attorneys revealed a heightened sense of purpose and pride—and a renewed determination to make their efforts count for more than just a means of making money.

The lawyers understood that they were both comfortable and energized by trying new things, and they built on this knowledge. Think of your own work, your change style, and your goals. Do you have the same understanding of you and your workstyle that helped them? You'll know you have it when you feel a sense of confidence that leads to excitement and commitment to your goals. Once all *your* energies are on the same track, you are free to look around and get those around you aligned.

Step 3 (Who's Where)

Nicole, a line supervisor at a Midwest sporting goods manufacturing company, posed a much more specific problem. She wanted to go on flex-time and work four ten-hour days per week rather than the five eight-hour days that was company practice. We encouraged her to focus on getting her own schedule adjusted rather than trying to get flex-time implemented company wide. By narrowing her focus, she could more easily identify the forces for and against the change she wished to initiate.

It is all too easy to plunge ahead enthusiastically with an idea that benefits you but might initially irritate someone else. To make sure this didn't happen to Nicole, we asked her to list the people who would be directly affected if she worked the different schedule. Next to the list, she was to put columns headed *For* and *Against*. Then we asked her to put a + under *For* if she believed the individuals listed there would support the change, a − under *Against* if she thought they'd oppose it. Then we suggested that she think about *why* each person would be for or against the change and how strong each one's feelings were. If she expected the person's feelings to be very strong and thought the person was in a position to do something about them, she was to put down a double + or a double − by that person's name. Here's her list:

Name:	For:	Against:
Ned, her boss		−−
Ruth, secretary		
Tim, security		−−
John, supervisor		−
Pat, nurse	++	

She gave Ned, her manager, a double minus. She felt he would be against her change because he'd have to clear it with his superior. And as the department manager, he had the power to enforce his position.

Nicole feared that John, her fellow line supervisor, would also be against the change because he'd have to alter his schedule if hers changed. She gave him a single minus.

She marked nothing for Ruth, the division secretary, whose work would be affected very little by Nicole's schedule.

Tim, the security guard, was another matter. Nicole was certain he'd be against the change because her longer hours might require some alterations in security procedures. "Besides, he's such a spit-and-polish, stick-to-the rules person," she said. She gave him a double minus.

Nicole added Pat's name to the list, not because she had any direct bearing on Nicole's job, but because Pat was the company's delegate to a community task force to clean up air pollution. Some companies in the area had already implemented flex-time to reduce air pollution caused by morning and evening rush hours. Pat could be a powerful ally, so she got a double plus.

Nicole ended with two pluses and five minuses. But she tried out the idea on Ned, her manager, anyway. She found that he was mildly interested in trying the plan for the entire department and thought Nicole would be a good test case. So she converted Ned's score to double plus because he was willing to try flex-time and had the power put it into effect. Then the score was four pluses and three minuses.

She talked first to her coworker, John, and got his consent to proceed. Next, she had lunch with Pat, who gave her some statistical information on how well flex-time had worked else-where. Thus fortified, she went back to Ned and found him quite amenable. At that point, she was home free. Incidentally, in a year's time, Nicole's company adopted flex-time in all departments.

Going through the Who's Where process enabled Nicole to get an estimate of how individuals might feel about flex-time and to estimate the relative strength of each person involved. Furthermore, asking the "how strong?" question often helps you identify the crucial point and/or person, the next step in successfully initiating change.

Step 4
(Crucial Point or Person)

Here's the problem a production manager named Stan brought to us. Hundreds of boxes were being destroyed just as they reached the end of the production line. He complained to his superiors about the quality of the employees he had been assigned. He felt they were lazy and irresponsible. Management was about to give these recalcitrants a lecture and a last warning, when a consultant asked, "Is there a pattern to these breakages?"

So Stan charted the breakages for two days and found that 95 percent of them occurred during the half-hour before lunch and the half-hour before shift changes. Upon closer observation, he realized that during these critical periods, the person who controlled the conveyor belt was moving in and out of position, getting ready for the shift changes. No one else had access to that lever, so there was no way for anyone else to stop it or slow it down.

You can see how valuable this insight was—and how watching for a pattern is an effective way of finding the crucial point for change.

Step 5
(Alignment)

Justin knew what the crucial point was and whose button to push, but he just couldn't figure out how to bring about alignment at his small manufacturing plant in Erie, Pennsylvania.

His company had been hit hard and early by the decline in the U.S. auto industry, and the impact had reduced company morale below zero. Besides, for many years, Erie had jokingly been called "Dreary Erie, the Mistake on the Lake." The lack of opportunity had recently driven Erie's young people to other areas. The laughing stopped and a gloomy despair settled in.

Justin's employees were suffering from this malaise. He came to our Change Workshop to find ways to reignite his company's will so he could turn things around and try again. A great opportunity had just surfaced—a chance to bid on a light rail system for a western city. But when Justin presented it to his employees, there was, as he described it, "no sign of life in the whole damned bunch." They felt they could not have the proto-type ready by the six-month deadline; they were sure they could never win the bid.

What could spark some enthusiasm—a common goal? We showed him videos of leaders setting forth a clear goal they wished to achieve in order to bring about a change in others. He found it particularly helpful to view Jack Nicholson's portrayal of Randle P. McMurphy in the movie *One Flew Over the Cuckoo's Nest,* especially the scene in which McMurphy leads his fellow inmates out of the asylum for an unauthorized boat ride. With his cocky confidence and belligerent assurance, he soon overcame their fears of being apprehended as he paraded them out of the hospital on the pretense that they were all doctors and not patients.

Their tentative and nervous behavior changed as he jauntily approached the guard questioning the group and introduced the first two inmates as "Dr. Roper and *the famous* Dr. Scanlon!" The patients copied Nicholson's confidence, straightened their backs, squared their shoulders, and gazed boldly at the guard. They really looked like famous surgeons and internists, and the guards imme-diately granted them access to the boat.

The bizarre-looking men began to view themselves as doctors. As they affected scholarly manners, they seemed to actually become intellectuals. As they began to feel in control of their lives, their physical presence changed. They stood erect; they almost sauntered; they smiled confidently.

This and other workshop examples demonstrated to Justin that both showing and emulating the desired behavior can cause mental and physical changes that in turn make the desired change real. Successful initiators of change provide a clear, simple, and consistent vision. They seem to be gifted in clarifying the change they want, with the result that others just naturally follow.

Justin went back to his dispirited people and held a company dinner in Erie's fanciest hotel. Spouses were invited, achievement awards were given. Following dinner, a motivational speaker talked about "Your ticket to success is you" and was followed by a choral group. In the closing moments, the whole company was led in singing "The Battle Hymn of the Republic."

"It was a moment to remember," he told us later. "All the employees were standing and singing in their best clothes, eyes aglow and happy. Then, I asked them to sit for a few last comments. I delivered a five-minute speech from the heart. I said that now was a turning point in the life of our company, and we had a great opportunity. If we got the contract, we'd have a company to be proud of. I thanked them for their years of devotion and able service, and told them how confident I was that we'd be one of the finalists—and what it would mean to them in personal and financial terms. But mostly, I emphasized how confident I was that we could build the prototype in six months because of their superior skills and experience."

Justin did three things that brought alignment. He established a clear vision; he outlined the steps it would take to achieve the vision; but most important of all, he helped his employees believe that success was probable with them as vital members of the team. He generated the vision and purpose to get the prototype completed on time. And it won the bid! They have the contract!

Step 6
(Staying the Course)

On your way to that goal or vision, you inevitably encounter detours, barricades, and deadends. You must find some way to stay on course yet make corrections to avoid meeting these roadblocks again. This resilience was demonstrated by three nurses at Case

Western Reserve who were redirecting their careers. All three were drawn to medicine by their desire to help people. But midway through training, when they were in their clinical year and involved with patients, they became aware of the limited power nurses often have.

"All I did during that clinical year was roll up beds and pass out pills. There was never time to give patients the kind of attention I know helps them get well," said Juanita.

She came to our workshop looking for ways to handle the ambivalence she was experiencing over her career direction. Her upbringing told her she should always finish what she started, yet her heart told her she didn't feel good about her present course. We asked her first to recreate her original vision of her career. She said, "Here I am, talking to patients and their families, listening carefully and evaluating the symptoms, making decisions that ease their pain or make them well."

Since the nursing role she had experienced was not consistent with that picture, we asked her to see who had that kind of responsibility and power. Juanita was not comfortable with the answer. "The doctors do . . . but I never even thought of being a doctor."

"Why not?" we asked, and that set her off in a slightly altered course that helped her achieve her original goal. She went back to the hospital and discussed her idea with her two frustrated colleagues. The more they talked about this different way of reaching their goal, the more they became resolved to apply for medical school. "It will take a little longer to get there—but our original vision will be fulfilled," they concluded.

At last report, Juanita and her friends had completed three years at Case Western's medical school, and they were well on their way to becoming a pediatrician, a family practicioner, and a psychiatrist, respectively. There are roadblocks and detours: They won't all graduate in the winter because their internships were scheduled at different times. But, Juanita says, "Even though it's rough at times, one of us is generally up enough to say, 'We're doing great, look how far we've come, only two more tough courses to take.'"

Juanita's story contains several hints you might want to follow when you're working towards a goal and confront a problem. To persevere try to:

1. Recreate your vision for clarification and inspiration (add the smell, color, feel, and sound of your goal for heightened perception).

2. Check your progress at short intervals to get the feedback you need to keep your courage up.

3. Give yourself rewards along the way (a movie on your day off or a call to a close friend about your progress).

Juanita and her friends were able to keep on course yet stay flexible—which is the final and ultimate test of the successful initiator of change.

Step 7
(Staying Flexible)

The one problem almost all workshop participants presented to us was that of staying flexible. They described how difficult it was for them to listen to people with styles very different from theirs and to do things in different ways when "their way" worked. And some who had tried new ideas and failed were afraid to risk again.

Tom Phillips could easily have fallen prey to such fears because he works in the sophisticated, competitive field of magazine publishing. In graduate school, he was sure he wanted to be an investment banker, but when he got out into the world, he found his ideas changing. As a result, he initiated a change that was both bold and brilliant.

Phillips is co-founder and publisher of *SPY* magazine, a monthly that combines a sophisticated literary style with the outrageous pillorying and punning ways of *National Lampoon* and *Mad* magazines. A baby boomer, Phillips was ready to follow much of his generation into yuppiedom when he decided he really didn't want to work on deals that were merely "rearranging capital, not creating anything new." Two Time/Life writers, Kurt Andersen and E. Graydon Carter, invited him to lunch hoping to entice him to find start-up capital for the magazine. But Phillips was so taken with their idea, he quit his job and invested everything he had in the project. "There was fantastic chemistry at that lunch. We never felt any doubts about it; we knew it was the right thing at the right time."

Andersen and Carter had noticed that as the baby boomers grew up, although they shed their sixties exteriors and got serious about materialism, they never lost their distaste for the establishment. These two understood the discomfort the boomers felt in now being a part of that establishment and saw an opportunity that might never present itself again. They design a magazine to take advantage of this change. *SPY* magazine tweaks authority, allowing its readers to make fun of materialism even as they enjoy it.

It uses biting humor, satire, and irreverence to describe the rich, the vacuous, the elite, and the influential. Typical *SPY* readers feel they haven't sold out entirely to the forces they rebelled against in their teens and twenties. Phillips and his two friends are having a wonderful time creating humorous havoc and making money in the process.

His example shows that you need not be middle-aged and "a member of the publishing club" to start a new magazine or to initiate a change. You *do* need an ability to detect opportunity and move fast to exploit it. You do need flexibility.

Phillips is one of the most flexible people we have ever met, but his is not a flexibility that comes from weakness; his is a resilience that comes from the strength of self-confidence and willingness to listen to others. Early success has not hardened his approach. He is continually open to the opportunities in the attitudes and activities of those around him. If you would do the same, you need to stay flexible yourself but also understand the flexibility of others.

The Flex Check

The second time around, Barney learned how important it is to understand the flexibility of others. An earnest young college

student working at McDonald's, Barney loved the bustling efficiency of the place and was full of suggestions for improving the
operation. But the manager deflected each and every idea with a
"That's not how we do it at McDonald's."

Fish sandwiches had just been added to the McDonald's menu,
and it was Barney's duty to prepare them. To his dismay, they were
not very popular. He watched with envy as his fellow employees
scurried around producing hundreds of Big Macs, shakes, and
fries, while he had only an occasional order to fill. Barney pointed
out to the manager that he could easily prepare the fish *and* man
the french fry station. The manager blew up and fired him.

Barney went on to a job in the chemistry lab at the university.
Once again, he confronted inflexibility when he developed a
method for washing test tubes that was actually superior to the
usual way. The lab professor refused to consider a change and
insisted that Barney wash tubes the "way we've always done it."
He did as he was told.

Barney learned that sometimes there are good reasons for
inflexibility and sometimes there aren't—but in either case, you'd
better be flexible enough to recognize the difference. Flexibility in
the real world often requires working within the confines of
another's inflexibility.

The Dynamics of Change

Thus far, *The Flexibility Factor* has focused on change at the
individual level. You have read how many individuals have
successfully responded to radical and gradual change and how
seasoned changemakers have initiated change. Now, let's step
back and look at the broader patterns all these changes follow. By
borrowing a tool from psychology, we can draw pictures of these
kinds of change. These visual images will help you see the
dynamics of change—how it grows and when it should happen.

Studies show that when people learn, they first have a slow
period of orientation, which is followed by rapid acceleration.
However, at a certain point, they learn more slowly. Psychologists
depict this process as a bell-shaped "learning curve." The dynamics of a change, whether it is manifested in one small alteration in

your thought process or in the course of life, can be expressed by the same bell-curve. The upward curve and rounded peak represent the cycle experienced by an individual or organization as the change begins, develops, and comes to fruition. But, like the learning curve, the change curve starts to tip downward. At the point of decline, you should make a new change to spark a new curve upward. To be skilled in change requires stopping at just the right moment, where you can see both the past and the future, and then moving to a new curve before the downswing begins.

When a radical change, such as getting fired from your job, occurs at the beginning of decline, you can renew your progress cycle by finding a better job or career. The imposed change actually helped you avoid the decay that normally occurs once the peak of the curve has been reached. This optimum point for change is shown on the curve.

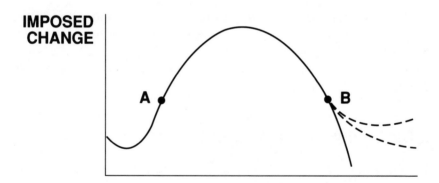

IMPOSED CHANGE

You can best adapt to gradual change by a series of small changes. While these seem less dramatic, they are sometimes more difficult to accomplish because they require constant vigilance and creativity. Switching between left and right brained tactics will prevent the flattening out of the curve that occurs during gradual change. If you have developed comfort with change styles other than your own and have an inventory of left- and right-brain strategies, you can stimulate gradual change in terms of this healthy cycle:

**ADAPTIVE
CHANGE**

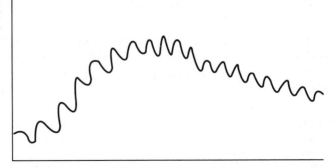

Notice that by alternating strategies when change is inching upward on the curve, you avoid the inertia that usually sets in once the peak is reached. The reward is long-term progress without dips and downward slides.

In initiated change, *you* make the decision to intervene at the point of decline. Awareness of this point can come through dissatisfaction with your present state or from a passionate need to create something new. You may even intervene before the peak is reached.

**INITIATED
CHANGE**

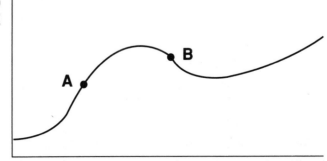

Initiated change may look the same as the other two kinds, but it is actually much more powerful because you are making the decision, reaping the rewards, and experiencing the thrill of doing it your way.

Whichever kind of change you're making, notice that you really can prevent the deterioration that often takes place in jobs and relationships. It takes an awareness of your strengths in dealing with the different kinds of change and the flexibility to apply them.

In the next section of the book, you will discover how these same abilities are used by organizations. You'll read about firms, corporations, government agencies, and educational institutions that experience the same kinds of changes you do. You'll find that to be successful and maintain their integrity, they, too, must respond to radical and gradual change; they, too, must initiate change. Their products are subject to the same change cycles individuals go through, and their actions also go through the same phases of development.

As you read the next section on organizational change, watch for the similarities between your personal experience with change and the experiences of the organizations. You may begin to feel that groups involved in change behave as individuals do. Read on to see if the macrocosm imitates the microcosm.

PART FOUR

Organizational Change

13

What Makes a Company Flexible?

The president of a large, staid, old bank stares with distaste at an elegant silver tray piled high with small bags of popcorn—favors for new checking account applicants. "Popcorn," he sniffs, then sighs with resignation and munches on a handful as he proceeds to his office.

The burly union leader places the latest list of demands on the negotiation agenda. The number one concern? Day care accommodations for employees' young children.

A middle-aged male executive complains, "I've worked my tail off for this company for twenty years, and who gets the vice presidency? A thirty-two-year-old female talk-show host."

The weary traveler who has just mastered the process of opening her hotel room with a computerized lock system is confronted by yet another challenge: an automatic ordering device for room service, telephone messages, and laundry. She calls the front desk and says, "Please, just give me my messages, I'm too tired to try to figure this thing out."

The aspiring junior manager dons the wardrobe of her profession her first day on the job. It is not the navy suit and crisp white shirt of yesteryear but the orange cap, slacks, and blouse of a fast-food outlet.

The retail store owner watches as an employee carefully opens a crate of sweatshirts. The employee mutters, "Next thing you know the Japanese will be primary producers of the American flag." The store owner replies, "This stuff isn't from Japan; it's from South Korea."

The dean of the graduate school adds an application to the accepted pile. A colleague is shocked. "A sixty-one-year-old retired accountant. Isn't he a little long in the tooth for graduate school?" The dean replies, "Listen, there used to be an abundance of young students eager to get into grad school, but those days are over."

Such scenes are being acted out in businesses and institutions all over this continent and throughout the world. They reflect a few of the startling changes of the past few years and the kairos in them: banks with a human touch, a broadened concern for the welfare of young children, high-tech efficiency in every area of life, ample management opportunities in service industries, vice presidencies for women, small countries earning a toehold in the world economy, and graduate school for sixty-year-olds.

These changes are both disquieting and exciting, and long before we're comfortable with them, other, even more dramatic ones, take hold. The pace of change is quickening and more so in the workplace than anywhere else.

Whether you work for a large company, a government agency, a major manufacturer, a school district, a retail store, your own business, or as a volunteer for a nonprofit corporation, you are surely faced with work changes. The force of these changes can bring new life to you and your associates, or they can be the beginning of the end.

Just as it is for the individual, flexibility is the key to managing the problems and opportunities that change brings to organizations. However, organizations become as entrenched in the past as individuals do. Even the American political and economic systems, which are inherently flexible, become nervous when confronted with change. The danger is clarified by Paul Kennedy, a Yale University professor, in his book *The Rise and Fall of the Great Powers:* "Since all societies are subject to the inexorable tendency to change, then the international balances can *never* be still . . . the only serious threat to the real and diverse interests of the United States can come from a failure to adjust sensibly."* We need to remember that our country and its economy have worked well for two hundred years precisely *because* they have been friendly to change.

In the forties, economist Joseph Schumpeter said, "Capitalism, then, is by nature a form or method of economic change and not only never is but never can be stationary."† Progress, according to Schumpeter, comes when your profits are frequently diminished by the inroads your competition makes, and you are forced to create a new product to regain them. So firms should continually leapfrog over each other for improved positions in a marketplace teeming with change. It is an arena in which a tug-of-war between the old and the new is always fought. Organizations start, grow fast, then decline as quickly as their products and services become obsolete. Destruction thus becomes a creative force for renewal. Schumpeter argues that this is as it must be for continued vitality. Seen this way, the unsettling mergers, divestitures, deregulation, takeovers, and global economy of the eighties are the agents for creative destruction, bringing the potential for increased prosperity and quality of life.

Organizations that are protected from change tend to become self-satisfied and ineffectual. To their detriment, industrial giants and such revered institutions as universities and churches have often been protected from change. Their many layers of fat (money, respect, power, and structure) have allowed them to remain comfortable while everything around them was changing. Today, all organizations are being shaken, and they must change to survive. And it's not all that bad. Change restores vigor and a zest for tomorrow.

Lester Thurow would agree. The spirited dean of MIT's graduate school of business, he gives lectures to business leaders

*Kennedy, Paul, *The Rise and Fall of the Great Powers* (New York, Random House, 1987).
†Schumpeter, Joseph, *Can Capitalism Survive?* (New York: Harper & Row, 1978).

all over the country on the dangers of old-fashioned attitudes. As he pointed out on *60 Minutes,* "Ford and Mitsubishi can work together to edge out General Motors, but General Motors and Ford can't cooperate against Mitsubishi—all because of our anti-trust laws set up in the 1930s, when we were worried about the survival of free competition. We need to change those laws if we are to maintain flexibility."

While one capitalist democracy (the United States) may be temporarily stunned by the pace of change in this century's culminating years, others (Japan, West Germany, and Singapore) have thrived on it. The creative destruction process envisioned by Schumpeter forty years ago has simply become global, and the capitalism of the eighties remains the political and economic system most likely to succeed.

What does this broad picture mean to you and the organization for which you work? Do the components of individual flexibility identified in the first half of this book have implications for organizational change? Can you apply the change techniques you've learned to the company or institution you work for? The answer to all three questions is yes. You'll learn how in this last section of the book, which focuses on organizational flexibility and its importance to a successful operation.

In this chapter, you will discover how friendly your workplace is to change. You'll read about companies, agencies, and other organizations that have successfully managed change—and about a few that became mired in pseudochange. Then you'll learn how an organization develops the ability to change just as a person does. Ultimately, you will find out how to make your workplace more flexible and, therefore, more likely to nurture the kairos in change.

The Climate of Your Organization

There's a special feel, an invigorating climate in the flexible organization. When you walk in the door, you can sense an openness to new ideas. There is the comfort of structure, a sense of purpose, and a system for getting things done. Yet there are lots of options, and people take the time to really listen. There is a feeling of mutual respect and a can-do attitude. Each person truly wants each product or service to be of the highest quality. Most of all, this flexible organization welcomes change, not change-for-change's-sake but productive change.

Think about the climate of your workplace. What sensations do you experience when you picture yourself at work? Pretend you are a client or supplier entering your place of business for the first time. What impressions do you get? Circle the words below that describe the climate of your workplace.

hot	warm	cold
sunny	overcast	snow flurries
dust storms	windy	blizzard
hazardous	partly sunny	showers
hurricanes	cool	sleet
clear	partly hazy	cooling
crisp	muggy	turbulent
humid	cloudy	windy
variable	foggy	temperate
mild	generally sunny	tranquil
tropical	improving rapidly	frigid
cold, with rain	cloudy but clearing	below zero
showers moving in	warming trend	misty

Do you see a pattern? The "weather conditions" in your office or plant tell you whether your operation is hospitable or inhospitable to change.

If it's extremely hot or cold, forces may be building towards a precipitous change. The warning signs may enable you to prepare for the turbulence ahead.

An office or business with a temperate and calm climate is the one least likely to change; it may gradually be becoming rigid.

Probably the climate most conducive to productive change is generally sunny but variable. It might feel like the climate in the training division of a large Texas multimedia corporation. Emily M., a program designer, gave us this weather report:

"It's a stimulating place to work. Staff members in other divisions are always asking how they can get transferred in because it seems we have so much fun here. There are four program designers, five support staff, and one director. Each of us has a lot of individual responsibility and authority, and we brainstorm and help each other out when it's needed. The support staff is on flex-time, and several coordinators are half-time, so there's a lot of coming and going and "creative" scheduling. Some times it looks like a circus, but it's a successful circus because we're all running our own show."

In contrast, Madeline Carlin, an interviewer for the California state employment services, described her office's weather conditions this way:

"It was like walking into a waist-high snowdrift, cold and tough going. We were told where we could and could not put plants, pictures, and paperweights, how we could arrange our desks, and how much time we could spend with each client.

"Part of it was the system. We had federal, state, and local guidelines, policies, and regulations to follow. We even had quotas. We had to interview so many people per day and place a certain percentage of them in jobs each week.

"But it was more than the system. It was the office manager, too. He claimed to have an open-door policy, but he sure didn't have an open mind. All the time you'd be explaining how a new way of doing things might help, he'd tap his pen on the desk and say 'uuum' in a way that told you he wasn't really listening and that he thought your ideas were unimportant.

"But, you know, I never felt the full impact of this place until one day, a neighbor came in the office. He'd been out of a job for six weeks and really looked down. When I saw him rushed through an interview, given the standard busy work to do, and then drag himself out the door, I realized how bitterly cold and unfriendly my office was. That's when I decided to move to a warmer climate."

Madeline had a very strong impression of the kind of climate she worked in. She also had identified some of the problems that made it unfriendly to change.

As you think about the climate in your workplace, you can probably see connections between the feel of the place and the prevailing policies.

Because policies and procedures tend to become entrenched over time, maintaining a favorable climate is difficult—but it is not impossible, as seen in the long career of Arthur C. Nielsen, Jr.

Changing Times at the A. C. Nielsen Company

By finding new ways of managing change, the A. C. Nielsen Company has thrived for more than a half-century. Although the company is best known for measuring television audiences, its activities span many fields. It has prospered in changing times by *responding to*, *adapting to*, and *initiating* change.

Imposed Changes

A. C. Nielsen, Jr., was hornswoggled into business when he was thirteen—by his father. Mr. Nielsen, Senior, was a pioneer in marketing research. During the Great Depression he saw his Chicago business decline from forty-five employees to six, and his prospective clients to one, in New York. Nielsen polled his employees, and they voted to spend the company's remaining funds to send him to New York in a last-ditch effort to get the account. But the company cashbox contained only enough money for a one-way fare. Enter young Mr. Nielsen. That night Art's father explained to his thirteen-year-old son the wonders of the capitalist system and pointed out that he could become a shareholder in the A. C. Nielsen Company. Young Arthur bought fourteen shares of company stock with the contents of his piggy bank, $52, just enough for his father's return fare from New York.

The senior Mr. Nielsen's trip was successful, and the company survived and later flourished, providing young Art with an opportunity to learn about every aspect of the business. His father insisted that Art work in every single department of the company. Furthermore, he couldn't leave one until he'd written a detailed report on its operation and included at least one idea for improvement. He accomplished this and his confidence grew with each assignment he successfully completed and each innovative department idea he prescribed.

Though challenging, this assignment was mild compared to his first assignment with the Corps of Engineers during World War II. His commanding officer said to him, "Lieutenant, we'll need an administration building to house 350 architects and engineers—in three weeks." "But sir, I've never built anything before," he responded. "Don't tell me your troubles, just do it" was the curt reply. Nielsen immersed himself in library books about construction, questioned every person he met who would discuss building methods, and worked round the clock. The project was completed in the prescribed three weeks, just barely. The experience, though harrowing, was another boost to his confidence. He had learned he could handle challenges well—even uninvited ones.

Adapting

From these rigorous beginnings, Nielsen went on to other experiences, using a variety of change-management styles, depending on the situation. When A. C. Nielsen Company paid a consultant $25,000 to advise the company on whether or not it should move its location, Nielsen was not happy with the answer.

"This consultant told us to stay where we were in the heart of downtown Chicago. He had the charts and the studies and the blarney. I looked at him—tall, handsome, a big full head of dark curly hair, a broad smile on his face, and a wide gold chain across his vest—and I thought, does he really know about traffic patterns and where people want to work and live? So I went out and got other opinions."

He went to the highway department and talked to train dispatchers to discover where traffic was heaviest and what trends were developing. He visited All-State Insurance headquarters to find out how they chose the convenient locations for their drive-in claims offices. He researched where the phone and utility companies were laying lines. He talked to clients and suppliers about their preferences.

The outcome: Nielsen Junior convinced his father that he should move the plant out of the increasingly congested confines of the city to Northbrook, where taxes were lower and access was easier—long before moves to the suburbs became common. His natural Relater style was bolstered by this success in adapting to change.

Initiating

In the fifties, one of the company's marketing services was the distribution of promotional samples of a client's product door-to-door. Since this was so expensive, few clients were interested. So Nielsen began distributing redeemable coupons instead and attracted many clients with this more versatile approach to marketing. The coupons could be distributed cheaply through the mail, magazines, and other distribution channels. But this success led to another challenge and opportunity: how to provide an efficient and inexpensive way to *process* the redeemed coupons without excessive cost to the client.

Nielsen struggled with this problem for months: He reflected, he analyzed, he concentrated on the problem. Then on a vacation in Hong Kong, he discovered the answer on a boat trip. He met the head of an Australian button factory who was setting up a production plant in Hong Kong. The Australian told him that on a previous trip he had noticed that there were many refugees in Hong Kong who needed work.

At once, Nielsen saw that he could use the same strategy for his coupon clearinghouse. When he returned home, he immediately began work on shifting the company's coupon sorting operations to Mexico. Eventually this led to the "twin plant" concept still used by A. C. Nielsen today, in which production plants with intensive labor needs are in Mexico and administrative operations are in the United States. While some criticize the model, what is important is that Nielsen's initiated a system that benefits people on both sides of the border. And Nielsen solved a serious problem: by thinking things through, reasoning out the pros and cons, and then keeping the problem in focus, he could come up with effective solutions.

In 1987, the company made another innovative change in one of its products, the rating services used by television stations to set advertising rates (the more homes tuned into a station at a given time, the higher the rate). The Nielsen Company developed the People Meter, a new device that can tell who is watching—not just that the set is on.

Although this refinement worried broadcasters, advertisers loved it and insisted the network ratings be based on it. Now they can tell whether the commercial they're paying prime-time rates for is reaching a target audience or is merely being heard from the bathroom or watched by the family cat. The improved monitor is a giant breakthrough in the technology of telemarketing and enables advertisers to reach very specific audiences. So broadcasters had to implement this change.

In 1985, Nielsen looked around and noticed a new kind of change. He realized that, to stay abreast in the telecommunications field, the company would need vast new resources. Nielsen's mother was ninety, he was sixty-four; and as one of the two primary stockholders, he recognized the inevitability of losing family ownership and control.

He was also aware that A. C. Nielsen Company was vulnerable to an unfriendly takeover. So he initiated another change and went courting. The Nielsen Company's subsequent marriage with Dun and Bradstreet is one of the happiest in corporate history, with a good fit of product and service lines, compatibile corporate cultures, and shared business goals. The synergy promises a bright future for both organizations.

The Corporate Change-Friendly Quotient Survey

Art Nielsen's experience shows how anticipating changing times, constantly adjusting company strengths, and vigilantly searching for the right strategy at the right time contributes to ongoing success.

To help you develop similar awareness of the conditions in your workplace, we have designed the test below. It is similar to the personal flexibility part of the Change-Friendly Quotient Survey. It can help you understand the flexibility in your organization and identify the change styles at work there.

The statements below are designed to provoke true and ready responses from you, so please go through this survey quickly without agonizing over your replies. Check *all* responses that you believe apply to the image or policies of your workplace, leaving blank the ones that do not apply in any way. Then, for each statement, write the number "1" by the response that is *most* like your place of work.

1. A logo that reflects my company's values would look like:

2. The celebrities who most closely personify my company's image are:
   a. _____ Margaret Thatcher and/or Walter Cronkite
   b. _____ Eddie Murphy and/or Mikhail Baryshnikov
   c. _____ Bill Cosby and/or Jane Pauley
   d. _____ Cher Bono and/or Luke Skywalker

3. In labor or contract negotiations, my company relies on:
   a. _____ legal advice
   b. _____ strength
   c. _____ connections
   d. _____ varied opinions

4. If my company's major competitor introduced a product making our primary product or service obsolete, management would:
   a. _____ analyze competitor's product or service for flaws
   b. _____ speed up production on secondary product or services
   c. _____ survey other companies in this field
   d. _____ push for more research and development

5. My company's policy toward training could be described as:

a. ____ mandatory
b. ____ specialized
c. ____ team-oriented
d. ____ enthusiastic

6. To manage change in a down-turn economy, my firm would:
   a. ____ tighten controls
   b. ____ readjust goals
   c. ____ get suggestions from staff
   d. ____ start new projects, methods

7. Regarding policies that deal with hiring, firing, and retiring, my office's approach is:
   a. ____ traditional
   b. ____ pragmatic
   c. ____ humane
   d. ____ progressive

8. If we just lost our primary client or customer, the item our management staff would immediately turn to would be:
   a. ____ the calculator
   b. ____ the client/customer list
   c. ____ the telephone
   d. ____ the company car/airplane

9. If my company's well-prepared, low-ball bid were rejected, our management would look for:
   a. ____ sabotage
   b. ____ a second chance
   c. ____ a savior
   d. ____ a bigger, better contract

10. Regarding dress codes, my company's style would resemble:
    a. ____ Brooks Brothers
    b. ____ The May Company
    c. ____ Levi's
    d. ____ The International Collection

11. If essential materials failed to arrive in time for a production deadline, our management would (in football terms):
    a. ____ call time out
    b. ____ punt
    c. ____ huddle
    d. ____ pass to the end zone

12. The word(s) that describe(s) our company's communication policy is (are):
    a. ____ orderly
    b. ____ network
    c. ____ circular
    d. ____ intuitive

13. A cliché describing our company's leadership would be:
    a. ____ the early bird gets the worm
    b. ____ out of the frying pan and into the fire
    c. ____ tail wagging the dog
    d. ____ today is the first day of the rest of your life

14. A magazine in which you are likely to find stories about my firm or company is:
    a. ____ *Scientific Digest* or a professional journal
    b. ____ *Business Week* or *Financial News*
    c. ____ *Time* or *People*
    d. ____ *Entrepreneur* or *Forbes*

15. At any given time, working at my office feels like being:
    a. ____ in the Pentagon
    b. ____ in a pressure cooker
    c. ____ in a three-ring circus
    d. ____ on a roller coaster

To Score: Add the total number of responses you checked and enter here____. Now add the number of first-choice responses in each line (a, b, c, or d) and enter below:

a. ____   b. ____   c. ____   d. ____

If most of your choices were a's, that means that from your

point of view your organization has a Reasoner's change style. This is the rational, organized approach to change typified by columnist George Will. The Reasoner style involves gathering lots of data, carefully analyzing it, and then taking measured steps toward the goal. An organization with this approach proceeds with change carefully and deliberately. Bechtel Corporation, the international engineering firm that relies on careful long-range planning and traditional sequencing of its engineering and construction projects, is an example of a Reasoner.

If your number-one choices were b's, your company's change style is that of the Refocuser, the changemaker who gathers lots of data, but then focuses intently on one approach, later shifting to another with the same concentration. Ted Koppel of *Nightline* typifies this method. An apt example in the corporate world is the Ford Motor Company, which, after thoroughly analyzing its declining market share, concentrated intensely on developing the Taurus/Sable product line of aerodynamic cars in 1984.

C answers represent the Relater way of making change— gathering opinions and ideas from many sources and involving many different people in the change. This organization freely uses consultants, marketing research, and community input to make decisions about change. Its public relations office is consulted early in any major move, because the Relater organization thrives on communication with its constituency. Barbara Walters is an example of a Relater. Sears and Company, the giant nationwide retailer, is an organization that relies on the good will and feedback from its customers to provide an ever-widening range of retail services.

The Risker is indicated if most of your first choices were d's. This change style is often seen in entrepreneurial companies and visionary, not-for-profit organizations that are on the cutting edge of change. As Sam Donaldson does, these companies are willing to risk and prepare for change as fully as time allows. This change style is clearly seen in the quick, deft moves of MCI, the long-distance telephone company you'll learn more about in the next chapter. MCI's bold moves led to the breakup of AT&T and opened telecommunications to many new enterprises.

The total of all the responses, which you entered on the first line above, indicates the overall flexibility of your workplace. There are 60 total responses, and any level higher than 35 suggests that your office policies are flexible and that many styles of change are used. A total between 25 and 35 indicates a company or office that has a moderate degree of flexibility, in addition to one typical approach to change, this company uses other styles. A total of 15 indicates limited options and inflexibility, especially if most of the 15 answers are in one column.

Obviously, the Corporate Change-Friendly Survey is subjective. But thinking of your workplace this way can help you gain a new perspective on your work. Besides, it's fun to think of your company as a personality. And your new perception of your organization can help you identify its strengths and weaknesses.

Shifting in the Workplace

The Corporate Change-Friendly Quotient Survey can also help you understand what styles you might need to add to your organization. For ultimate flexibility, organizations must have all four styles represented. Just as individuals shift among Reasoner, Refocuser, Relater, and Risker change styles, so flexible organizations use different ways of managing change at different periods and under different circumstances.

An example of shifts in change style is evident in the history of the Young Men's Christian Association (YMCA), which operated in the traditional, rational mode of the Reasoner for many years. Founded as a quasi-religious organization, it had a clean-cut, wholesome image, a limited membership, and a conservative approach to change.

Then, during the seventies, the results of the baby boom of the fifties filled YMCA swimming pools and membership roles, and its change style shifted to that of a Risker. With the hiring of younger, more innovative staff and managers, the Y emerged in the forefront of the holistic health movement and offered classes in aerobics, low cholesterol diets, and stress-reduction methods.

Once these and other innovations were in place, the Y gradually moved to the Relater style, broadening its base to all ages and enlisting the aid and advice of volunteers. This was a most fortunate move, because public support was reduced in 1981 and non-fee-producing health care programs cut deeply into YMCA finances.

And now, in the late eighties, once again the YMCA is finding it necessary to take a different approach to change and is using the Refocuser style. To find a new niche in the current recreational climate of change, administrators are reviewing YMCA history and refocusing on its original purposes and tenets, in part because of competition from jazzy health clubs, the emergence of the "couch potato" attitude, and a swing back to a more conservative family style. The Y is pulling in, cutting back, and concentrating more intently on fewer, but higher quality programs and services, with more intense coverage of the traditional programs and services it is best known for.

No doubt the YMCA will shift between change styles again and again as it heads into the twenty-first century. Organizations that survive and prosper through radical or gradual change are those that behave like the Y. In looking at your own workplace, you can be heartened if you see similar shifts. You may also notice several change styles simultaneously at work. This, too, is an encouraging sign of flexibility.

In study after study, we and other researchers have found that flexibility in change style is a key predictor of an organization's success. In the retail world, "80 percent of the success of a sales representative lies in situational sensitivity and style flexibility," according to the National Retail Merchants Association in *Managerial Psychology* (1981).

In these and many more articles and studies, the keys to success for individuals and organizations are open-mindedness and flexibility. The Corporate Change-Friendly Survey's view of your organization's flexibility should help identify areas that can be improved to ensure future success. Your company's change style can also help you understand the T.E.A.M. tasks of *Trust, Ego-identity, Action,* and *Method* in organizational terms.

Trust, Ego-identity, Action, and Method (T.E.A.M.)

Remember the descriptions in Chapter 5 of how the full development of these skills throughout life leads to the ability to make successful change? Remember how getting a handle on *trust* helped Tom Gable overcome the loss of his hand and find the library career he'd always wanted? Do you recall how Edward, the Burrel Finch vice president, was finally able to break away from his "big daddy" employer—how he discovered the real Edward and fulfilled his real *ego-identity* as a creative film entrepreneur? Remember Anna, the diligent worker, who stopped thinking of herself as second banana and in a bold *action* became a television executive by integrating her trust in herself and the world with her strong sense of identity? Finally, do you recall that blue-blooded Malcolm developed a *method* to reach the life he wanted to lead after his life was galvanized by confinement in a Cuban prison?

These four skills are just as important to organizations as they are to individuals. And in a similar way, each skill evolves from the one before it. First, the organization must have *trust* in its product or service and its market. If you don't believe your widgets are quality products and that there's a market for them, then you'll never get sales rolling. But when an organization trusts its own value, the feeling is infectious. The client's trust level goes up in response, and the client's confidence in turn enhances the firm's self-trust.

Second, as this sense of trust rises, the organization's image is clarified, and its *ego-identity* is established for all to see. This clearly defined image establishes a marketing niche for the firm, energizes its productivity, and allows development of the third skill, *action.*

Action means that the company's widgets are selling well, operating profits are increasing, and morale and confidence are soaring. Repeated sales, products, and successful actions then lead to the development of the fourth quality, *method,* a systematic and reliable way of ensuring that action is repeated regularly. The more completely each developmental task is mastered, the more fully each quality will emerge and allow for full development of the next quality.

This interdependence of the four developmental qualities for overall business success can be seen in the corporate history of IBM. Even though its initial success had been with huge mainframe computer systems for large businesses, IBM nevertheless belatedly entered the field of micro and personal computers. Being second after years of leadership might have been too humiliating to some old, established firms, but IBM was confident and flexible. It *trusted* its abilities to develop and market a good product, and its strong ego-identity gave the company the confidence to make a late entry into PCs. Although its response was slow, IBM nevertheless took decisive *action* to enter the personal computer market. Its microcomputers and PCs quickly gained wide acceptance, thus validating its *method* for product development and marketing. IBM's mastery of the T.E.A.M. qualities is continuing to bear fruit. In early 1988, the company announced a breakthrough in the development of computer chips. It has developed fast chips that will enable users to access data much more quickly. While the trend for years had been to produce smaller chips that store more and more data, this shift of emphasis from size to speed is a major competitive breakthrough.

Companies that have not developed a similar mastery of change might find it difficult to make major changes in production and marketing.

From the individual's stories of earlier chapters, you learned how each developmental skill builds on the previous one. When any stage of development is skipped or is incomplete, the subsequent stage is harmed. Have you heard the old song that begins, "There's a hole in de bucket, dear Liza, dear Liza." Well, like that bucket, the human psyche also gets holes in it, when the crucial qualities of trust, ego-identity, action, and method are not mastered. Similarly, when a company has several small holes or one large hole in its corporate psyche, its ability to change successfully is impaired. The company often spends a great deal of time, money, and energy plugging holes instead of making productive changes. Here are some examples:

Trust

When a business first starts up, its primary task is to develop *trust:* the trust of its clients, trust between management and employees and among employees, trust in the marketplace, and trust in its own products or services. When trust is lacking, it's almost impossible to move the business ahead.

A case in point arose out of the acquisition in 1982 of Video Concepts, Inc., the pioneer in retail home-video equipment stores, by the Jack Eckerd Corporation, one of the country's premier retailers. The number of Video Concepts stores had grown in two years from eight to seventy-five under the entrepreneurial leadership of Larry Welch, a fiery, ambitious salesman of thirty-five, who managed to leverage tremendous growth without regard for financial controls. By begging and borrowing money from any possible source, Welch hoped to open Video Concepts stores in every major U.S. market and thus preempt all competition in the home-electronics retail business. Eckerd was more than able to provide the needed financial backing for Video Concepts' continued expansion. It was a Fortune 500 company, with access to capital markets and retailing expertise gathered in slowly developing a chain of 1,200 drug stores over many years.

But the marriage between Eckerd Drugs and Video Concepts faltered immediately after the honeymoon—largely from lack of trust. Stuart Turley, CEO of Eckerd, demanded tight inventory controls, polygraph testing, and balance-sheet accuracy in *all* retail operations, including Video Concepts. It soon became apparent that Larry Welch's swashbuckling, growth-for-growth's-sake style of doing business was anathema to Turley. How can you trust Video Concepts, when bills are not paid promptly, employees don't wear the same style name tags, and inventory in stock does not match the books? And how can you trust Eckerd, when necessary capital for expansion and lease acquisitions for new locations are delayed, creating the risk that dormant competitors will awaken before you can get your marketing act together?

Trust did not exist. Turley fired Welch. Eckerd could not develop Video Concepts and finally sold it at a loss. But imagine what could have happened if Turley and Welch had only understood and appreciated each other's contributions from the start. Think what could have happened if they had been able to blend their left- and right-brained talents, their financial strength and marketing wizardry, into the foremost home-electronics chain in the country. Think what could have happened if they had built customer trust in their products and marketing approach. Could Eckerd and Video Concepts have preempted the entire home-electronics business that eventually exploded?

Ego-identity

The second T.E.A.M. quality essential to organizational development is *Ego-identity*. In business, the term means that a firm is strongly identified with a specific product or service. It is well known by its customers as well as its suppliers, and its standing in relationship to its competitors is clear. Confused or incorrect ego-identity affects a company's ability to set or achieve goals and may harm the drive and morale of its management and employees, and ultimately, its clients or customers. It is also important for departments within an institution to have a clear sense of identity both for purposes of morale and for knowing their precise roles within the organization.

Likewise, the nonprofit agency must know where it fits into the marketplace. How else can it have a clear sense of whom it serves, in what way it serves, and how it differs from its competitors? "Competitors" and "marketplace" may seem inappropriate terms to apply to the non-profit groups. However, it is especially deadly for groups that use volunteer workers to be unclear about their purpose, place, and goals. Even universities and symphony orchestras operate in competitive environments and need a clear sense of identity.

For example, Suffolk State College, a northeastern urban institution, has suffered an identity crisis several times during its thirty-five-year history. It was established in a major metropolitan area as an extension service for Suffolk University, its parent organization located in a nearby college town. As the extension service grew along with the city it served, this urban campus became a full-fledged, degree-granting college. Today, however, most residents and alumni still refer to it as the "Extension Center."

Further aggravating its identity problem is the fact that a respected private university is also located in the college town of Suffolk. Both share the Suffolk name, but the private school is better known. The resulting confusion affects the morale of staff, faculty, and students.

To make matters worse, when higher education was growing in the seventies, the state legislature built a community college adjacent to the beleaguered Suffolk State. Classrooms are now shared, as are parking space, recreation facilities, and library services. This forced marriage strains relations among faculties, staffs, and students. What's more, Suffolk State suffers the indignity of being confused with its young, upstart competition, and buildings added to accommodate *both* institutions are commonly thought to belong to the community college.

Recently, a marketing-oriented administration launched an advertising and public relations campaign to clarify the image and to shore up the ego of Suffolk State. Perhaps soon, its students and employees will feel good about the fine education Suffolk provides and less defensive about the community college it shares space with and the private university it shares a name with.

Action

The third T.E.A.M. quality, action, enables the organization to operate, produce, and make decisions in an expeditious manner.

As with the individual, the ability to act properly and at the ideal time rests mainly on the organization's earlier successful experiences with trust and ego-identity. The ability to take effective action, rather than getting involved in energy-depleting pseudochange, is imperative for companies faced with the challenges of change, such as harsh economic times.

An organization with trust and ego-identity in place has the confidence to take action when it is needed, not just when it seems easy. However, the company lacking trust and identity will often "rearrange the deck chairs" when confronted with a problem that requires action.

An unfortunate example of ineffective action is found at Bellcorp, a privately owned restaurant chain run by the son of its founders, a husband and wife team who built the chain over twenty years by careful expansion, adapting services to the prevailing needs of travelers, and progressive employee training programs that emphasized customer service. As at many other privately held corporations, Bellcorp's developmental growth reflects that of its primary stockholder and officer, Jay Cochran, the son of the founders. Unfortunately for Bellcorp, that developmental growth has been stunted by lack of trust and ego-identity.

Jay's parents always wanted him to be a concert pianist, so they sheltered him from the family business. By using some connections, they got him into the Juilliard School of Music, even though he'd have been happier at the local business college. They applauded his attempts at musical performance rather than his interest in the company. Although he loved music and was an adequate musician, Jay's performance was never of concert quality, and he knew it. But rather than disappoint his parents, he stayed in a field he was not suited for. They shooed him away from the restaurant kitchens and the corporate sales office with reminders that he was a musician not a dishwasher. He minored in accounting, but he was never privy to company books or talk about the business. In short, he never developed a sense of trust in his business skills or identity with the restaurant business.

Jay's parents felt that their chain would always enjoy success with them at the helm. What they did not plan for was their death in a boating accident when Jay was in his late twenties. Nor was Jay prepared to take the action necessary to be head of a sprawling fast-food and restaurant chains. To his credit, he took on the burden of leadership with determination and grit but was, and fourteen years later still is, very ill at ease with the responsibilities of chief executive officer.

In a time when restaurants must find new ways of servicing a tight and changing economy, the ability to act, listen, observe, and make resolved decisions is keenly needed. To cope with the changing needs of travelers, Bellcorp's competitors have developed special offerings such as food takeout service. Even the no-frills fast-food restaurants have low-calorie items and offer pasta. But there have been no similar actions at Bellcorp, only change, change, change—pseudochange that produces nothing more than new personnel and organizational charts.

Early on, Jay decided to hire an operations manager and to free himself to develop new sites and services—a good idea that fell short in its execution. In the last eight years, he has hired not one but five new operations managers but has never given any one of them the authority needed to run the operations.

Jay also says he wants a strong, talented marketing officer and property managers, but then dismisses anyone with new ideas. Invariably, he finds he cannot trust them to do the job the way he thinks his parents would have done it. The revolving doors in his restaurants are constantly spinning with the entering and exiting of Bellcorp managers. Jay sets up training meetings, consultations with universities, and trips to food chain conventions. At each meeting, he darts in impatiently and is gone five minutes later. Jay lacks the self-trust and self-image of an entrepreneur.

Jay claims Bellcorp is an effective changemaker that adds new sites, services, and approaches to marketing. But the enormous amount of time and energy that he expends in pseudochange keeps him from true and productive change. These actions serve only to relieve his underlying anxiety and undeveloped trust and identity.

Bellcorp's case shows that when any one of the T.E.A.M. skills is missing, the flexibility and health of the individual or company is at risk. Jay never developed trust in his abilities, either in music or management. Furthermore, he didn't know enough about his parents' business to trust the staff and the successful methods already in place. Without trust and a clear sense of the chain's identity, his actions were inappropriate and damaging. As the business deteriorated under his tutelage, he panicked and actively changed things with the hope that the actions would turn the business around. But he had slipped into the wrong kind of action. Without the first two qualities as a foundation, his actions were without direction. Every task seemed as if it were being done for the first time, because he was never able to develop a reliable, workable method for keeping his company flexible in a changing environment.

Method

The success of the fourth quality, *method,* rests heavily upon the other three. People and organizations both develop it by fully experiencing trust, ego-identity, and Action skills and then finally integrating them into a method—a system for doing things that really works.

It is easy to see how a person might muddle through life without developing a system for getting things done. Because individuals are often protected by relatives, friends, and circumstances, they sometimes get by without such skills. It might seem that there is no similar protective device available to the corporation, but a quick look beneath the surface reveals several possibilities. Some businesses are founded at a time when they can't possibly fail, no matter how inadequate their organizational methods are.

For example, after World War II, consumer goods were in such short supply that almost any manufacturer could succeed. Sometimes, too, a corporation with a patented product or untapped market will survive despite the absence of organizational methods.

But to achieve continuing success, the organization needs a tried and true method, which is built, of course, upon a strong foundation of trust, ego-identity, and action. Such is the case of Gates Rubber Company, a corporation as flexible in managing change as its flexible products—automobile belts and hoses—are world-renowned.

Gates's method, since its beginning decades ago, has been to develop a loyal, stable work force to provide reliable, quality products for its customers. From the outset, it offered a menu of employee benefits that no one else had even thought of at the time. This attracted and kept solid, dependable employees.

Gates also personalized relations with its employees through birthday cards, Christmas parties, and such social services as a medical clinic and exercise classes. Other improvements to this method were added along the way, but always with the emphasis on ways to keep employees and thereby provide the best products and the finest customer service. This method worked, and it still works.

Gates Rubber Company was founded in 1911 by Charles Gates, Sr. That was three generations ago, and the Gates plant was located at the southernmost edge of Denver, in flat, dry grasslands. Today, that plant is surrounded by a crosstown interstate highway, an elegant mall for designer clothes, a residential area, and a renovated shopping district.

The corporation developed gradually under a family dynasty, with only two CEOs over seventy-seven years. The company earned a trusted, solid image in the community and a strong sense of identity.

But growth changed to decline when the automobile industry began to suffer reverses in the late seventies. Gates's vaunted fanbelts and car tires were no longer as much in demand. The employees had also changed. A new generation of workers was not as interested in birthday cards and health-care plans; they were more interested in variety of work and personal challenge. In response to the change, Charles Gates, Jr. (the second-generation leader of the company), listened to options for adapting to this new economy and kind of people. The consensus was to "diversify and broaden your base and get some riskier managers in here."

Diversify and broaden it did! The Gates Rubber Company took actions that complemented its method. It moved into land development, microcomputers, Lear Jets, and a host of other businesses. These actions very likely saved it from the failure that many automobile-related companies suffered during the sluggish mid-seventies.

Today, Gates Rubber Company is undergoing more broad changes. "What worked yesterday won't necessarily work tomorrow. We've listened to our customers and have switched some directions," says Charles Gates, Jr. "For example, we're building small plants right next to our customer's plants in Iola, Kansas, and Monks Corner, South Carolina, so we can easily provide for their 'Just in Time' inventory needs," he continues. "And we've acquired Uniroyal, which provides us with the next dimension in synchronous belts."

Furthermore, Gates is establishing plants in other countries so that rises and falls in the American dollar can be balanced. It has acquired two large plants in Spain to more efficiently serve its European customers. It has refocused on its strengths: it is limiting production to automotive parts, the business it knows best and is best known for. It has sold its company health programs to Cigna Insurance so that its management resources are not spread into non-specialty areas.

"Probably the most difficult change we've made is to move all manufacturing out of Colorado," Charles admits. "Of course, we still have research and development, marketing, administration, and corporate headquarters here in town, but at one time, we employed 20,000 people in the area, and now we're down to 2,500. But if you're going to survive in the kind of global, changing economy we have today, you must be light on your feet. We must respond quickly to our customers—and we have to be close to them to do that. Furthermore, we're staying flexible. Look for us to make more changes every time they're needed.

"And even more important, we have achieved flexibility with a tried and true method of keeping a qualified and loyal work force—smaller, yes, with different motivations, yes, but still a human resource that delivers the best products and customer service we can provide."

Gates fully learned all the skills of normal development during the business ups and downs of the past fifty years and thus was able to successfully manage change.

The contrast between the Gates Rubber Company and Bellcorp clearly demonstrates the difference between productive change and pseudochange. It also demonstrates how the skills of trust, ego-identity, action, and method can bring flexibility to the organization. Both Gates Rubber and Bellcorp are facing change. But Bellcorp becomes more static each day and is in decline. Gates is on the upswing through flexibility built on mastery of trust, ego-identity, action, and method.

The Flexibility of U.S. Corporations

How typical is Gates? Do most U.S. firms have the same kind of flexibility? Certainly those that survived the economic ups and downs of recent history do. Even the companies with unlimited capital (deep pockets) have needed an inner resilience to withstand the watershed change of the mid-eighties.

And then, some organizations survived accidentally, reeling from one response to another, sometimes making it because of the greater incompetence of their competitors. Such incompetence and disarray is deeply disturbing. Americans expect more of themselves and their institutions and have been thoroughly shaken by the demise of many venerable organizations and the loss of our dominance of the world economy. (The oil embargo made us realize how dependent we are on other, much smaller countries. The perpetual Mideast crisis is a constant reminder of how vulnerable we are to terror and trouble. Foreign competition clarifies that we do not have a divine right to be number one. And even the environment is informing us that our resources are not infinite, that the earth can become uninhabitable.) Although the country was founded on the concept of flexibility (the checks and balances system, for example), we had had everything "our way" so long that we found organizational change threatening and depressing.

But as we adjusted to our losses, corporations began to recover. What first began as merely responding to drastic changes just to survive became thoughtful, initiated change. Today we see strong signs that organizations in the United States have gotten the change message and have the flexibility to do it. Here are some ways we've noticed they've increased their flexibility factor in recent years.

- In the early eighties, many companies established production facilities in Japan, Korea, and Taiwan because of lower labor costs and less government intervention in labor issues. According to *Forbes,* the Conference Board, and the Department of Labor, among others, the trend has shifted in the late eighties. Not only are U.S. corporations bringing production and jobs back home, the Japanese are opening factories in the United States.

- The United States has changed the emphasis in its economic structure from traditional manufacturing to high technology.

- We've gone from big to little. Small business provides seventy percent of the jobs in the United States. Entrepreneurship is at an all-time high, with women owning double the number of sole proprietorships they did ten years ago. Large business has had to trim down and, like a person who's been on an exercise program, feels the better for it. Operating at peak efficiency is an enduring benefit of "trimming the fat." Responsibilities, chain of command, and goals are clearer in trim companies, and the sense of commitment is greater.

- Conglomerates are out, and specialization is in. This enables an organization to focus on doing what it does well.

- Large corporations have moved from vertical to horizontal integration to save on capital investment. For instance, rather than owning and managing all aspects of an operation, they are using independent consultants and small businesses to provide state-of-the-art expertise and specialized products. Other savings come from JIT (just in time) inventories that enable corporations to cut costs on parts and materials storage. And sharing other companies' employees lowers overhead—for instance, by reducing the number of employees eligible for long-term benefits.

- Small companies are staying flexible through a similar process, "outsourcing," in which they swap specialists with other companies. Outsourcing enables them to be on the cutting edge of innovation without a huge investment.

- U.S. corporations are going multinational. When the dollar goes down, the mark or the yen usually goes up; when production costs increase in one location, they may go down in another. Having facilities in many locations worldwide keeps these corporations financially flexible.

- U.S. corporations are learning to work with shorter production cycles. The time between birth and death of a product these days can be extremely short. So these flexible planners are taking the long view but fitting small, short-cycled products into their plans. In the words of Alan Hassenfeld, president of Hasbro, Inc., the world's largest toy company, "We have got to be able to stop on a dime if we think there's trouble." Even when there's no trouble, such agility is a must in any business that will respond to quickly shifting consumer tastes.

Strong corporations are aware that all of these trends are subject to reversal. They have learned that nothing is forever—except change. They welcome change and plan for it. It is heartening to observe that U.S. organizations are rising to the challenge of changing times.

When we began this book, we hoped to find examples here and there in our consulting work that would exemplify our theses about organizational change. Instead, we encountered many companies, agencies, and institutions that responded to, adapted to, or initiated change in flexible ways. But we never dreamed that *one* organization would illustrate all the "ideal" characteristics of flexibility—and then some. Read all about the ultimate flexible organization and its leader in the next chapter.

14
Strategies of a Flexible Organization

Think for a moment of a family group: a mother, a father, several children, and perhaps an uncle or grandmother. See yourself belonging to such a group living under one roof for a period of time. Now, imagine that a social worker comes to your family, removes one person, and gives you a replacement with the comment, "We've found a wonderful home for him, and you'll just love this new person."

Reflect on this scene for a while; experience your emotions and those of your loved ones. Think about how you'd feel toward the replacement and toward the social worker who intervened. Think how you'd feel if you were asked to move out of your bedroom to accommodate the new person.

How would this sit with you and other members of your family? All of you might be quite unhappy. If you were the person being moved, you might actually become ill from the change. If you remained in the family, you'd probably pine for the family member you lost and be reluctant to accept the new person— especially if she was demanding or troublesome in some way.

Now switch your viewpoint: Think how you'd feel if you had always had such changes going on in your household. What if your family entertained talented and interesting guests for extended periods of time? What if you had cultural exchange students or foster children living with you and you loved their company? What if favorite aunts, cousins, and grandpas frequently took up residence with you? What if your siblings were always coming and going to and from college, Europe, and the Peace Corps? In such a family setting, where change is normal, happy, interesting, and exciting, you might *welcome* the scene that opened this chapter.

When you are accustomed to change—and when it has been a rewarding, beneficial experience—you are much more likely to discover the kairos in it. The same dynamic is at work in an organization. The more an office or plant is involved in stimulating, rewarding change, the more likely it is to be a productive, flexible, and positive place. So the trick is to find some way of maintaining a climate that is friendly to productive change—one in which work is fun, change is the norm, and flexibility reigns!

Bill McGowan, copresident of MCI Communications, Inc., has created just such a climate. When you walk into the MCI flagship offices in Washington, D. C., there's an instant feel of friendliness, *joie de vivre,* and openness. Perhaps it is McGowan's open door: As you arrive he calls "come on in," and waves you into his office. Never mind that you are ten minutes early, and he's on the phone. He tries to switch to a conference call and cries out, "Help, Melanie, the phone monster has got me." This leader of a multibillion dollar telecommunications company hasn't yet mastered the art of switching to a conference line! What he has mastered—and inspired in his company—is flexibility. This flexibility has enabled MCI to respond to radical changes, to adapt to more gradual change, and to initiate successful change as it continues its climb.

We have observed that successful organizations have a variety of ways of dealing with the different kinds of change (imposed, gradual, and initiated) and nowhere is this more evident than at MCI. In structure, ambience, and operation, MCI personifies flexibility. The techniques used there to cope with change are not called "loss," "immersion," "poll-taking," or "replacement," yet they are all in use.

Though we'd read of MCI's historic challenge to AT&T's

monopoly over telephone service, and we had been affected by AT&T's divestiture, we were unaware of MCI's relevance to our flexibility theme when we first worked for them as consultants. At seminars for MCI's Eastern Division in Atlanta and later at their think tank and corporate offices in Washington, D.C., we met scores of executives, managers, supervisors, and support staff and got a feeling for MCI's way of doing business. As we learned more about MCI, we saw experiences to verify that flexibility is indeed the key to successfully managing change. Join us now as we place flexibility markers along MCI's road to success.

Responding to Change

Any imposed change causes discomfort because something is lost. Even if the change is perceived as a step forward, you feel a loss. If you get a job promotion, you've still lost the comfort of your old one. When you win your battle, you lose the excitement of the fight. In Chapter 9, we prescribed the Loss Technique to take you through the experience of mourning your loss so that you can get on with finding opportunity in it.

Organizations experience grief just as profoundly as individuals, and the wise ones recognize and deal with it. For example, when plants were closed, corporations across the United States held mock funerals to help employees handle the loss. Kodak and Storage Technology held relocation fairs after severe cutbacks. After filing for bankruptcy or reorganization, some organizations went through group therapy sessions to help their employees manage grief.

MCI was well into its twentieth year before it experienced a big loss, but it was a doozy. In 1986 MCI lost $448 million. Then Bill McGowan, MCI's founder and CEO, had a heart attack so severe he eventually had to have a heart transplant.

McGowan was the man who had led the fight in the late sixties and the seventies to wrest exclusive control of long distance telephone service from AT&T. After years of slogging through governmental regulations and the "leave well enough alone" attitude of the general public, he finally won the right to offer long-distance service to the general public in 1978. Not only that, but MCI also received a 55 percent discount on long distance inter-connection to compensate for AT&T's years of monopoly.

This ruling and others by the FCC eventually led to AT&T's divestiture and the development of free competition among several long-distance carriers (primarily MCI and Sprint). Profits soared at MCI until 1986, when they and the other new long distance carriers lost the 55 percent discount. At the same time, AT&T cut long distance rates. This put MCI in a double bind: It had to absorb higher expenses *and* cut rates to stay competitive.

To do so, MCI reduced employment by 15 percent, made a stock buyback, and slashed capital spending for 1987 by $100 million. Loss, loss, loss. Then, four days before Christmas, the second blow came: McGowan had a nearly fatal heart attack. Grief, grief, grief.

"We were all stunned by the thought of trying to operate without our feisty, buoyant CEO," recalls an MCI employee. "Here we were, facing off against AT&T, a half-dozen long-distance and specialized phone competitors, and an unpredictable economy, and suddenly McGowan is taken from us. We went through all the stages of profound grief."

First, *Denial:* "It's not all that bad, he'll be back in a week or two," employees said to each other. And to disguise their real concern, there were feeble jokes about his recent marriage, such as "guess the strain of all that night work was nearly too much for him."

Then, *Anger:* "Why did this have to happen now, just when we need him most?"

Next, *Bargaining:* "If he can just make it through this, we'll never let him overload himself again."

Followed by *Depression:* "Maybe the honeymoon is over . . . maybe it's a sign that we're going downhill just like Bill's health."

And then, finally, *Acceptance:* "Things will never be the same as they were before. We'll just have to do a lot of this stuff without him."

But as with most things at MCI, the grief was brief, and the mourning was completed quickly, because a flexible system was in place that allowed, even encouraged, grieving and then turned even this loss into a gain.

In part, MCI adapted to McGowan's absence and the need to cut expenses quickly because of an Executives in Residence, flexibility factor that McGowan had implemented in 1980. This system allows retiring executives to serve as consultants to the company for as long as they wish.

One such retiree was V. Orville Wright, former MCI president who had retired two years before, when he was sixty-five. When Wright's wife died, he returned to MCI on a limited basis in the Executive program. "At the time of Bill's heart attack, Wright was current on everything and, so, shifted easily into becoming 'co–chief executive.' I say 'co' because Bill's presence was still with us; he was still sending ideas and energy from his hospital bed," says Executive Vice President Dick Liebhaber.

But the year ahead was not easy for McGowan or MCI. The company's profits continued to decline, as did McGowan's health.

His initial recovery was normal; he returned home late in January and kept in touch with the office through their electronic mail system. He did all the right things: gave up his three-pack a day cigarette habit, watched his diet, and joined an exercise group of recovering heart-attack patients. He soon noticed, however, that though all the other exercisers were feeling and looking better everyday, he wasn't. Instead, McGowan lost weight, energy, and appetite. That's when he began to investigate the possibility of a heart transplant.

"All signs were negative, 'contra-indicated,'" he says, laughing, "which is a euphemism for: I was too old, too flabby, and too far gone. Besides, they thought I'd never get a heart in time." But McGowan had faced impossible odds before.

Two months later, he had a heart transplant. Six months later, he was back at work but with a new approach. Instead of seventy-hour work weeks he limits himself to forty hours a week; instead of taking on every responsibility and task he sees, he and Wright divide them. They are truly co-executives. Life is better than ever for McGowan and for MCI. He thinks his absence was good for all concerned. His description of this six-month period is typically self-effacing and realistic: "They got used to it, and I got used to it."

The morale and energy at MCI are at peak levels today. The

employees successfully responded to two radical changes and have more than survived. They took their losses and grew stronger. As financial analyst Robert Morris III, of Prudential-Bache Securities, said in the *Washington Post:*

"MCI was a child of Bill McGowan's and when he got sick the kids grew and went to college. On his return he has found he has a more mature, disciplined, responsible company to work with and that is exhibited in its improved cost controls, its disciplined approach to entering markets, and in its improved earnings and revenue growth."

Change Styles and the Long Haul

The change styles of McGowan and Wright are important to McGowan's new approach and MCI's continuing good health.

In Flexibility Factor terms, McGowan is a Risker and a Relater. He gathers information from all kinds of people and then integrates it into audacious concepts. He is a charismatic, intuitive leader. Wright provides the calming balance of a Reasoner and Refocuser. He is quiet and reserved compared to McGowan, but acts with the conviction and confidence that his solid technical skills and management experience give him. Wright is an engineer who bases decisions on detailed facts and figures. While his actions are just as bold as McGowan's, they have an air of contemplation about them.

The division of duties in their co-managing plan fits their different styles well: McGowan is in charge of corporate development and is the primary contact point on finance, regulations, and public affairs—all of which require the visionary, persuasive skills of the Risker and Relater. Wright oversees marketing operations, engineering, field operations, and budgets and thus uses the analytical, planning, disciplined skills of the Reasoner and Refocuser.

*Tucker, Elizabeth, "There's Long Distance Ahead, But MCI Profits Are Back," *Washington Post,* Oct. 26, 1987.

This balance between the change styles of McGowan and Wright helped the company survive recent radical changes and to prosper during its midlife growth. From the beginning, they appreciated what each brought to the management table. Contrast their experience with Turley and Welch, the entrepreneurs who wanted to market video rentals through the existing Eckerd stores. Welch had the marketing pizzazz, and Turley had the financial know-how. Their differing change styles might have made a great combination, but neither adapted to the other, so their potential was never realized.

Early on, McGowan realized that he was good at starting companies and providing general direction but not so good with the daily, nitty-gritty management. So, once the company was up and running in 1975, he coaxed Wright to join forces with him. Their genuine regard for each other's strengths seems to have kept the company flexible over the long haul.

Although McGowan represents the most noticeable flexibility factor in MCI's leadership, Wright's presence is always an influence. An indication is the frequent comment about him: "Wright's the man who taught us how to fly."

Wright served as president in the ten years before his retirement. He and McGowan worked with and off each other. The constant tug between styles kept the ideas flowing and the energy high.

There are other players in the MCI drama whose change styles helped to keep the company constantly moving upward and forward. The president and chief officer of operations, Bert C. Roberts, Jr., is a reserved engineer, who clearly is a Reasoner. He puts his time and trust in logic and the bottom line. He provides the structure and coherence that any organization needs.

Dr. Peter Keen, tall, red-haired, with white-rimmed preppy glasses and tons of enthusiasm, at first seems like a Risker. But soon he takes on the look of a Refocuser who concentrates his considerable research abilities on highly specialized areas. These include MCI's new Smart Card, a card that contains all the data from the holder's current cards, thus eliminating the need to carry a pocketful of charge cards. He has also developed the hybrid manager concept, which holds that the most needed manager of the future will be a hybrid, a person with strong business skills and computer literacy, or a computer whiz familiar with business. Keen writes and teaches about this concept to "cross pollinate" such skills and produce hybrid leaders. A former faculty member at the Harvard Business School, the Massachusetts Institute of Technology, and Stanford University, Keen heads MCI's think tank in Washington D.C.

Connie Paquette of Minneapolis crosses many geographic and departmental boundaries to coordinate the numerous services she manages for large corporate accounts. Her Relater style is perfectly suited to her job: to orchestrate the resources of the company for the customer, but also to be an effective advocate for the customer's interests within MCI.

Laurie Tolleson is MCI's southeastern director of external affairs and a quintessential Risker. She is willing to stick her neck out, make split-second decisions, and take the consequences. Although quiet at first encounter, with blond hair, freckles, and low-key style, Tolleson loves nothing better than running flat out with an idea that excites her. Unlike many Riskers, though, she has unrelenting follow-through. She is multiskilled and talented—as are all the players we observed at MCI.

At MCI and in other such successful collaborations, each person appreciates the contributions of people with other change styles. And the benefits are great. The more options the organization has at each juncture, the more likely it is to find the kairos in change.

Gradual Change

Having the four change styles constantly interacting in leadership and other levels of the corporation has helped MCI avoid the trap that many companies fall into as they experience gradual change over the years. Many organizations are innovative and energetic in the beginning, but little by little, even the innovations become standard operating procedure. McGowan was determined to avoid the slide into mediocrity that he'd seen at other companies, such as: the weekend retreat for creative problemsolving that becomes a tradition and eventually produces nothing but traditional ideas; the flexible schedule that deteriorates into chaos as each employee "does his own thing"; and the bright young public relations director who slips into alcoholism as he courts the same media contacts at the same parties and power lunches week in and week out.

An organization employing a constant shift among change styles can avoid such traps by keeping the policies and actions of the organization vital and effective. The leadership of MCI had the counter-balancing change styles of McGowan and Wright to keep the operation flexible through the years of gradual change. Wright was the calm at the center of McGowan's storm of visionary leadership. MCI also used all four change styles constantly throughout the company.

We have observed that other companies, partnerships, collaborators, and teams that work well over time have the same sort of dynamic. In team building sessions, we noticed a natural attraction between left- and right-brained dominants. This collaboration of styles and brain preferences helps the organization or group adapt to gradual change without losing energy. The push and pull between them seems to keep the organization vital and creative.

Such shifting between left-brain and right-brain ways of thinking occurs when a variety of change styles are active within an organization.

Change Cycle

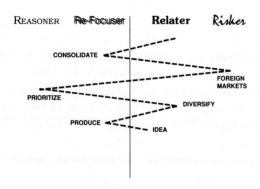

At MCI, a series of shifts from left to right and back happened during the financing of the world's second-largest telecommunications network. MCI people realized that, to build a system that would really make money, it would have to serve the whole country. To do so, they would have to merge all the independent affiliates sprinkled throughout the Midwest. This would take major funding—not just venture capital but a real commitment from an established financial institution. How could MCI get it? The company didn't have the analytical data required by such institutions, so it made a complete shift and appealed to the intuitive, emotional, right brain part of the bankers.

Jimmy Miller, chairman of Blyth & Company's bank fund, had never financed a start-up company before, but, like everyone else, he *fell in love* with the MCI idea. He got excited and saw financing it as his last hurrah of a great career. And Blyth shifted between two very different ways of operating to underwrite MCI's public offering. To produce the bank balances required, he cajoled MCI's major suppliers into investing one dollar for every two from products sold to MCI, so that healthy back-up funds were apparent when the stock went public. Balancing out that strategic left-brained approach was the enthusiastic and energetic way he sold the idea to the public. Even though MCI had no product to sell, Miller sold the dream.

Each step in MCI's financing history shows adaptability and timing—a shifting from right to left or left to right at just the *right* time for success.

When we consult with organizations on how to become and stay flexible, we try to help them achieve this kind of balance in thinking and change styles. To do so, we help them clarify the differences in change styles among the managers, board members, and other employees and then have them practice alternate ways of handling change. We ask them to practice techniques that will use various change approaches. We were pleasantly surprised to find that MCI already used change strategies similar to those we described in Chapters 10 and 11 and use in our consulting work. Here is evidence of those similarities:

Loss

Although loss is rare at MCI, the climate there is clearly hospitable to open grieving, as is illustrated by employees' reactions to Bill McGowan's heart attack, which we described earlier.

Immersion

Bill McGowan immersed himself in seven different professional roles to get MCI into the long-distance business. He first plunged into the task of fully understanding and then acquiring venture capital. Next, he immersed himself in the regulations of the FCC relative to AT&T. He then moved on to saturation in the art of lobbying, which was necessary to get a hearing for his point of view. He says:

"I learned more about law and lobbying than I really wanted to know. We even moved our offices to D.C. so we could be close to the whole process. Then, when we needed capital investment, I submerged myself in the banking business. When we finally got to the construction process, I learned everything I could about that too. I found you can never get enough information. I ask questions of everyone, everywhere I go. I read four hours a day, and when I'm starting a new project, I jump in with both feet until I know everything I can about it.

"It works for others, too. Account executives at MCI go live with their accounts for weeks. They actually move to the client's headquarters and work side by side with the marketing people, the administrative staff, the comptroller, and so on. That's how our account executives understand the real telecommunication needs of a company. You have to be out there in the field to truly service the customer," he concludes.

Poll-taking

Poll-taking is everywhere at MCI. From its inception, Bill McGowan has polled legislators, lawyers, customers, and friends for their communications needs as well as for ideas. Dick Lieb-haber polls other companies—even those in other countries—for production techniques.

Peter Keen also uses poll-taking to keep up with a huge variety of trends. He seldom reads in the field of telecommunications because his friends and colleagues inform him when anything new develops. Instead, he polls other resources. He reads magazines and trend sheets, anything he can find on music, and twenty-two college newspapers. He attends meetings on new construction techniques and other topics he's interested in. From these varied sources, he gets general knowledge and opinions and keeps his thinking broad. If Peter does feel the need to learn something specific, he calls three experts in the field and asks each of them to ask three others who also have an insider's view of the issue in question. From these nine sources, he is able to get all the information he needs for that time.

The Replacement Technique

This technique involves replacing an old way of thinking or behaving with an entirely new one—the exact message MCI sent to potential customers in 1980. Through marketing research, the company had found that, when phone bills increased, rather than blaming AT&T for high long-distance charges, customers blamed themselves for talking too long. This insight helped MCI devise its motto: "You're not talking too much, just spending too much." This different perspective struck home with thousands of customers who quickly shifted to MCI.

An example of replacing an old concept with a new one is in the design of MCI's electronic mail service, which sends messages and graphics to a receiver's computer terminals. Other companies' systems required that both parties have a terminal and that the senders pay a regular subscription rate. If MCI's mail customers do not have compatible terminals, the message is simply delivered by first class mail or courier service. Furthermore, there is a sender's fee only when a message is actually sent, and then the fee is based on the message's length. This new way of using electronic mail has broadened MCI's appeal to potential customers and made it the largest service of its kind.

These are just a few examples that show how the Loss, Immersion, Poll-taking, and Replacement techniques are being used at MCI. We also found variations of Internal Brainstorming and Inside Outs in use. They are the two techniques that allow you to constantly shift between your brain's two hemispheres. At MCI they were commonly used from the beginning.

McGowan used an Inside Out to rethink dividends. Unlike most other company chairmen, who thought paying dividends was a show of corporate strength, McGowan believed just the opposite. He had observed that companies paid dividends when they had stopped growing and could not attract investors. To McGowan, a healthy company reinvests in itself rather than paying dividends—especially in such a capital-intensive business as telecommunications.

Another Inside Out was the unheard of approach of telling the truth in international negotiations. When MCI was trying to establish telecommunication networks in the United Kingdom, France, and elsewhere, representatives of one country would ask what position another country was taking with MCI. Seth Blumenfeld, the frank, straightforward MCI negotiater, would say quite honestly, "They don't want to talk with me" or "We're not getting anywhere." Seth's contacts assumed he was just being sneaky and that a deal was at hand. Not to be outdone, they would push for a settlement, making concessions to MCI in the process.

Ben Dida, an account executive, repeatedly uses Internal Brainstorming to anticipate MCI's "fast-change" management style. "I know better than to get MCI corporate officers interested in a project if I haven't thoroughly massaged it first," he says. "That group is so fast and intuitive, they'll often say, 'let's do it' at a first hearing. It's a little scary to propose an idea and a few minutes later have approval *and a budget.* I learned to look at all sides of the issue and check the pros and cons thoroughly before I opened my mouth."

No doubt so many kinds of approaches are active at MCI because its work climate encourages and empowers its employees to act in a courageous, creative way.

Initiating Change

Many of the changes at MCI were initiated by Bill McGowan, and as we studied his descriptions of them, we found that he regularly implemented the seven steps to initiating successful change described in Chapter 11. His actions tell it all: .

1. *Know and be comfortable with your change style.* Bill likes to move fast, to take action, and to lead. The family style set by his father's innate leadership and his mother's intelligence gave Bill the confidence to enjoy change.

2. *Feel excitement and commitment to the change.* Bill reports that he was thrilled at the prospect of challenging AT&T. Not only was he initiating a potentially profitable change, the challenge was a first for anyone. "I was told, 'You can't change AT&T's hold; it's a monopoly.' But I thought, 'Where is it written that they have control over *long-distance lines?* Where are their contracts?' It turned out that *there were no FCC regulations regarding long-distance calls,* so my hunch was right.

"Once I knew we had a legitimate claim, I started thinking about all the uses for telephone lines that could be developed . . . things not yet thought of. It could be a breakthrough as important to history as the cotton gin and the steam engine were to the Industrial Revolution. I was and am excited and committed to discovering all the ways telecommunications can speed our mastery of the Information Age."

3. *Know who's where—who supports and who opposes the forces for change.* "I found there were multiple interests involved," says Bill. "Of course, AT&T was against me, and it had financial and legal power. The regulations just naturally cause inertia and so they were against me, too. Some powerful legislators were opposed just because the law had been in place for so long. But on the other hand, there were those in favor of deregulation, such as Alfred Kahn of the Federal Reserve, and Tim Wirth, the Democratic congressman from Colorado. Then, too, some players' opinions were unknown: How would big business feel about it, and what about the public at large?

4. *The crucial point.* It's important to find the right time and place to act. "There were many crucial points, but the first was when I discovered that none of the FCC regulations under which AT&T operated gave it exclusive rights to long distance operations," Bill notes. "I knew then where to apply the heat. This led to a court battle in which MCI was granted equal access to long-distance lines."

5. *Alignment—getting support and commitment from others.*
McGowan may have followed a precept of Stan Scheinman, MCI's
financial genius. Scheinman's simple but fool-proof first rule of
business is "Create enough economic benefits for many people,
and they will allow what you want to happen." McGowan made
sure everyone had something to gain each time he proposed a
deal . . . and he got alignment.

6. *When you encounter barriers and setbacks, continue moving toward your goal; persevere, don't retrace steps, find new ways to
get there.* As Bill recalls, "In 1964, we needed a greater range in
frequencies for our long-distance connections. We wanted to build
our own network of towers, but were denied permission. So we
took a different tack. We tried to buy existing quality lines but
found that the 'old boy network' that controlled intercontinental
lines wouldn't sell to us. Once more, a shift in strategy worked! We
bought some 'dog lines' just to get into the network, and then later
we were able to upgrade them."

Though throughout MCI's history there have been countless
examples of persevering and keeping its eye on the goal even when
knocked off, perhaps the most dramatic is what happened in 1985.
On June 25, 1985, McGowan was forced to change the entire face
of the telecommunications industry once again. With the court's
award from the settlement of the suit with AT&T reduced to only
$113.4 million instead of the original requested $2 billion, MCI
struck a history-making deal with IBM. MCI bought IBM's entire
Satellite Business Systems, and IBM got 16 percent of MCI's
stock.

Because its main business is long-distance telecommunications, MCI also sold its paging and cellular subsidiaries and
teamed up with IBM. It once again refocused and is keeping the
company eye on its primary goal.

7. *Stay flexible.* Below are eleven principles on which MCI
operates, as expressed by Bill McGowan in conversations with us.
They could rightfully be titled:

Tenets of the Flexible Organization

1. "WE MOVE FAST and don't require reports and studies

to validate what we need to do. We trust gut feelings. Consensus is too slow for us. Individuals have the power to make decisions and take actions in our organization. When a move is successful, it is noted and rewarded; when it fails, the effort is rewarded and the method revised.

"There's real time, and there's MCI time which is like dog time. That is, we do a lot of living in each hour. 'Dog time' refers to the fact that one year of a dog's life is equivalent to seven years of a human. In other words, it is common practice at MCI for projects to be completed, decisions to be made, and action to be taken seven times faster than anywhere else."

2. "WE ARE COUNTERCYCLICAL. Whatever is normal, expected, or traditional, we change. If big is the trend, we go small; if new is in, we go old.

"When everyone else is centralizing, we're decentralizing and sometimes both at once. When others beef up advertising, we cut back."

3. "WE INSTITUTIONALIZE CHANGE. Employees change jobs every two years. This holds down 'empire building' and raises the energy level for the work they're currently perform-ing. We refuse to establish antichange procedures. There are no lockstep promotions, no organizational charts, no job descriptions at MCI. There are no rule books or policy pronouncements to mandate what happens tomorrow."

4. "WE ENCOURAGE INITIATIVE by giving both respon-sibility and authority. Employees can do almost anything as long as they believe it is in the best interest of the company." (A typical employee comment: "McGowan believes in you so much, you're sure you can succeed.")

5. "WE LIKE HIGH TURNOVER. When people get stale or can't fit into a particular job, they should move to another. To encourage constant self-appraisal on this score, we make it easy for employees to move to other functional areas and encourage cross training. If a valued employee cannot find a position that chal-lenges him or her, we make it possible for the employee to leave MCI and come back when the time is right. The individual can

take other jobs, return later, and still have full credit for the time applied toward retirement and other benefits."

6. "WE SOMETIMES DECIDE NOT TO DECIDE. At times, we apply a little 'positive procrastination' and decide not to make a decision for a while. Because the pace of change in the telecommunications industry is so fast, it is sometimes more beneficial to watch until we feel the technological developments have been perfected before we invest in the sexiest new product. A wrong modem marketed on a nationwide basis could be a billion dollar mistake."

7. "WE ARE NOT PRETENTIOUS KNOW-IT-ALLS. We know we can't do everything well all the time. We admit our mistakes, and we try to do what we do best. Ideas are judged on the basis of their merits, not who proposed them. We are egalitarian—no caste system, no formalities. We develop managers who listen and respect others. No one is too big to hear honest comments. 'No' men and women are prized here."

8. "WE INSIST THAT WORK HAS TO BE FUN. Orville Wright is the company model for this tenet. He quit his executive management job at IBM without another one lined up because "it wasn't fun any more." He and many others believe that a job is more than money, title, or public recognition. Fun to Wright is knowing he's making a difference."

9. "WE ENCOURAGE ALL THINKING AND CHANGE STYLES HERE. We purposefully encourage diversity in our staff: By keeping our senior executives available through the Executive in Residence Program, we get continuity and experience. By hiring computer wizards and keyboard experts, we get innovative technical abilities. Through the Graduate Program, we get the visionary ideas of students. And, yes, we also take those with the resumes from Wall Street who keep us up-to-date with financial expertise."

10. "WE KNOW THAT NOTHING IS FOREVER EXCEPT CHANGE. We realize that decay sets in as soon as an idea or organization is born. We're prepared for a twenty-year run here—and ready for a quick end or a complete revision."

11. "WE LEARN MORE FROM THE FUTURE THAN FROM THE PAST. I like to think this way: It's February, 1990; what do I wish I'd done in February, 1989? I see the carpet a little more worn, the desk with some new dents in it, and I imagine specific actions I wish I'd taken. It's amazing how much that helps me plan for the future."

Before you can apply these tenets at the organizational level, you need to make them your own. Return now to each tenet and see how it might be converted to:

Tenets of the Flexible Person

1. I MOVE FAST because I relish change and have confidence in my ability to deal with it. This confidence comes from acknowledging the successes I have experienced. I enjoy change because I attend to my physical and emotional needs even when I am extremely busy with my work.

2. I AM COUNTERCYCLICAL. I don't automatically accept every new trend that comes along. Before I undertake a new health regimen or style, I explore how appropriate it is for me. I investigate new medicines and medical procedures. Sometimes I do the reverse of what is *au courant* just for the fun of it. I read offbeat literature and magazines; I mentally reverse news headlines to avoid "group think."

3. I INSTITUTIONALIZE CHANGE. Trying new foods, magazines, and ways of doing things is a habit with me. Each year I commit myself to one new interest (Red Cross volunteer work, the history of Kuwait, etc.) and establish one new tradition (celebrating the Chinese New Year, giving a gift to an elderly aunt).

4. I ENCOURAGE INITIATIVE by allowing myself to undertake new projects without assurances of success; if I fail, I give myself credit for trying. When I am involved in a difficult task, I allow myself full rein so that I have the maximum chance for success. By doing so, I know I give it my best shot and can be comfortable with the outcome—whatever it is.

5. I LIKE A HIGH TURNOVER IN MY ACTIVITIES AT WORK AND IN MY PRIVATE LIFE. I can let go of responsibilities and tasks and either not replace them or take on different ones. I discard items and ideas that are no longer useful to me. I give away books, clothing, and other items, sometimes even while they are in prime condition. I don't have to maintain harmful relationships. I consciously watch for interesting individuals to add to my social circle and try to add new elements to existing relationships.

6. I SOMETIMES DECIDE NOT TO DECIDE. I might have been looking for a new job or shopping for a new car for several months and then put the whole idea on hold for a week or forever. Often, when I allow myself to procrastinate or not to finish a project, I find an underlying reason for doing so that I wouldn't have recognized had I doggedly pursued it to the end. It's similar to forcing yourself to read a book to the end, even when you know it is a waste of time.

7. I DON'T HAVE TO BE PERFECT. I do not seek perfection. I can and do recognize mistakes I make and try to keep a sense of humor about them. By being open with friends and associates about my failings, I need not feel guilty or driven to covering them up. As a result, I find they are more tolerant of my imperfections, and I of theirs.

8. I INSIST THAT MY LIFE BE FUN. I will not force myself to perform tasks over a long period of time that are not fun to me. I build amusing elements into my work life. I take the "play" side of my life seriously; I value it and insist that it has equal time.

9. I ENCOURAGE ALL THINKING AND CHANGE STYLES. I surround myself with colleagues, friends, and relatives of all kinds. I truly listen to the opinions of young and old, rich and poor, educated and ignorant, titled and unrecognized. The variety of ideas I hear stimulates my thinking and gives me a broad view of issues, and in the long run, it enables me to accept and initiate change.

10. I KNOW THAT NOTHING IS FOREVER EXCEPT CHANGE. Even though I constantly seek stability and balance in my life, I realize that disequilibrium is an ever-changing constant. Even though I enjoy the present and revere some elements of the past, I know that if change does not occur, I will lose my zest for the future.

11. I LEARN MORE FROM THE FUTURE THAN FROM THE PAST. Periodically, I look ahead one month or one year and try to discover what I should be doing currently. I prepare for the future by asking myself, "It's July 1990: What do I wish I'd done in December 1989? What actions might I have taken to make this future picture look exactly the way I'd like it to be?" Then I take those actions and make those changes.

Applying these tenets to your personal and work life will increase your flexibility. While you will likely prefer and feel most comfortable with the change style you identified as your first choice in the Change-Friendly Quotient Survey, practicing the tenets assures increasing comfort with a variety of approaches.

A brief review of MCI's history reveals a variety of ways of managing change. Bill McGowan was an experienced change-maker and therefore equipped to initiate the change that would make it a megacorporation with an impact upon the daily lives of millions. Once the company was fully in the telecommunications world, it profited from the many change styles encouraged by the company's flexible climate.

In this chapter you have seen how MCI has successfully managed all three kinds of change—imposed, adapted, and initiated—by being flexible. You've read about some of the specific strategies the company used and how they relate to those we have recommended throughout the book. Our strategies and techniques are based on common sense and current usage. They are not secrets. They are not magic. You can see from MCI's story that, while they don't always occur in the order described in the book, all elements are there. Since no two organizations have exactly the same structure and experience, each company must chart its own course.

As you consciously begin applying these techniques to your

organization, you will find yourself becoming more tolerant of change—and more than enthusiastic about it.

Pushing Four

You first discovered your usual way of handling change in the Change-Friendly Quotient Survey; you next became acquainted with other ways of handling change, and then you experienced using them. If you apply all four approaches—reasoning, refocusing, relating, and risking—when you confront or effect change, you have available at least four options. By pushing yourself to use all four options, you will probably gain more than the three new ones. The sum will be greater than the parts. The act of pushing for all four options will carry you into a state of creative plenitude.

Without change, there would be little reason to try new ideas and there would be little reason to call upon our creative resources. So all the while that you are responding to imposed change and adapting to gradual change, you are being pushed to be inventive.

However, the luxury of gradual change may be on its way out. Businesses come and go quickly these days, as do products and conventional wisdom. To cope with the stress of constant change, we need an expanded ability to make sense of vast amounts of information, an expanded range of options so we can control our lives.

There are those who think these skills are already developing and that we humans already have access to expanded abilities through hypnosis, meditation, intuition, telepathy, and even aerobic exercise. The site of such skills is thought to lie in the frontal lobes, the twin portions of the cortex that are about the size of a walnut and lie behind the forehead. Presently, they house such executive skills as planning.

In fact, some say that not too far down the road, we will all have the bulbous foreheads of the space creatures portrayed in *Close Encounters of the Third Kind* because of this progress that our brains are making.

Dr. Barbara Brown, sometimes called the "mother of biofeedback," challenges her medical colleagues and other researchers to take seriously the evidence biofeedback offers about the "paranormal" abilities humans exhibit during clairvoyance, under hypnosis, and in moments of creativity. She has had such experiences herself and believes that they cannot be denied just because science has found no way of quantifying or verifying them.

Dr. Jonas Salk is another medical doctor who sees change taking place in the human brain. This developer of the Salk vaccine for polio has shifted his energies to the human brain and theorizes that our brain is currently evolving: "And it must. Our old ways of thinking may soon be as outdated as the dinosaur."†

None of this is difficult to believe if you look at the research and invention underway today in the fields of astronomy, computer science, and medicine. And what about the challenges ordinary people meet each day? Think of the awesome array of skills you use just to get through the day: finding your way home through a monumental traffic jam; keeping in touch with friends and family during a six-month work project that requires seventy-hour weeks; operating automatic tellers and mechanized postal stations. Think of the astonishing performance of dual-career couples who maintain a good relationship. Add children to that, and you realize you don't have to be an inventor to invent at the world-class level!

So take stock of the breadth of options and abilities you already have. Take heart from your accomplishments. See how far you've come since you first came into this world. See how many skills you've tested in this book. See how many new ones you've added. And continue to develop. The words of the French philosopher Henri Bergson help put this sense of development into perspective: "To exist is to change; to change is to mature; to mature is to create oneself endlessly."

Today's technology, which seems threatening to many, actually frees us to develop these broader mental skills, just as the harvester freed farm hands to move to the cities and eventually go

†*Parade* magazine, Nov. 4, 1984.

to Harvard. At one time the most significant inventions of the Information Age, telecommunications and the computer, seemed poised to destroy the kinds of work we do and reduce us to performing menial jobs for meager wages. Since then, the climate has brightened. Isaac Asimov, the scientist, writer, and futurist, sees unprecedented opportunity in these changes. When asked to predict what humans would do now that work is changing from muscle to machine, he said: "What will be left, then, for human beings to do? Only everything—everything human, that is; everything that involves insight, intuition, fancy, imagination, creativity. The twenty-first century will be the first in which the natural creative potential of human beings generally will be utilized and encouraged from the first."‡

You are on the leading edge of this kind of progress; you can help make Asimov's prediction come true. Beginning now, commit yourself to increasing your flexibility each day so that you can find the kairos in change.

‡Asimov, Isaac, "1984, What Now?" *Omni* magazine, Jan. 1984.

CHANGE

Change always brings out our **Creativity**,
whether through **Hardship**,
Adaptation,
or something **New**. And in every change
there is opportunity for **Growth**
and **Excitement**.

Epilogue
After the Change

When we reached the end of *The Flexibility Factor,* we felt uneasy. From our experience with *Whole-Brain Thinking,* we knew we might be grieving for a loss; it hurts to let go of your "brain child." But this time there was something else bothering us. We felt unfinished, unsatiated. Finally, we realized we wanted to know what had happened to all the people in the book whose stories illustrated the characteristics of and techniques for change. We wondered how are they doing after the change. While many have scattered, we were able to follow up on most of them.

Just in case you, too, are curious about *The Flexibility Factor's* changemakers, here's what we learned about them:

Paris, the playboy turned family man, is considering offers from architectural design firms in San Diego and Boston, where construction is booming. He finished school, and his wife is completing a nursing degree while running a day-care home. And they have a third child.

Anna continues her success in the telecommunications field and has a congenial relationship with Kurt. After their divorce, he returned to Germany, where their daughters visit him each summer. Because of his photography experience in the United

States, he gained a heightened status in Europe and enjoys the kind of recognition he always longed for.

Malcolm, whose mettle was tested in a Cuban jail, is spending a great deal of time these days in Washington, lobbying for a multibillion dollar nuclear power contract. His volunteer efforts are at a similar high level. He is involved in policymaking and program design for national drug abuse control.

Bob, the hospital administrator whose pseudochange style involved him in nonstop opinion polling, has made several major decisions. He married the woman he had courted for ten years and took retirement a year later. He seems relieved and happy at last.

Nigel, the Houston lawyer who got off the treadmill when business got bad, is busier than ever now. His more humane approach to law has brought more and new clients; he has two new partners and two secretaries to share the load. He no longer has the radio show but plays basketball and volleyball regularly with his broadcast friends. And he just bought a ski house in Vail.

Doris is the computer analyst who turned cold when she got fired. She was successful as an independent computer consultant, but she missed the contact with colleagues that a larger business setting offers. Recently, she accepted a position with an airline in Europe. She loves the new challenge and the self-confidence she gained from operating her own business.

Mary, the clotheshorse who wanted a baby and a career, is more than fulfilling her goals. Her son is 16 months old, she represents four designer lines and is active in Junior League, and her Mother-Baby Shoppe concept is nearing fruition. How can she do all this? A full-time nanny and a husband who loves fatherhood.

Jessica, the tennis player with the stubborn backhand, still finds it the weakest part of her game. But she is a 4.0 (B+) player and perseveres. Her occasional brilliant games keep her excited about tennis and the time when she will make a lasting breakthrough.

Larry, the chronic entrepreneur whose bent for pseudochange kept him from reaping the rewards of his many projects, has mellowed. He is renovating an old house he bought with a modest inheritance. He has a garden and a horse. His visions are still exciting: He's negotiating a deal to get back into the helicopter business. Why? He sees the oil market strengthening and helicopters as a primary method for prospecting oil.

Gretchen, who researched her prospects for child-bearing too long, has recently adopted a six-month-old child. Both she and her husband are on maternity leave and loving every minute of it.

Melissa, the human resource manager who didn't listen to her intuition and got fired, has become a training consultant. There were some rough moments financially, but now she is building a strong client list, she says, by listening intuitively and acting quickly on her gut feelings.

Harriet, the country girl, has her degree in computer science and a job with the Department of Agriculture in Washington, D.C. She fords the streams of bureaucracy with an air of innocence and a sense of commitment. She's not sure where she's going, but she's enjoying the voyage.

You read daily the updates on the more public stories we've used in the book: the *Challenger* shuttle investigations go on; RJR–Nabisco is perpetually in the middle of the controversy over smoking; and billion-dollar takeovers. Chrysler prospers, with a few glitches along the way; MCI's earnings are growing rapidly; *SPY* magazine is the darling of sophisticated New Yorkers; and the Neilsen television rating system is the standard for the entire industry. The other major party in the MCI drama, AT&T, has also benefited from the changes divestiture brought. While their cuts in employment were painful, many who were forced to take early retirement happily struck out in new directions. Most who remain enjoy the challenge that competition brings and the flexibility that has necessarily developed within the company.

Gates Rubber Co. continues its customer-friendly ways: a case in point is their response to the request of a Cornish farmer for rubber boots for his cows whose hooves crack during winter. The Gates factory in Scotland is now producing the foot-high Hobble Boot with two buckles and a sole in the shape of a hoof.

It's been easy to follow-up on Gary Hart: His coverage of the Russian summit and the U.S. political conventions was carried by major newspapers worldwide. However, you may have missed a few details: he left the Denver law firm of Davis, Graham, and

Stubbs to form an international consulting group with an emphasis on the Soviet Union. And he was recently heard to say, "I'm still trying to figure out what I want to do when I grow up." Even the most bitter experience need not ruin your life or limit its possibilities. With such an attitude, he's bound to find kairos in change.

The stories of changemakers rarely have storybook endings. In fact, they're never quite finished because life is open-ended and change is forever. But all of these people have profited from their change experiences in some way. As you apply what you've learned about change from life and from this book, keep in mind that you may not achieve exactly what you set out to accomplish, because change brings so many unexpected twists and turns. But relish these surprises, and know that with each experience you become more and more successful in making change work for you.

Index